PATRICK SUPPES

PROFILES

AN INTERNATIONAL SERIES
ON CONTEMPORARY PHILOSOPHERS
AND LOGICIANS

EDITORS

RADU J. BOGDAN, *Stanford University*
ILKKA NIINILUOTO, *University of Helsinki*

EDITORIAL BOARD

VOLUME 1

PATRICK SUPPES

Edited by

RADU J. BOGDAN

Stanford University

D. REIDEL PUBLISHING COMPANY

DORDRECHT : HOLLAND / BOSTON : U.S.A.
LONDON : ENGLAND

Library of Congress Cataloging in Publication Data

Main entry under title:

Patrick Suppes.

    (Profiles; v. 1)
    Bibliography: p.
    Includes index.
    1. Suppes, Patrick Colonel, 1922–   —Addresses, essays,
lectures. 2. Philosophers—United States—Biography—Addresses,
essays, lectures. I. Bogdan, Radu J. II. Series: Profiles (Dordrecht);
v. 1.
B945.S95P37   191   78–21095
ISBN 90–277–0950–5
ISBN 90–277–0951–3 pbk.

Published by D. Reidel Publishing Company,
P. O. Box 17, Dordrecht, Holland.

Sold and Distributed in the U.S.A., Canada, and Mexico
by D. Reidel Publishing Company, Inc.
Lincoln Building, 160 Old Derby Street, Hingham,
Mass. 02043, U.S.A.

TABLE OF CONTENTS

EDITORIAL INTRODUCTION   vii
PREFACE   ix

Part One   1
PATRICK SUPPES – A Self Profile   3

Part Two   57
CARLOS-ULISES MOULINES & JOSEPH D. SNEED –
  Suppes' Philosophy of Physics   59
R. DUNCAN LUCE – Suppes' Contributions to the
  Theory of Measurement   93
ROGER D. ROSENKRANTZ – Suppes on Probability,
  Utility, and Decision Theory   111
RICHARD E. GRANDY – Suppes' Contribution to
  Logic and Linguistics   131
WILLIAM H. BATCHELDER & KENNETH WEXLER –
  Suppes' Work in the Foundations of Psychology   149
DEAN T. JAMISON – Suppes' Contribution to Education   187
PATRICK SUPPES – Replies   207

Part Three   233
BIBLIOGRAPHY OF PATRICK SUPPES   235
INDEX OF NAMES   259
INDEX OF SUBJECTS   262

EDITORIAL INTRODUCTION

The aim of this series is to inform both professional philosophers and a larger readership (of social and natural scientists, methodologists, mathematicians, students, teachers, publishers, etc.) about what is going on, who's who, and who does what in contemporary philosophy and logic. PROFILES is designed to present the research activity and the results of already outstanding personalities and schools and of newly emerging ones in the various fields of philosophy and logic. There are many Festschrift volumes dedicated to various philosophers. There is the celebrated *Library of Living Philosophers* edited by P.A. Schilpp whose format influenced the present enterprise. Still they can only cover very little of the contemporary philosophical scene. Faced with a tremendous expansion of philosophical information and with an almost frightening division of labor and increasing specialization we need systematic and regular ways of keeping track of what happens in the profession. PROFILES is intended to perform such a function.

Each volume is devoted to one or several philosophers whose views and results are presented and discussed. The profiled philosopher(s) will summarize and review his (their) own work in the main fields of significant contribution. This work will be discussed and evaluated by invited contributors. Relevant historical and/or biographical data, an up-to-date bibliography with short abstracts of the most important works and, whenever possible, references to significant reviews and discussions will also be included.

Since rigorous argumentation and a rational approach to philosophical problems are among the most worthwhile trends in contemporary philosophical thought, PROFILES will give priority to surveys of the work of authors and schools of thought that meet these standards. However, this preference allows for a broad spectrum of philosophical and methodological viewpoints. As a vehicle of information about, and systematization of, contemporary philosophical and logical knowledge, PROFILES will strive to report on any major contribution to that body of knowledge, be it personal or collective. PROFILES will also report on research and new projects that, although still esoteric and even tentative, may be expected to become seminal and influential in some field of philosophical or logical studies. The sooner the information about such new ventures is disseminated and systematized, the greater will be its impact on undergraduate and graduate students, researchers, teachers on all levels, editors, publishers, university and foundation managers, etc.

The editors will welcome information on personal and collective research in progress, Ph.D. theses, surveys and monographs dealing with individual philosophers and schools of thought working in contemporary philosophy and logic.

We expect to publish one or two volumes yearly.

RADU J. BOGDAN

Stanford University

ILKKA NIINILUOTO

University of Helsinki

PREFACE

By the very nature of this series the profilees need no introduction. The volumes themselves are designed to provide one. But there are some things to be said about the making of this volume.

The volume has three major parts. Part One contains the *Self Profile* written by Patrick Suppes. It is an intellectual autobiography, a presentation of his professional activity, a summary of its results up to the present, i.e. close to mid-1978, and an occasion for reflection and review. We have decided to classify Suppes' research and publications into the following major fields: (i) foundations of physics, (ii) theory of measurement, (iii) decision theory, probability, and causality, (iv) foundations of psychology, (v) philosophy of language, and (vi) education and computers. Of course, many of Suppes' works go beyond this classification while many others fall into two or more of these fields. Still the classification reflects Suppes' main areas of scientific and philosophic interest.

In Part Two, distinguished contributors review and discuss Suppes' work and results in each of the above fields. Replies by Suppes conclude this part. Part Three is a complete bibliography of Suppes' published and forthcoming works. Some of the most important publications are concisely presented by their author. In order to save space and achieve some homogeneity all references, in Suppes' *Self Profile* and *Replies*, to works of which he is the, or an, author can be found in this final bibliography. The contributed papers have self-contained bibliographies whereas the parts written by Suppes contain only references to works of other authors.

This volume inaugurates a series whose prehistory should be briefly told. Some years ago, while in Romania, I started a series of handy, informative volumes intended to acquaint a national audience of students and scholars in philosophy and related disciplines with the state of philosophy abroad and with some of its most active practitioners. With the enthusiastic and consistent support of Dr. Mircea Ioanid, a man of great vision and deeds to whom I am deeply indebted, several volumes were published. When, due to various circumstances, the original enterprise had to be abandoned, a new international edition took off in a new format with a new publisher. But the original intent of PROFILES survives.

Through their confidence, encouragement and advice, many people have helped PROFILES in its new life. It is a tribute to the widespread support that we had and have that my fellow editor Ilkka Niiniluoto and myself find it difficult to list the names of all those to whom we are grateful and indebted. Without some of them this first volume would hardly have been possible. Although extremely busy, Patrick Suppes was an ideal profilee to work with. He faced the editorial constraints with grace, added many suggestions, and supported the whole enterprise in many ways.

Marguerite Shaw did much more than typing and correcting most of the manuscript, putting together the bibliography, and helping at each stage of the editorial process. I can hardly imagine this volume without her wonderful assistance. And I can hardly imagine my work during this period without the love and understanding of my wife, Catalina.

Stanford, May 1978   RADU J. BOGDAN

PART ONE

PATRICK SUPPES

SELF-PROFILE

I have divided this autobiography into three main parts: education, research, personal reflections. The second part on research is the longest
and most substantial.[1]

1. Education

I was born on March 17, 1922, in Tulsa, Oklahoma, and grew up as an
only child; my half brother George was born in 1943 after I had entered
the army. My grandfather, C. E. Suppes, moved to Oklahoma from Ohio
in the early part of this century. He and my father were independent oil
men, intelligent and competent in their business but not well educated.
My mother died when I was four and a half; I was raised by my stepmother,
who married my father before I was six. She also had not had much
formal education, but her interest in self-improvement was strong, and
she encouraged me in a variety of ways to pursue my intellectual interests,
in spite of my father's ambition for me to follow him and his father in the
oil business.

My interest in philosophy was generated early by my stepmother's
devotion for more than a decade to the Christian Science of Mary Baker
Eddy. From about the age of eight to fourteen years I attended Sunday
school and church regularly and studied the works of Eddy as well as the
Bible. The naive epistemological idealism of Eddy's writings stirred my
interest, which turned to skepticism by the age of thirteen or so. I can
remember rather intense discussions with fellow Sunday-school students
about how we were supposed to reconcile, for example, the bacterial theory

Bogdan, R.J. (Ed.) 'Patrick Suppes' 3–56.

of disease with the purely mentalistic views of Eddy. No doubt our arguments were not at all sophisticated, but our instinct to distrust the flagrant conflicts with common sense and elementary science was sound.

I attended the public schools in Tulsa and was graduated from Tulsa Central High School in 1939. My public school education was more influential on my development than is often the case, mainly because I was a participant in what is known as the Tyler eight-year study of the Progressive Education Association. On the basis of examinations given in the sixth grade, able students were selected to participate in a six-year experiment of accelerated education. In many respects the most competitive and ablest classes I ever attended were those in high school. One of the important aspects of this special educational venture was the extended attempt to get us as young students to talk about a wide range of current events and everything else that interested us. As is often the case, this led into some unusual lines of effort. I can remember very well being chagrined at fourteen if I were not able to name the senators from every state in the union.

The high school courses in mathematics, chemistry and history were excellent, but physics and English were relatively mediocre. The English course was so dominated by the idiosyncrasies of the teacher we had for two years that we became experts in her life and tribulations rather than in the more essential matters of grammar and composition.

I began college at the University of Oklahoma in 1939 but, after the first year, found the intellectual life too pedestrian compared to the much more exciting high school years. In the second year I transferred to the University of Chicago, but, under the *laissez-faire* approach of Chicago, neglected my academic work so completely that my family insisted on my attending the University of Tulsa for my third year, where I majored in physics. At the beginning of my fourth year I was called up in the Army Reserves (this was 1942) and returned to the University of Chicago as a senior in uniform. I undertook there an intensive course in meteorology and received a BS degree from the University of Chicago in 1943. Knowledge of meteorology has stood me in good stead throughout the years in refuting arguments that attempt to draw some sharp distinction between the precision and perfection of the physical sciences and the vagueness and imprecision of the social sciences. Meteorology is in theory a part of physics, but in practice more like economics, especially in the handling of a vast flow of nonexperimental data.

From Chicago I was sent to the South Pacific for two years of duty in

1944 and 1945. After a short period of adjustment, I found the isolation and serenity of the Solomon Islands quite attractive. I occupied myself with swimming, poker, Aristotle, and a couple of correspondence courses in mathematics and French. After a year of living on a small island, occupied only by military troops, I was transferred to Guam, which seemed relatively civilized but less conducive to intellectual work.

I was discharged from the Army Air Force in 1946, and after some months of deciding what to do, changing my mind any number of times, and spending more than half a year working for my father in the oil fields near Artesia, New Mexico, I entered Columbia University as a graduate student in philosophy in January of 1947 and received a PhD in 1950.

As an undergraduate I moved too often to be strongly influenced by any one teacher. I do remember certain impressive individuals, including Richard McKeon at Chicago, who lectured on Aristotle, Norman Steenrod, who taught my first course in calculus, and Professor Tanner at the University of Tulsa, from whom I learned elementary Greek.

The situation was different in graduate school. I was influenced by Ernest Nagel more than by anyone else and I still relish the memory of the first lecture of his that I attended in 1947. I came to philosophy without much background in the subject, since my undergraduate training was primarily in mathematics and physics. But Nagel's skeptical, patient and detailed analysis of F. H. Bradley and John Dewey, in the first course I took from him, won my attention and interest from the start. I have recorded these impressions in more detail in my account of Nagel's lectures on Dewey (1969e). In those days, interdisciplinary work was very much favored in the Department of Philosophy, and consequently I continued to learn a good deal more mathematics and physics. I still remember with great pleasure the beautiful and penetrating lectures of Samuel Eilenberg on topology and group theory, and I remember well the course in relativity theory I took from L. H. Thomas. Thomas was a terrible lecturer, in sharp contrast to the brilliance of Nagel or Eilenberg, but he knew so much about the subject and was in such total control of the theory and relevant data that it was impossible not to learn a great deal and to be enormously impressed by the organization and presentation of the lectures.

In those years Columbia was swarming with returning veterans, and in certain ways we veterans had our own ideas about what should be taught in graduate school. We organized in 1947 or 1948 an informal seminar on von Neumann and Morgenstern's theory of games, partly because we did not seem to be able to find a course on the subject, but also because Columbia's graduate school immediately after the war was so vastly overcrowded that the kind of individual attention graduate students now receive at Stanford, for example, was simply unheard of in almost all departments at Columbia. I felt myself extremely lucky to have as much personal contact as I did with Ernest Nagel. Friends of mine in the History Department saw their adviser only a few hours during their entire graduate-school career, including completion of the dissertation.

Considering my relatively extensive research efforts in psychology from about 1955 onward, it is somewhat surprising that I took no work in psychology either as an undergraduate or as a graduate student, but there was a feature of my education that made it easier for me to pick up what I needed to know without prior systematic training. As an undergraduate I wandered about in several different fields, and because of the easygoing policy of the Department of Philosophy in those days at Columbia I spent a good deal of time in nonphilosophical courses. I thus developed early the habits of absorbing a wide variety of information and feeling at home in the problem of learning a subject in which I had not had much prior training or guidance.

Because of my background and interests in physics I wanted to write a dissertation about the philosophy of physics, in particular to give a modern axiomatic treatment of some branch of physics, but as I got deeper into the subject I realized that this was not the kind of dissertation that was considered appropriate in philosophy. The Department at that time was primarily historically oriented, and Nagel advised me to consider a more informal approach to the foundations of physics. What we finally agreed on was a study of the concept of action at a distance, and a good deal of the dissertation was devoted to an analytical study of this concept in the works of Descartes, Newton, Boscovich, and Kant. I was able to come closer to my original interest in a chapter on the special theory of relativity, but certainly what I had to say in that chapter was no contribution to the axiomatic foundations of the subject. I did find the historical work absorbing and have continued over the years to retain and, on occasion, profitably to use the knowledge about the history of philosophy and science I first systematically acquired as a graduate student at Columbia. The part of my dissertation I published, with only minor modifications, was the material on Descartes (1954a). But I have relatively recently used much more of the dissertation material in a long article on Aristotle's theory of matter (1974b), in which I also review the theories of matter of Descartes, Boscovich, and Kant.

Earlier, but still long after the dissertation was written, I used some of the material on Kant in a Festschrift article for John Herman Randall, Jr. (1967h). Randall's lectures in the history of philosophy were a great occasion at Columbia, and it was a pleasure to say something in detail about Kant's philosophy of science as an extension of Randall's interpretation in the Festschrift volume. Randall, like a lot of other philosophers mainly interested in the history of philosophy, did not have a strong analytical turn of mind, but his lectures were a memorable experience. As I said in the opening paragraph of my Festschrift article for Randall, "The wit, the literary quality, and the range of learning exhibited in these lectures were famous around Columbia long before the time of my own arrival. As a young scientist turned philosopher, the most important general thing I learned from Randall was not simply to read the great modern philosophers in terms of a close explication of text, but also to realize that they must be interpreted and considered against the background of the development of modern science." The contrast between Nagel's analytical and dialectical skill and Randall's sympathetic and impressionistic account of ideas was dramatic, but I can rightly claim that I learned a great deal from both of them although I was clearly more influenced by Nagel.

Another person whose intellectual habits influenced me at Columbia and who was of quite a different sort than any of the others I have mentioned was Paul Oskar Kristeller. He was interested in the fine details of historical scholarship, famous of course for his work in Renaissance philosophy, but I was more influenced by the seminar on Kant that he and Randall gave. Kristeller's meticulous insistence on a textual basis for every interpretation suggested in the seminar, and his decisive way of handling the text, were a model of scholarship that I admired and learned from, even though Kristeller always modestly insisted that he was in no sense a Kantian specialist.

I received my PhD from Columbia in June of 1950 but my education scarcely stopped there. Although I began teaching upon arrival at Stanford in the fall of 1950, where I have been ever since, almost as soon as I could I also began to think about research in the philosophy of science. My problem was that I did not really know much about how to do any serious research and writing, since my graduate education did not involve the personal supervision of research of the kind so familiar to graduate students today. I was neither forced nor encouraged to produce early in my graduate career a publishable paper nor to become acquainted with the 'how-to-do-it' aspects of research.

I was, however, full of energy and brimming over with ideas. I thrashed around for a few months but fortunately I soon became acquainted with J. C. C. McKinsey, a logician who had recently joined the Department of Philosophy at Stanford. McKinsey served as my postdoctoral tutor. It was from him that I learned the set-theoretical methods that have been my stock in trade for much of my career. It was not, however, just set-theoretical methods as such that McKinsey taught me but also a passion for clarity that was unparalleled and had no precedent in my own prior education. I remember well his careful red-penciling of the initial draft I gave him of my first article on the theory of measurement (1951a). McKinsey was just completing a book on the theory of games and consequently also had some of the interests that were of importance to me as my own interests in the social sciences began to blossom.

But there were other people at Stanford and Berkeley who continued my education in those early years at Stanford. With McKinsey's encouragement I attended Alfred Tarski's seminar in Berkeley. McKinsey always claimed that he had learned everything he knew from Tarski. This was not true, but after attending Tarski's seminar I understood why he liked to say this. Tarski was a ruthless taskmaster. I think he probably got the most out of his students of anyone I have known. His seminar provided perhaps the best example I know of vicarious learning. A student who made a poorly prepared seminar presentation was so ruthlessly and mercilessly questioned that the other students did not need any hints about the state of preparation they should achieve before making their own presentations. Tarski, as one of the great examples of the Polish school of logic, was unwilling to go forward on a single point unless everything covered thus far was completely clear – in particular, unless it was apparent to him that the set-theoretical framework within which the discourse was operating could be made totally explicit. It was from McKinsey and Tarski that I learned about the axiomatic method and what it means to give a set-theoretical analysis of a subject.

McKinsey died in 1953, and our collaborative work on the axiomatic foundations of empirical sciences was brought to a sudden stop. Another learning experience that influenced much of my later work was the summer research position I had early in the fifties for a couple of years with David Blackwell and M. A. Girshick while they were writing their influential book *Theory of Games and Statistical Decisions* (1954). As I remark later, I did not learn as much from them as I should have, but what I did absorb played an important role in a number of my early papers.

In later years I have learned a great deal from many persons who are mentioned below. Rather arbitrarily I have terminated this section on my education as of about 1954, but it seeems important to mention those who have taught me much of what I know about psychology because, although my allegiance to philosophy had continued strong throughout all these years, for a considerable period I published more papers in psychology than in philosophy. Much of this work was due to the influence of William K. Estes, R. Duncan Luce, and Richard C. Atkinson. My joint work with each of them is discussed later at appropriate points.

II. Research

I have grouped the discussion of my research under seven headings: foundations of physics; theory of measurement; decision theory, foundations of probability, and causality; foundations of psychology; philosophy of language; education and computers; and philosophy and science. Where details warrant further organization, appropriate subheadings are also introduced. There is some arbitrariness in the classification, but I do not think any serious confusions will arise. The number of topics on which I have worked is large and it would be foolish to claim that I have contributed in a fundamental way to all of them. On the other hand, each of the main headings represents an area that has been the focus of my interests at some period over the past several decades.

Foundations of Physics

As already mentioned, my doctoral dissertation lay within the philosophy of physics. In particular, I studied the problem of action at a distance as it had occurred in 17th- and 18th-century physics and philosophy, especially in the writings of Descartes, Newton, Boscovich, and Kant. The final chapter dealt with the problem in the special theory of relativity. Working on it strengthened my earlier desire to give an axiomatic formulation of classical mechanics in the spirit of modern mathematics rather than 'physical' axiomatizations common in physics. Serious joint work on this project began soon after my arrival at Stanford, in collaboration with J. C. C. McKinsey, and is represented in four papers we wrote on the foundations of physics prior to McKinsey's death in 1953 (1953a, 1953b, 1953c also with A. C. Sugar, and 1955b). Shortly thereafter I wrote with Herman Rubin a similar paper (1954c) on the axiomatic foundations of relativistic particle mechanics. It is a long and very complicated piece of work that has not been read, I suspect, by very many people.

My main interests soon turned to research on decision theory and related problems in the foundations of psychology but I have continued through the years to have an interest in physics, and an irregularly spaced sequence of papers has reflected that interest.

Special relativity
In 1957 I organized jointly with Leon Henkin and Alfred Tarski a symposium on the axiomatic method with special reference to geometry and physics. Working with Henkin and Tarski on the organization of this symposium was an exhilarating experience. My own paper (1959a) was concerned with the derivation of the Lorentz transformations of special relativity from an explicit but minimal set of assumptions. Essentially, the aim of the paper was to give an elementary derivation of the Lorentz transformations, without any assumptions of continuity or linearity, from a single axiom concerning invariance of the relativistic distance between any two space-time points connected by an inertial path or, put another way, from the assumption of invariance of segments of inertial paths. Important new results on the derivation of the Lorentz transformations have since been published by Walter Noll (1964), E. C. Zeeman (1964), and others.

The elegant aspect of Noll's paper is that he axiomatizes Minkowskian chronometry using coordinate-free methods. More importantly, Zeeman shows that it is not necessary to assume invariance of time-like intervals as I did, but that it is sufficient to assume the preservation of order, that is, the relativistic partial ordering of one point being after another is sufficient. Like many simple and beautiful ideas, it is surprising that this did not occur to someone sooner. The key to the results is already present in the early work of Robb (1936), which shows that the binary relation of being after is a sufficient conceptual basis for the kinematical theory of special relativity.

In the final section of my 1957 paper (1959a) I discuss the possibility of introducing a relation of signaling in order to fix the direction of time. It is obvious that this can be done very directly in an *ad hoc* fashion. What is needed, however, is some natural approach that is fully satisfying from an intuitive and a conceptual standpoint. In his article, Noll makes some remarks about this, and he raises the question of whether his approach solves the problem I raised. Essentially, Noll introduces a directed signal relation that is asymmetric, and of course if we postulate that the numerical representation must preserve the direction of signals passing from earlier to later events, the direction of time is guaranteed. I find this approach unsatisfactory since this is an arbitrary stipulation in the definition of isomorphism, and we get just as good an isomorphism from a structural standpoint if the direction in time is reversed. At the time it did not seem feasible to give such an analysis, but recently I have been rethinking and, more importantly, learning a great deal more about optics. It now seems to me that natural qualitative postulates differentiating signals being received and being sent should be feasible, although such postulates must go beyond the purely kinematic aspects of the special theory of relativity to include some substantive assumptions, even if of a general nature, about physical optics.

After a gap of some years, my interest in classical physics (in which I include special relativity) was revived while working on Chapter 10 of *Foundations of Measurement* (1971a). This chapter is concerned with dimensional analysis and numerical laws. I think I made some contributions to the chapter, but almost surely I learned more than I contributed, especially from Duncan Luce. The rather technical material in this chapter on the algebra of physical quantities and on dimensional analysis, including the question of why numerical laws are dimensionally invariant, has not been much picked up by philosophers of science, but I think that in due time it will be.

Quantum mechanics

Most of the effort that I have put in on the foundations of physics since 1960 has been devoted to quantum mechanics, and this continues to be a current active intellectual interest. Almost everything that I have written about quantum mechanics has been intertwined with questions related to the foundations of probability, especially as to how probabilistic concepts are used in quantum mechanics. My first paper on the subject (1961c) was concerned with the absence of a joint distribution of position and momentum in many standard cases. I shall not enter into the technical details of the argument here, but I do want to convey the basic philosophical point that I continue to find the real puzzle of quantum mechanics. Not the move away from classical determinism, but the ways in which the standard versions seem to lie outside the almost universal methodology of modern probability theory and mathematical statistics. For me it is in this arena that the real puzzles of quantum mechanics are to be found. I am philosophically willing to violate classical physical principles without too many qualms, but when it comes to moving away from the broad conceptual and formal framework of modern probability theory I am at once uneasy. My historical view of the situation is that if probability theory had been developed to anything like its current sophisticated state at the time the basic work on quantum mechanics was done in the twenties, then a very different sort of theory would have been formulated.

It is worth recording a couple of impressions about this because they indicate the kind of changes that can take place in one's attitudes as the years go by. Initially I was much impressed by the mathematical formulation of foundations given by von Neumann in his classical work and, later, by Mackey (1963), whose book has also become classical in its own way. No doubt I was originally struck by the mathematical clarity and sophistication of this work, but in later years I have become dissatisfied with the unsatisfactory conceptual basis from a probabilistic standpoint of the way in which the theory is formulated. I shall give here just two examples to indicate the nature of my conceptual dissatisfaction. Von Neumann stresses that we can take the expectation of the sum of any two operators, even though they are conjugate, that is, do not commute. But once this is said, the natural question is to ask about the underlying probability space that justifies the exact probabilistic meaning of the expectation. A similar question arises with respect to Mackey's treatment. Mackey takes as fundamental the concept of the probability that a measurement in a given state of an observable will lead to a given value. This seems innocent enough, but when the fundamental postulates of the theory are stated in these terms, what seems missing from what one would expect in a standard causal physical theory is any clarity about the relation between observables. The axioms he gives would seem to concentrate too deeply on the relatively simple properties of the probability of a given measurement on a given observable and not enough on the causal dependencies between observables. (It is important to remember that I am not really making a technical argument here but trying to give the intuitions back of arguments that I think can be formalized.)

A detailed analysis of the kinds of requirements that a satisfactory probabilistic theory of quantum mechanical phenomena should have is laid out for the simple case of the harmonic oscillator in a relatively recent paper by Zanotti and me (1976m). As I write this autobiography I am struggling to develop in a much deeper way than I have previously a thoroughgoing probabilistic interpretation of interference phenomena in quantum mechanics, especially as produced by the classical two-slit experiment.

Until recently I thought that the most important philosophical problems of quantum mechanics could be analyzed in the nonrelativistic framework characteristic of the early development of the subject. An effort to understand the place of probability concepts in relativistic quantum mechanics has abruptly changed my mind. The meshing of probability and relativity seems to be badly worked out for even the most elementary problems. One sign of the difficulty is the superficiality of the development of probabilistic concepts in relativistic quantum mechanics. An extensive search of the literature, for example, has not revealed a single discussion of particular distributions. The multivariate normal distribution is invariant under linear transformations, and the Lorentz transformations are linear, but the proper space-time hyperplane on which the distribution is defined needs to be correctly chosen to be Lorentz invariant as well. As far as I know, discussion of these 'first' questions does not yet exist, which I find very surprising.

Although I continue to be fascinated by the conceptual problems of quantum mechanics and I think of it almost as a responsibility of any philosopher of science with wide interests to know a good many of the details of what is surely the most important scientific theory of the 20th century, I find that my own work here is less satisfying to me than other areas I discuss later, just because I do not anticipate making a scientific contribution to the subject. In the case of the theory of measurement or psychology, for example, my contributions have as much a scientific as a philosophical flavor, and I find that this suits my temperament better – independent of whether the scientific contribution is of greater or less significance than the philosophical one.

Theory of Measurement

In my first published article (1951a) I gave a set of independent axioms for extensive quantities in the tradition of earlier work by Hölder and Nagel. My contribution was primarily to weaken the assumptions of Hölder's axioms and also to prove that both the axioms and the concepts used were independent.

Looking around for other topics in measurement, and returning to the earlier interest in the theory of games and utility theory, it soon became apparent that there were more outstanding problems of measurement in psychology than in physics. One of my first efforts in this direction was a joint article with my student Muriel Winet (1955d). We gave an axiomatization of utility based on the notion of utility differences. The idea of considering such utility differences is a very old one in the literature, but an explicit and adequate set of axioms had not previously appeared. In 1956 I published two other articles which fell between decision theory and measurement theory. One was on the role of subjective probability and utility in decision making. In this article (1956b) I used the results of the joint work with Winet to provide an axiomatization alternative to that given by Savage in his book *Foundations of Statistics* (1954). And in the second article, my colleague Donald Davidson and I gave a finitistic axiomatization of subjective probability and utility (1956c).

Shortly after this I began to think more generally about the foundational aspects of theories of measurement and was fortunate to have as a collaborator the logician and mathematician Dana Scott, who was at that time a graduate student in mathematics. (Scott is also one of the Berkeley-Stanford persons from whom I learned a great deal, beginning when he was an undergraduate in a course on the philosophy of science I taught at Berkeley in 1952, along with Richard Montague. What a pair to have in such a course!) Scott and I tried to give a general framework for theories of measurement and to obtain some specific results about axiomatization. This article was published in 1958, a year or so after it was written. The framework that Scott and I set up has, I think, been of use in the literature, and probably the article with him has been the most important article in the theory of measurement that I have written, although the chapter in the *Handbook of Mathematical Psychology*, written with J. L. Zinnes and published in 1963, has perhaps been more influential, especially in psychology.

My most important recent effort has been the extensive collaboration with David Krantz, Duncan Luce and Amos Tversky in the writing of our two-volume treatise *Foundations of Measurement*, the first volume of which appeared in 1971. At the time of writing this autobiography, we are hard at work on Volume II. My present feeling is that when Volume II is published I shall be happy to let the theory of measurement lie fallow for several years. It is, however, an area of peculiar fascination for a methodologist and philosopher of science like myself. The solution of any one problem seems immediately to generate in a natural way several more new problems. The theory nicely combines a demand for formally correct and explicit results with the continual pursuit of analyses that are pertinent to experimental or empirical procedures in a variety of sciences but especially in psychology, where the controversy about the independent measurability of psychological concepts has been long and intense. The theory of measurement provides an excellent example of an area in which real progress has been made in the foundations of psychology. In earlier decades psychologists accepted the mistaken beliefs of physicists like Norman Campbell that fundamental measurement in psychology was impossible. Although Campbell had some wise things to say about experimental methods in physics, he seemed to have only a rather dim grasp of elementary formal methods, and his work in measurement suffered accordingly. Moreover, he did not even have the rudimentary scholarship to be aware of the important earlier work of Helmholtz, Hölder, and others.

The work of a number of people over the past several decades has led to a relatively sophisticated view of the foundations of measurement in psychology, and it seems unlikely that any substantial retreat from this solid foundation will take place in the future. I am somewhat disappointed that the theory of measurement has not been of greater interest to a wider range of philosophers of science. In many ways it is a natural topic for the philosophy of science because it does not require extensive incursions into the particular technical aspects of any one science but raises methodological issues that are common to many different disciplines. On the other hand, by now the subject has become an almost autonomous technical discipline, and it takes some effort to stay abreast of the extensive research literature.

Although important contributions to the theory of measurement have already appeared since we published Volume I of *Foundations of Measurement*, I do think it will remain as a substantial reference work in the subject for several years. What is perhaps most important is that we were able to do a fairly good job of unifying a variety of past results and thereby providing a general framework for future development of the theory.

Having mentioned the seminars of Tarski earlier, I cannot forbear mentioning that perhaps the best seminar, from my own personal standpoint, that I ever participated in was an intensive one on measurement held jointly between Berkeley and Stanford more than ten years ago when Duncan Luce was spending a year at the Center for Advanced Study in the Behavioral Sciences at Stanford. In addition to Luce and me, active participants were Ernest Adams, who is now Professor of Philosophy at Berkeley and was in the fifties my first PhD student, and Fred Roberts, who was at that time a graduate student in mathematics at Stanford and is now a member of the Department of Mathematics at Rutgers University. William Craig also participated on occasion and had penetrating things to say even though he was not as deeply immersed in the subject as were the rest of us. Our intensive discussions would often last well beyond the normal two hours, and it would not be easy to summarize all that I learned in the course of the year.

There is also a pedagogical point about the theory of measurement, related to what I have said just above about measurement in the philosophy of science, that I want to mention. The mathematics required for elementary examples in the theory of measurement is not demanding, and yet significant and precise results in the form of representation theorems can be obtained. I gave several such examples in my textbook in logic (1957a) and also in my paper 'Finite Equal-interval Measurement Structures' (1972d). I continue to proselytize for the theory of measurement as an excellent source of precise but elementary methodology to introduce students to systematic philosophy of science.

Decision Theory, Foundations of Probability, and Causality

Decision theory

It is not easy to disentangle measurement theory and decision theory because the measurement of subjective probability and utility has been such a central part of decision theory. The separation that I make will therefore be somewhat arbitrary. My really serious interest in psychology began with experimental research on decision theory in collaboration with my philosophical colleague Donald Davidson and a graduate student in psychology at that time, Sidney Siegel. Davidson and I had begun collaborative work with McKinsey in 1953 on the theory of value and also on utility theory. We continued this work after McKinsey's death, and it is reflected in Davidson, McKinsey, and Suppes (1955a) and in the joint article with Davidson (1956c) on the finitistic axiomatization of subjective probability and utility, already mentioned. The article on the measurement of utility based on utility differences, with Muriel Winet, was also part of this effort.

Sometime during the year 1954, Davidson and I undertook, with the collaboration of Siegel, an experimental investigation of the measurement of utility and subjective probability. Our objective was to provide an explicit methodology for separating the measurement of the two and at the same time to obtain conceptually interesting results about the character of individual utility and probability functions. This was my first experimental work and consequently in a genuine sense my first real introduction to psychology. The earlier papers on the foundations of decision theory concerned with formal problems of measurement were a natural and simple extension of my work in the axiomatic foundations of physics. Undertaking experimental work was quite another matter. I can still remember our many quandaries in deciding how to begin, and seeking the advice of several people, especially our colleagues in the Department of Psychology at Stanford.

I continued a program of experimentation in decision theory as exemplified in the joint work with Halsey Royden and Karol Walsh (1959i) and the development of a nonlinear model for the experimental measurement of utility with Walsh (1959j). This interest continued into the sixties with an article (1960g) on open problems in the foundations of subjective probability. Then in 1961 I drew upon my interest in learning theory to try to create a behavioristic foundation for utility theory (1961a), and I also made an attempt in that same year to explain the relevance of decision theory to philosophy (1961b).

The most important effort in this period was the writing with Duncan Luce of a long chapter, 'Preference, Utility and Subjective Probability' (1965i), for Volume III of the *Handbook of Mathematical Psychology*. The organization of a large amount of material and the extensive interaction with Luce in the writing of this chapter taught me a great deal that I did not know about the subject, and I think the chapter itself has been useful for other people. It is also worth mentioning that large parts of the joint effort with Krantz, Luce and Tversky in writing our two-volume treatise on the foundations of measurement have been concerned with decision theory.

In the latter part of the sixties I wrote several articles in the foundations of decision theory, oriented more toward philosophy than psychology. Three of the articles appeared in a book on inductive logic edited jointly with Jaakko Hintikka, my part-time philosophical colleague at Stanford for many years.

One article dealt with probabilistic inference and the concept of total evidence (1966j). Here I advanced the argument that under a Bayesian conception of belief and decision there was no additional problem of total evidence, contrary to the view held by Carnap and also Hempel. According to this Bayesian view, which I continue to believe is essentially right on this matter, if a person is asked for the probability of an event at a given time, it will follow from the conditions of coherence on all of his beliefs at that time that the probability he assigns to the event automatically takes into account the total evidence that he believes has relevance to the occurrence of the event. The way in which total evidence is brought in is simple and straightforward; it is just a consequence of the elementary theorem on total probability.

A second article in the volume (1966e) set forth a Bayesian approach to the paradoxes of confirmation made famous by Hempel many years ago. I will not outline my solution here but much of the philosophical literature on the paradoxes of confirmation has taken insufficient account of the natural Bayesian solution, at least so I continue to think. A third article in the volume (1966f) dealt with concept formation and Bayesian decisions. Here I attempted to set forth the close relations between formal aspects of the psychology of concept formation and the theory of Bayesian decisions. I now think that the ideas I set forth here are the least interesting and the most transitory of those occurring in the three articles. The general idea of value in this article concerns the relation expressed between concept formation and the classical problem of induction. For those restricted settings in which no new concepts are needed but for which an induction about properties is required, a Bayesian approach is sound and can meet most, if not all, of the conceptual problems about induction that I regard as serious. On the other hand, a Bayesian viewpoint toward induction does not provide a general solution because it does not incorporate a theory of concept formation. Genuinely new inductive knowledge about the world requires not only a framework of inductive inference of the sort well worked out in the contemporary Bayesian literature but also a theory about how new concepts are to be generated and how their applicability is to be dealt with. This large and significant aspect of the general problem of induction seems to me still to be in a quite unsatisfactory state. In my own thinking, the problem of induction and the concept of rationality are closely tied together, and as I point out in the article on probabilistic inference mentioned above, the Bayesian approach still provides a very thin view of rationality, because the methods for changing belief as reflected in the introduction of new concepts or in the focus of attention are not at all adequately handled. The outlines of any future theory that will deal in even a partially satisfactory way with the central problem of concept formation are not at all visible, and it may even be that the hope for a theory that approaches completeness is mistaken.

Distributive justice

For a variety of reasons, the literature on decision theory has been intertwined with the literature on social choice theory for a very long period, but the focus of the two literatures is rather different and I have certainly had more to say about decision theory than about the normative problems of social choice or distributive justice. To a large extent, this is an accident of where I have happened to have had some ideas to develop and not a matter of *a priori* choice. I have published two papers on distributive justice (19661, 1977a). The main results about justice in the first one, which were stated only for two persons, were nicely generalized by Amartya Sen (1970). The other paper, which was just recently published, looks for arguments to defend unequal distributions of income. I am as suspicious of simplistic arguments that lead to a uniform distribution of income as I am of the use of the principle of indifference in the theory of beliefs to justify a uniform prior distribution. The arguments are too simple and practices in the real world are too different. A classical economic argument to justify inequality of income is productivity, but in all societies and economic subgroups throughout the world differences in income cannot be justified purely by claims about productivity. Perhaps the most universal principle also at work is one of seniority. Given the ubiquitous character of the preferential status arising from seniority in the form of income and other rewards, it is surprising how little conceptual effort seems to have been addressed to the formulation of principles that justify such universal practices. I do not pretend to have the answer but I believe that a proper analysis will lead deeper into psychological principles of satisfaction than has been the case with most principles of justice that have been advanced. I take it as a psychological fact that privileges of seniority will continue even in the utopia of tomorrow and I conjecture that the general psychological basis of seniority considerations is the felt need for change. A wide range of investigations demonstrate the desirable nature of change itself as a feature of biological life (not just of humans) that has not been deeply enough recognized in standard theories of justice or of the good and the beautiful.

Foundations of probability

The ancient Greek view was that time is cyclic rather than linear in character. I hold the same view about my own pattern of research. One of my more recent articles (1974g) is concerned with approximations yielding upper and lower probabilities in the measurement of partial belief. The formal theory of such upper and lower probabilities in qualitative terms is very similar to the framework for extensive quantities developed in my first paper in 1951. In retrospect, it is hard to understand why I did not see the simple qualitative analysis given in the 1974 paper at the time I posed a rather similar problem in the 1951 paper. The intuitive idea is completely simple and straightforward: A set of 'perfect' standard scales in introduced, and then the measurement of any other event or object (event in the case of probability, object in the case of mass) is made using standard scales just as we do in the ordinary use of an equal-arm balance. This is not the only occasion in which I have either not seen an obvious and simple approach to a subject until years later, or have in fact missed it entirely until it was done by someone else.

On the other hand, what would appear to be the rather trivial problem of generalizing this same approach to expectations or expected utility immediately encounters difficulties. The source of the difficulty is that in the case of expectations we move from the relatively simple properties of subadditive and superadditive upper and lower measures to multiplicative problems as in the characteristic expression for expected utility in which utilities and probabilities are multiplied and then added. The multiplicative generalization does not work well. It is easy to give a simple counterexample to straightforward generalization of the results for upper and lower probabilities, and this is done in Suppes (1975a). I have continued to try to understand better the many puzzles generated by the theory of upper and lower probabilities, in joint research with Mario Zanotti (1977j).

Partly as a by-product of our extensive discussions of the qualitative theory of upper and lower probabilities, Zanotti and I (1976n) used results in the theory of extensive measurement to obtain what I think are rather elegant necessary and sufficient conditions for the existence of a probability measure that strictly agrees with a qualitative ordering of probability judgments. I shall not try to describe the exact results here but mention the device used that is of some general conceptual interest.

Over the years there have been a large number of papers by many different individuals on these matters. Essentially all of them have formulated conditions in terms of events, with the underlying structure being that of the Boolean algebra of events and the ordering relation being a binary relation of one event being at least as probable as another. The conditions have turned out not to be simple. The important aspect of the paper with Zanotti is our recognition that events are the wrong objects to order. To each event there is a corresponding indicator function for that event, with the indicator function having the value one when a possible outcome lies in the event and the outcome zero otherwise – as is apparent, in this standard formulation events are sets of possible outcomes, that is, sets of points in the probability space. We obtain what Zanotti and I have baptized as *extended indicator functions* by closing the set of indicator functions under the operation of functional addition. Using results already known in the theory of extensive measurement it is then easy to give quite simple necessary and sufficient axioms on the ordering of extended indicator functions to obtain a numerical probability representation.

Recently we have found correspondingly simple necessary and sufficient qualitative axioms for conditional probability. The qualitative formulations of this theory beginning with the early work of B. O. Koopman (1940a, 1940b) have been especially complex. We have been able drastically to simplify the axioms by using not only extended indicator functions, but the restriction of such functions to a given event to express conditionalization. In the ordinary logic of events, when we have a conditional probability $P(A|B)$, there is no conditional event $A|B$, and thus it is not possible to define operations on conditional or restricted events. However, if we replace the event A by its indicator function A^c, then $A^c|B$ is just the indicator function restricted to the set B, and we can express in a simple and natural way the operation of function addition of two such partial functions having the same domain. The analysis of conditional probability requires considerably more deviation from the theory of extensive measurement than does the unconditional case: for example, addition as just indicated is partial rather than total. More importantly, a way has to be found to express the conceptual content of the theorem on total probability. The solution to this problem is the most interesting aspect of the axiomatization.

The move from events to extended indicator functions is especially interesting philosophically, because the choice of the right objects to consider in formulating a given theory is, more often than I originally thought, mistaken in first efforts and, as these first efforts become crystallized and familiar, difficult to move away from.

Apart from technical matters of formulation and axiomatic niceties, there are, it seems to me, three fundamental concepts underlying probability theory. One is the addition of probabilities for mutually exclusive events, the second is the concept of independence of events or random variables, and the third is the concept of randomness. I have not said much here about either independence or randomness. A conceptually adequate formulation of the foundations of probability should deal with both of these concepts in a transparent and intuitively satisfactory way. For any serious applications there is a fourth notion of equal importance. This is the notion of conditionalization, or the appropriate conceptual method for absorbing new information and changing the given probabilities. I have ideas, some of which are surely wrong, about how to deal with these matters and hope to be able to spend time on them in the future. However, rather than try to sketch what is still quite premature, I want to end with some general comments about the foundations of probability and decision theory.

It has been remarked by many people that logic is now becoming a mathematical subject and that philosophers are no longer main contributors to the subject. Because of its more advanced mathematical character this has really been true of probability from the beginning. The great contributions to the foundations of probability have been made by mathematicians – de Moivre, Laplace, von Mises, and Kolmogorov come quickly to mind. Although there is a tradition of these matters in philosophy – and here one thinks of Reichenbach and Carnap – it is still certainly true that philosophers have not had a strong influence on the mainstream of probability theory, even in the formulation of its foundations. On the other hand, I strongly believe in the proposition that there is important and significant work in the foundations of probability that is more likely to be done by philosophers than by anyone else. The various interpretations of foundations, ranging from the subjective view of the classical period through the relative frequency theory of the first part of this century to propensity and other views of late, have probably been discussed more thoroughly and more carefully by philosophers than by anyone else. I see no reason to think that this tradition will come to an end. The closely related problems of decision theory are just beginning to receive equal attention from philosophers after their rapid development by mathematical statisticians in the two decades after World War II.

It is important for philosophers to be familiar with and to know the formal and technical developments by mathematicians and statisticians. It is unfortunate that there has been a tendency for philosophers to pursue their own special formalisms that do not relate well to the mainstream of work. Such formalisms tend to be, from a mathematical and conceptual standpoint, too elementary to come to grips with complex problems of applications or to offer sufficient complexity of structure to handle the main problems of interest to those pursuing technical issues. What seems to me to be the right role for philosophers in these matters is to be able to comment on and to use the concepts that are actively developed in most cases by others. I do not see as viable a special philosophical approach to probability, and my views on this matter are consonant with what I think about other issues in the philosophy of science or in philosophy generally.

Causality

Because my own approach to causality is probabilistic in character, I have included it in this section. It is hard to think of a philosophical topic that has received more attention historically than that of causality. It has already become clear to me that what I have had to say (1970a) has got to be extended, revised, and deepened, in order to meet objections that have been made by other people and to account for a variety of phenomena that I did not consider in any detail. Causality is one of those concepts that plays a major role in a variety of scientific disciplines and that can be clarified and enriched by extensive philosophical analysis. On some subjects of a probabilistic kind I find it hard to imagine how I, or another philosopher, could improve in a substantial way on what has been said with clarity and precision by probabilists and statisticians – the concept of a stochastic process is a good example. This is not true of the concept of causality. A good many statisticians use the concept in various ways in their research and writing, and the concept has been a matter of controversy both in the physical sciences and in the social sciences over the past several decades. There is a major place in these discussions for philosophical analyses of causality that join issue firmly and squarely with this extensive scientific literature.

A recent article by Woods and Walton (1977) emphasizes a point that is something of a minor scandal in philosophy. This is the absence of clear and definite elementary principles for accepting or rejecting a causal relation. The teaching of elementary logic depends upon extensive use of material implication and other truth-functional sentential connectives, in much the same way that beginning students of physics are taught Newtonian and not relativistic mechanics. We unfortunately do not at the present time have the same tradition in philosophy about a range of concepts that lie outside of formal logic. Causality is perhaps the prime example. I mention the point as a matter of pedagogy but in fact it is a matter of philosophy proper, because there has not been sufficient development or agreement about the developments that have taken place to provide a set

23

of transparent systematic concepts that can be used in introductory teaching.

There are one or two systematic points about causality I would like to comment on here without entering into technical details. The first is the objection to my characterization of causality in terms of probability. A standard remark about this characterization is that all kinds of spurious relations will satisfy the definition of *prima facie* cause. According to my formulation, an event *A* is a *prima facie* cause of event *B* if *A* occurs earlier than *B* and the conditional probability of *B* given *A* is greater than the unconditional probability of *B* alone. It is properly pointed out that many kinds of events are connected in the sense of this definition by a *prima facie* causal relation, for example, the lowering of the barometer and the rain that follows, and yet we all immediately reject the falling of the barometer as a *prima facie* cause of the rain. I see the situation here as no different from that which applies to logical inference. The machinery is set up to be indifferent to our intuitive facts about the world, so that we can make logical inferences that seem silly. Standard examples are easy to give and are familiar to everybody. The same point is not as easily accepted about causality, but it is my claim that this is a virtue and not a defect of a general theory of causality. It should be universally applicable; intuitive counterexamples simply reflect the fact that the formal theory is indifferent as to what intuitive knowledge or substantive theory is being called upon.

Moreover, the full formal theory has appropriate devices for eliminating falling barometers as causes of rain. The standard notion to use here is that of a spurious cause. Showing that other events account for the change in conditional probability when the barometer is not present or broken provides the intuitive evidence we all accept for the absence of a causal relation between falling barometers and rainfall. The second point, related to this one, is that the notion of spurious cause itself and the closely related one of genuine cause must be relativized to a particular conceptual framework. This is made especially clear when one wants to prove a theorem about causality within the framework of a particular scientific theory. In my 1970 monograph I did not make the relativization to a particular framework an explicit part of the definitions. It is obvious how this can be done and perhaps in many cases it should be done. I do think that the insistence on relativizing the analysis of cause to a particular conceptual framework is a point on which to make a stand. Absolutists, who think they know the full truth and do not need such relativization, have the burden of providing forceful examples. I know of no interesting ones myself. I take this point as no different than the point that the systematic formal concept of truth is relative to a model and not in any sense appropriate to reality taken straight.

There is another and more interesting point raised in conversations on various occasions by Nancy Cartwright, Paul Holland, and others. It is that the full notion of causality requires a sense of experimental manipulation. There are many ways of formulating the idea. Holland likes to say that, from a statistical standpoint, without random assignment of individuals to experimental groups an unimpeachable causal inference cannot be made. My most immediate reply is that ordinary talk and much scientific experience as well does not in any sense satisfy these conditions of experimental design, that is, the causal claims that are made in ordinary talk or in much of science have not arisen from well-designed experiments but from quite different circumstances – in fact, from circumstances in which no experiments have taken place and in many cases are not possible. The great classical example is celestial mechanics. From the time of the Babylonians to the present, we have seen a variety of causal theories to account for the motion of the planets, the moon, and the stars. In the case of some terrestrial phenomena that are not themselves directly subject to experiment but for which an analysis can be built up in terms of experimental data, we are faced with a rather more complicated decision about what we regard as proper extrapolation from experiment. In fact, one underhanded way to meet the objections raised by Cartwright and Holland is to point out that the use of scientific theories outside the experimental domain and the power of the application of science depend upon sustaining causal claims in nonexperimental settings. Are we to conduct experiments on extendability in order to establish a justification of using the results of experiments in nonexperimental settings? It would not be difficult to set up a straw man of infinite regress by literal pusuit of this line of thought. My own view is that, rather than claiming that only in experimental settings can we really make proper causal claims, we should formulate theorems that are applicable to experimental settings but not to others. It seems to me one kind of theorem we might want to insist upon is that for experiments whose theory of design is adequate we should expect to be able to prove within a framework of explicit probabilistic concepts that all *prima facie* causes are genuine. We would not expect such a theorem to hold in general in nonexperimental settings.

Kreisel has pointed out to me that the *general* theory of causality is unlikely to be of much scientific significance once specific scientific theories are considered. Indeed, the interest of such theories is to provide a testing ground for the correctness of the general notions. On the other hand, not only ordinary talk but much highly empirical scientific work does not depend on a well-defined theoretical framework, and for these cases the general theory of causality can provide useful analytic concepts.

Foundations of Psychology

I have already remarked on my earliest experimental work in psychology in connection with the test of various concepts and axioms of decision theory. I shall not refer further to that work in this section. Because of my extensive work in psychology over the past two decades, I have organized my remarks under four headings: learning theory, mathematical concept formation in children, psycholinguistics, and behaviorism.

Learning theory

Either in my last months as a graduate student at Columbia or shortly after my arrival at Stanford in the fall of 1950 – I cannot remember which – I developed my first interest in learning theory. As might easily be surmised, it began with trying to understand the various works of Clark Hull, not only the *Principles of Behavior* (1943) but also the relatively unreadable work written earlier in collaboration with the Yale logician Frederick Fitch and others (Hull, Hovland, Ross, Hall, Perkins, & Fitch, 1940). Part of my interest was stimulated by some very bright graduate students in psychology who attended my lectures in the philosophy of science. Probably the most influential was Frank Restle. I was a member of his dissertation committee, but I am sure I learned more psychology from him than he learned from me.

My serious interest in learning theory began, however, in 1955 when I was a Fellow at the Center for Advanced Study in the Behavioral Sciences. Restle was there, but even more important for my future interests was the presence of William K. Estes. In his own and very different way, Estes has the kind of intellectual clarity I so much admired in McKinsey and Tarski. We began talking seriously about the foundations of stimulus sampling theory, which really began with Estes's classical paper (1950). It became apparent to me quite soon that stimulus sampling theory was from a conceptual and mathematical standpoint much more viable and robust than the Hullian theory of learning. No really interesting mathematical derivations of experimentally testable results could be made from Hull's axioms. The great virtue of stimulus sampling theory was that with variation of experimental conditions new experimental predictions could be derived in an honest way without the introduction of *ad hoc* parameters and with the hope of detailed experimental test.

Perhaps it will be useful to say something more about the contrast between Hull's theory and stimulus sampling theory. The mere use of mathematics and especially of mathematical symbols in a theory is no guarantee that anything of mathematical or scientific interest is being done. In Hull's theory the feeling is too much that each experimental result, or almost each remark about an experiment, is being given a direct translation into mathematical symbols. In contrast, no powerful and simple set of theoretical postulates from which specific results can be derived, once initial and boundary conditions are described, is even remotely approached. The translation from ordinary mathematical statements into the still more formal apparatus of mathematical logic as exemplified in the 1940 work of Hull and others cited above is still more mistaken if the only objective is a translation. One of the great lessons of logic in the 20th century is that formal systems themselves as deductive instruments are not of as much conceptual importance as the mathematical study of properties of such systems, but it is precisely the mathematical analysis of psychological theory that is not even touched upon in Hull's work. Hull, on the other hand, is in good company in this mistaken move. It has taken some time for the situation to become clarified as a result of the large body of important work in mathematical logic and metamathematics in this century. In Volume III of Whitehead and Russell's *Principia Mathematica* (1913) a detailed theory of measurement is developed; but from a formal standpoint their results are elementary, the notation is so forbidding and the welter of symbols so profuse that very little use has subsequently been made of the material.

In order not to seem too dogmatic about this point, it is worth noting that the interest in the use of formal systems has returned in new guise in the form of programming languages, but here the orientation is very different from that to be found, for example, in Hull's *Mathematico-Deductive Theory of Rote Learning*.

In contrast to Hull's theory, stimulus sampling theory works in a way very analogous to that of physical theories. The initial probabilities of response correspond to initial conditions in a physical problem, and reinforcement schedules correspond closely to boundary conditions.

The fruits of extensive collaboration with Estes in 1955–1956 did not appear until later. In fact, we have published only two articles together (1959e, 1974q). The first article appeared as a technical report in 1957 and the second one first appeared as a technical report in 1959. The collaboration with Estes in writing the two long technical reports, later condensed into shorter papers, has been one of my most satisfactory research efforts in psychology. In a genuine sense these two reports combined a concern for axiomatic foundations with a focus on new scientific results.

While Estes and I were together at the Center, he introduced me to his former graduate student, Richard C. Atkinson, and we arranged for Atkinson to spend the following academic year at Stanford as a research associate. He and I undertoook an extensive series of investigations into the application of stimulus sampling theory to two-person interactions. The initial fruit of this collaboration was my first experimental article in psychology (1958a). (Unlike most psychologists, I published an experimental book (1957b) before publishing an experimental article.) Atkinson and I expanded this first effort into an extensive series of studies, which were published in our book, *Markov Learning Models for Multiperson Interactions* (1960b). It was a great pleasure to me to work in this area of application of learning theory. It combined my fundamental interest in learning theory with my earlier interest in game theory, and I found that I had a natural taste for elaborate analysis of experimental data. (The book with Atkinson is much richer in data analysis and the testing of models than is the earlier book with Davidson and Siegel.) I think I work best with someone like Atkinson, who is extremely well organized and very good at designing and running experiments. I like to get into the action when the analysis of the data and the testing of theory are to be the focus. Working with Atkinson has the additional advantage that he is also an able theorist and has plenty of ideas of his own.

This was the period in which my theoretical interests in learning theory were flourishing. I also worked at this time on mathematical aspects of learning processes, particularly a study of their asymptotic properties in collaboration with John Lamperti, who was then a member of the mathematics faculty at Stanford. This work appeared in two publications (1959h, 1960i).

I spent a fair amount of time on the generalization of learning theory to a continuum of responses. The first step was to generalize the linear model (1959b), and the second step was to generalize stimulus sampling theory (1960h). In collaboration with Raymond Frankmann, Joseph Zinnes, and later Henri Rouanet and Michael Levine, extensive tests of learning theory for a continuum of responses were made in publications between 1961 and 1964. With Jean Donio, who like Henri Rouanet was at that time a young French scientist working with me, I worked out the generalization in another direction to a continuous-time formulation of the theory. I am still pleased with the character of this work. It took a certain amount of mathematical effort to get things straight, and some of the detailed empirical predictions were quantitatively accurate and surprising. It is especially in predicting something like the continuous distribution of responses that untutored intuition fails in providing anything like an accurate idea of what the results will be. The need of theory to make non-trivial predictions becomes especially evident. On the other hand, I do not think that this work has had very much impact in psychology. The developments have not been folowed up in the directions that could have led to more powerful results, but I do not think we were walking down a blind alley in this research effort. The kind of approach developed will almost surely turn out to be of use in several directions when a larger number of psychologists with strong mathematical training and quantitative empirical interests come onto the scene to study the theory of motor skills and a variety of perceptual phenomena in detail.

Mathematical concept formation in children
In 1956 my oldest child, Patricia, entered kindergarten and my interests in applications were once again stimulated, in this case to thinking about the initial learning of mathematical concepts by children. In collaboration with Newton Hawley, who was and still is a member of the mathematics faculty at Stanford, we began the following year, when our daughters were both in the first grade, the informal introduction of constructive geometry. At that time very little geometry was taught in the primary grades. A brief description of this first effort is to be found in Hawley and Suppes (1959g), but, more importantly, we went on to write two textbooks for primary-grade students in geometry, which have since been translated into French and Spanish (1960c, 1960d).

This practical interest in the mathematics curriculum in the schools almost inevitably led to trying to understand better how children learn mathematical concepts. Once again because of my continued collaboration with Estes, I was fortunate to get Rose Ginsberg, who was just completing a PhD at Indiana with Estes and C. J. Burke, to join me at Stanford as a research associate with the express purpose of studying concept formation in children. This work resulted in a number of publications with Ginsberg (1962d, 1962e, 1963c) and also a number of publications of my own, of which I mention especially my monograph *On the Behavioral Foundations of Mathematical Concepts*, appearing in the Monograph Series of the Society for Research in Child Development (1965e), and also my article on the same topic in the next year in the *American Psychologist* (1966g).

In this work in mathematical concept formation in children, Ginsberg and I were concerned to apply, as directly and as naturally as possible, stimulus sampling theory to the learning of such concepts. We met with more success than I initially expected. The ability of relatively simple models of stimulus sampling theory to account for the learning of simple mathematical concepts in great detail is, I think, a surprising fact and an important one.

In 1960, I was finishing my textbook on axiomatic set theory and the question naturally arose of the relation between the set-theoretical foundations of mathematics provided by Zermelo–Fraenkel set theory and the learning of mathematics by children. If I had not been finishing that textbook at the time I might well not have embarked upon a number of the experiments that Ginsberg and I undertook to test the formation of elementary concepts about sets – for example, identity and equipollence – as well as elementary geometrical concepts. A practical fruit of these investigations was the undertaking of a new series of elementary mathematics textbooks entitled *Sets and Numbers*, which was published over several years in the sixties.

In recent years the interest in mathematical concept formation has melded into my work on computer-assisted instruction, which I discuss in a later section.

Psycholinguistics

Another natural area of application of stimulus sampling theory is language learning. Again I was fortunate to get another former student of Estes and Burke from Indiana, Edward Crothers, to join me as a research associate at Stanford. We undertook a systematic series of experiments in second-language learning; this effort led to several publications but especially to a book in 1967, *Experiments in Second-language Learning*, which reported a large number of investigations on various elementary aspects of learning Russian.

At the same time, given my philosophical inclinations and training, it was natural for me to become interested in the broader range of controversies in psycholinguistics. To some extent the first chapter of the book with Crothers summarizes the kind of attack on the problems of language learning to be expected from a behavioral standpoint. I also attempted in the writing of this chapter to provide a partial answer to the many criticisms that were being made of behavioral theories by psycholinguists.

Two years later I published a more thoroughly worked out answer in my article 'Stimulus-Response Theory of Finite Automata' (1969g). In this article I showed that from simple principles of conditioning one could obtain the kind of language behavior of which a finite automaton is capable. I made no attempt to relate the theoretical developments to the detailed and subtle learning that takes place in a child, but rather argued that the presumed theoretical limitations of stimulus-response theory were misunderstood by a number of linguistically oriented critics. I have continued to be involved in this controversy and some of my most recent articles are concerned with it (1975b, 1977d).

I have emphasized in my writings on this subject that the challenge to psychological theory made by linguists to provide an adequate theory of language learning may well be regarded as the most significant intellectual challenge to theoretical psychology in this century. At the present time numerous difficult problems of providing a completely adequate scientific theory of language learning and language performance are enough to make even the most optimistic theorist uneasy. In very developed areas of science or mathematics, it is familiar to find the statement made that certain kinds of problems are simply far beyond the resources currently available but that certain more restricted problems are amenable to serious attack and likely solution. For example, in quantum chemistry there is, with present intellectual and computing resources, no hope of making a direct attack on the behavior of complex molecules by beginning with the first principles of quantum theory. A problem as easy to formulate as that of deriving from first principles the boiling point of water under normal atmospheric pressure is simply beyond solution at the present time and is recognized as such. Within mathematics there are classical open problems in elementary number theory, group theory, differential geometry, and in fact almost any developed branch of mathematics. Psycholinguistics will be a far happier and more productive subject when the same state of developed theory has been reached. A frontal attack on the problem of giving a complete analysis of the speech of even a three-year-old child is certainly outside the range of our conceptual tools at the present time. What seems essential is to recognize this fact and to determine the appropriate range of significant yet possibly solvable problems that should be studied.

One approach that has already been fruitful and will be significant in the future is the attempt to write computer programs that can understand and learn a natural language. Such enterprises must at present be restricted to a small fragment of a natural language, but the thorough investigation of such small fragments seems to me a promising arena for making progress in the way that is characteristic of other domains of science. I do not mean to suggest by this that study of natural language should be restricted to computers – certainly not. There will continue to be a significant and important accumulation of fact and theory about the language learning of children. Our understanding of these matters will deepen each year, but what is not yet clear is the direction theory will take so as to be adequate to the limited domains of understanding we master. I recognize the inadequacies from an empirical standpoint of what can presently be said about language learning within a stimulus-response framework or a more sophisticated version of S–R theory in terms of procedures and internal data structure, but I also believe in emphasizing the theoretical thinness of any of the proposals about learning that come from the linguistic side of psycholinguistics. In fact, practically none of the ideas originating from linguistics about language learning has been sufficiently developed in a systematic fashion to permit any sort of theorem, asymptotic or otherwise, to be proved.

Some may say that it is scarcely required of an empirical theory that it be precise enough to permit the proving of asymptotic theorems, but in the present context it seems to me an important consideration. The actual empirical phenomena are too complicated for anyone coming at them from *any* theoretical viewpoint to provide a detailed account. One test of a theoretical proposal is whether its structure is rich enough to permit in principle the learning of language as the amount of exposure or experience goes to infinity. A good recent effort in this direction that does permit a theorem to be proved, even if the concept of meaning underlying the theory is not at all realistic, is to be found in Hamburger and Wexler (1975) – and I am pleased to claim Wexler as a former doctoral student of mine.

Toward the end of this period in the sixties I also got involved in the detailed empirical study of children's first language. The initial work in this area was in the construction of probabilistic grammars (1970b) followed by the construction of model-theoretic semantics for context-free fragments of natural language (1973e). I have been especially skeptical of the semantical concepts used by linguists. The long and deep tradition of semantical analysis in logic and philosophy provides, in my judgment, a much sounder basis for the analysis of the semantics of natural language. In my address as recipient of the American Psychological Association Distinguished Scientific Award in 1972, I tried to lay out the virtues of the model-theoretic approach to the semantics of children's speech (1974m). This is an issue that is still before us, and it would be too easy for me to enter into the substantive debate in this essay. I cannot refrain, however, from a few remarks.

The concept of meaning has a much longer history in philosophy and logic than it does in psychology or in linguistics. It is possible to begin the philosophical story with Aristotle, but Frege and Tarski will do as modern points of departure. The important thrust of this work has been to describe how the meaning of a sentence is to be built up from the meaning of its parts. In Tarski's case this takes the form of giving an explicit recursive definition of truth. One of the reasons for the large disparity between this developed logical literature and what goes under the heading of meaning in psycholinguistics is, I believe, the concern in psycholinguistics primarily for the meaning of individual words. In Roger Brown's recent book (1973) he talks a good deal about the meanings of individual words and even about the meaning of imperatives, but what he does not really face at any point is the Fregean task of trying to understand how the meaning of a complex utterance is built up from the meaning of its parts. Without this there can be no serious theory of meaning, and until this is thoroughly recognized by psycholinguists I am skeptical that a satisfactory psychological theory of meaning for use in studying the first language of children can be developed.

I have undertaken additional large-scale empirical work on children's language in collaboration with my former students, Dr. Robert Smith and Dr. Elizabeth Macken, as well as with Madeleine Léveillé of the Laboratory of Experimental Psychology in Paris. The first fruits of this collaboration are to be found in the reports by Léveillé, Smith, and me (1973g; 1974t), and in two recent articles, one with Macken (1978f) and one by me (in press–b).

Of all my work in psychology, that concerning the syntax and semantics of children's first language has had the closest relation to broad issues that are current in philosophy, and for this reason alone I expect my interest to continue unabated. I have more to say on these matters in the section on philosophy of language.

Behaviorism

In spite of my recent interest in psycholinguistics I have certainly been identified in psychology with behaviorism, and I have written several philosophical pieces in defense of behaviorism. It should be clear from many other things I have to say in this essay that I do not believe in some Skinnerian form of behavioristic reductionism. In fact, the kind of methodological behaviorism, or what I have sometimes labeled neobehaviorism, I advocate is antireductionist in spirit, and wholly compatible with mentalistic concepts. The central idea of methodological behaviorism is that psychology as a science must primarily depend on behavioristic evidence. Such evidence is characterized in terms of stimuli and responses described in terms of psychological concepts. It is certainly possible to ask for physiological and, indeed, physical or chemical characterizations of both stimuli and responses. In some kinds of work, characterization of stimuli at a physical level is highly desirable, as for example in some detailed studies of visual perception. On the other hand, I strongly believe that a reduction of psychology to the biological or physical sciences will not occur and is not intellectually feasible. I am not happy with leaving the statement of my views at this level of generality, and I consider it an intellectual responsibility of methodological behaviorists like myself to reach for a deeper and more formal statement of this antireductionist position. What are needed are theorems based on currently reasonable assumptions showing that such a reduction cannot be made. I think of such theorems as being formulated in the spirit in which theorems are stated in quantum mechanics about the impossibility of deterministic hidden variable theories.

Given my earlier work, as reflected for example in my paper on the stimulus-response theory of finite automata (1969g), it may seem paradoxical for me to be arguing for such impossibility theorems, but the thrust to develop a psychological theory of computable processes is to be understood as an effort to bring the theory of language and other complex psychological phenomena within the framework of methodological behaviorism.

As I have urged more than once in the past, stimulus-response theory of behavior stands in relation to the whole of psychology in much the same way that set theory stands to the whole of mathematics. In principle it offers an appealingly simple and rigorous approach to a unified foundation of psychology. It is worth examining the extent to which a stimulus-response 'reduction' of the rest of psychology is feasible. The first difficulty is that most of the other parts of psychology are not formulated in a sufficiently general and mathematical form, contrary to the case of mathematics where what was to be defined in set-theoretical terms already had a relatively precise characterization. Because I am not persuaded that the reductionistic approach is of much interest at the present time, I turn to stimulus-response theory itself and its internal difficulties.

Although I shall not enter into the technical details here it is not difficult to show that given an arbitrary Turing machine a stimulus-response model of behavior with only simple principles of stimulus sampling, conditioning and reinforcement operating can be constructed that is asymptotically (in time) isomorphic to the Turing machine. The tape of the machine is represented by some potentially infinite sequence of responses, for example, responses to the numerals as stimuli. From this asymptotic representation for any Turing machine, we can construct a universal stimulus-response model corresonding to a universal Turing machine that will compute any partial recursive function. Thus in principle we can claim the adequacy of stimulus-response theory to give an account of the learning of any computable process, and presumably any human cognitive or affective behavior falls within this context.

From a sufficiently general philosophical viewpoint this stimulus-response representation of any behavior no matter how complex is of some interest. It shows, just as does the representation of all of classical mathematics within set theory, how simple the primitive concepts of a powerful theory can be when there is no severe limitation on the means of construction. In particular the representation provides an abstract reduction of all concepts of behavior to the simple set required for the formulation of stimulus-response theory, but the word *abstract* needs emphasis because we certainly have no idea how to carry out the actual reduction of most interesting behavior.

The basic representation of a universal Turing machine by a stimulus-response model brought to isomorphism at asymptote requires learning procedures that consist only of conditioning and change of conditioning of responses to given stimuli. But there is a severe weakness of these asymptotic results. Nothing is said about the learning rate. To match human performance or to be of real conceptual interest, the learning of appropriately simple concepts must not be too slow. Take the case of first-language learning in the child, for instance. A rather extravagant upper bound on the number of utterances a child has heard by the age of five is ten million. A learning rate that requires three orders of magnitude of exposure beyond this is not acceptable from a theoretical standpoint, but the highly simplified inadequate representation of the genetically endowed structures and functions the child brings to the task is evident. A richer theory is required to deal with them, but almost certainly there will be no fully satisfactory theory developed at any time in the foreseeable future.

Philosophy of Language

I have already said something about my interest in language in the section on psycholinguistics. Much but not all of my formal work on the theory of language has been related to psycholinguistics. Some overlap of the earlier section will be inevitable, but I concentrate here on the work that is more or less independent of psycholinguistics. My paper on model-theoretic semantics for context-free fragments of natural language (1973e) was partly generated by thinking about children's language but also by the formal problem of putting together the kinds of grammar that have become current in linguistics and computer science with the kind of model theory familiar in logic. The general approach has been anticipated by Knuth (1968) but he had not brought to the surface the model theory, and I did not become aware of his paper until I had worked out the essentials. My paper was first circulated as a technical report in 1971, and the ideas were applied with great thoroughness and extended by Robert Smith in his dissertation (1972), written under my direction. The basic philosophical point is that we can provide a standard model theory for context-free fragments of English directly without any recourse to the model theory of first-order logic. Because of my conviction that this can be done easily and naturally, I have continued to argue for the inappropriateness of first-order (or second-order) logic as an analytical tool for the study of the semantics of natural language. I summarize some of the further developments in later papers. Before doing so I want to note that the restriction to context-free grammars is not essential. One can work out a corresponding model-theoretic semantics for transformations that map trees into trees in the standard linguistic fashion, but because there is a great deal of work to be done just within a context-free framework I have not worked out many details from a wider perspective.

In my address (1973b) as outgoing president of the Pacific Division of the American Philosophical Association, I applied these semantical ideas to develop a general notion of congruence of meaning. I characterized this view as a geometrical theory of meaning because I developed the viewpoint that different weak and strong notions of congruence are appropriate to catch different senses of 'identity' of meaning. Moreover, it seemed to me then and it still seems to me that there is much to be learned from geometry about the concept of congruence and the related concept of invariance that is applicable to the theory of meaning. We have long ago abandoned the idea of one true theory of geometry; we should do the same for meaning.

The most important idea in the paper is to tie closely together the notion of congruence of meaning and the particular syntactical structure of expressions. Without such an explicit use of syntax I am deeply skeptical that any satisfactory general theory of meaning can be found. In particular, the features of similarity of meaning between two expressions seem to me lost in any translation into first-order logic, and just for this reason I am doubtful of the appropriateness of the standard notions of logical form. In fact, I suppose my view is that there is no serious notion of logical form separate from the syntactic form of an expression itself.

On the other hand, I accept as of great importance the crude notion of congruence characterized by logical equivalence of expressions. This extensional concept of congruence is the robust and stable one needed for much scientific and mathematical work. Of course, for most systematic contexts a weaker notion of equivalence is used, one in which the notion of consequence is broader than that of logical consequence, because of the assumption of various background theories – all of classical mathematics in the case of physics, for example.

There is a point concerning identity of meaning that I did not develop explicitly enough in that address. In geometry we have a clear notion of identity for geometrical figures but it is not a notion that receives any real use compared to the importance of the notion of congruence for the particular geometry under study. It seems to me that this is very much the case with meaning. I am not unhappy with a very psychological approach to meaning that takes the meaning of a term to be unique at a given time and place to a given individual. Thus in crude terms the meaning of a proper name in this sense might well be taken to be the set of internal programs or procedures by which the individual that uses or recognizes the proper name attaches properties or relations to the object denoted by the proper name. These procedures or programs internal to a particular

37

language user are private and in detailed respects idiosyncratic to him. The appropriate notion for a public theory of meaning is a notion of congruence that is considerably weaker than this very strong sense of identity. If the viewpoint I am expressing is near the truth, the search for any hard and fast sense of identity of meaning is a mistake. It rests hidden away in the internal programming of each individual. What we are after are congruences that can collapse these private features across language users to provide a public and stable notion of meaning.

In fact, this way of looking at the matter is in a more general philosophical way very satisfying to me. I have come to be skeptical of the long philosophical tradition of looking for various kinds of bedrocks of certainty, whether in epistemology, logic, or physics. Just as the natural notion of a person is not grounded in any hard and definite realization, and certainly not a physical one because of the continual fluctuation of the molecules that compose the body of the person, so it is with the meaning of expressions. In terms of what I have just said about an ultimately psychological theory of meaning at the deepest level, I also disagree with Frege's attempt to separate in a sharp and absolute fashion logic from psychology.

From a formal standpoint, my work on the semantics of natural language has recently taken a more radical turn. I now believe that the semantics of a significant fragment of ordinary language is most naturally worked out in a framework that is an extension of relational algebras as developed earlier by Tarski, McKinsey, and others. Moreover, the notation for the semantics is variable free, using only constants and operations on constants, for example, taking the converse of a relation, the image of a set under a relation, etc. In a recent paper (1976c) I work out the details of such an approach to the standard quantifier words, whether in subject or object position. Such a view runs against the tide of looking upon quantification theory in first-order logic as one of the prime logical features of natural language. But as has been known implicitly since the time of Aristotle, much natural language can be expressed within Boolean algebra and it is not a large step from Boolean algebras to relational algebras of various sorts. One of the points of my 1976 paper is to prove that if we use the standard linguistic parsing that makes quantifiers part of noun phrases – so that we treat *all men* in the sentence *All men are mortal* as being a simple noun phrase and have a tree structure that reflects this – then it is not possible under obvious and natural conditions to have a Boolean semantics of the sort that has been familiar for a hundred years for such utterances. The previous history of Boolean semantics did not emphasize that the syntax and semantics had to go together. The proof of the theorem depends upon this intimate marriage of model-theoretic semantics and context-free grammars. The line of extension to quantifiers in object position brings in relational algebras in an obvious way, but the elimination of any quantifier notation in the underlying semantical notation is based on the same concept as in the case of quantifiers in subject position.

This same framework of ideas is developed in considerable detail in a paper on attributive adjectives, possessives, and intensifying adverbs, by Macken and me (1978f). The full set of subtleties to be found in the ordinary use of adjectives, possessives, and adverbs is beyond the competence of any theory to handle completely at the present time. I do think we make a reasonable case for the kind of model-theoretic semantics without variables that I have described as providing a more detailed and intuitive semantical analysis than any of the theoretical approaches previously published.

In a paper I am just now finishing I go on to consider logical inference in English. To my surprise I have been able to find practically no papers dealing with such inferences in a direct fashion. The reason for the absence, I suppose, is the slavish adherence to first-order logic in too much of the tradition of semantical analysis of natural language. A semantics that fits more hand in glove with the syntax of the language is required to generate the proper feeling for rules of inference, even though, as a technical tour de force, translation back and forth into a formal language is possible.

My own program of research in the philosophy of language is firmly laid out in broad outline, if not in all details. I want to understand in the same way I believe I now understand quantifier words the many other common function words in English. I have already spent some time on the definite article and the possessive preposition *of*, and I would like to do the same for the other high-frequency prepositions like *to, in, for, with, on, at, by*, and *from* – I have listed these prepositions in their order of frequency of occurrence in a large corpus collected by Kucera and Francis (1967). The frequency of these simple prepositions is among the highest of any words in English but their semantical theory is as yet in very unsatisfactory state. Detailed analysis of their semantics is undoubtedly too empirical a problem for many philosophers deeply interested in language. I do not know whose work it is supposed to be – perhaps the empirical flavor of it seems antithetical to what philosophy should be like – but my own empirical bent in philosophy is nowhere more clearly reflected than in my attitude toward the philosophy of language. I do not think it is the only task, but for me it is a primary task, to provide a formal analysis that is faithful to at least the main function words in English when used in a serious and systematic way – I would of course like to have a theory for all possible uses but that seems out of reach at the present time. Frege himself had little to say about such matters and seemed rather suspicious of natural language as a vehicle for communicating exact thoughts. This same Fregean attitude has continued to hold an important place in the philosophy of language, but it should be apparent that I consider this aspect of Fregean philosophy a clear and definite mistake. I can think of no more appropriate task for philosophers of language than to reach for an exact and complete understanding of the prepositions I just mentioned, quantifier words, the tenses of simple verbs, and the like. As long as there is one definite intuitive usage that remains semantically unanalyzed, we have not completed the main task of any semantical theory of language. I do want to emphasize how complex and subtle I consider this task to be. I am sure it will continue to be an active topic in philosophy a hundred years from now.

Education and Computers

In the section on mathematical concept formation in children I mentioned the beginning of my interests in education in 1956 when my oldest child, Patricia, entered kindergarten. I cited there the work in primary-school geometry. An effort, also noted but briefly, that was much more sustained on my part was work in the basic elementary-school mathematics curriculum. This occupied a fair portion of my time between about 1956 and the middle of the sixties and led to publication of a basic elementary-school mathematics textbook series, *Sets and Numbers*, which was one of the more radical of the 'new math' efforts. Unlike many of my colleagues in mathematics and science who became interested in school curriculum after Sputnik, I had a genuine interest in the psychological and empirical aspects of learning and a traditional interest in knowing what had been done before.

When I began working on the foundations of physics after graduate school, I was shocked at the absence of what I would call traditional scholarship in the papers of philosophers like Reichenbach that I read, or even more of physicists who turned to philosophical matters such as

Bridgman and Campbell. There was little or no effort to know anything about the previous serious work in the field. I found this same attitude to be true of my colleagues from the sciences who became interested in education. They had no desire to know anything about prior scholarship in education.

I found I had a real taste for the concrete kinds of questions that arise in organizing a large-scale curriculum activity. I shall not attempt to list all the aspects of this work here, but since, beginning in the mid-fifties, I have written a large number of research papers concerned with how students learn elementary mathematics and I have had a fairly large number of students from education or psychology write dissertations in this area. Most of the work in the last decade or so has been within the context of computer-assisted instruction, to which I now turn.

Computer-assisted instruction
In the fall of 1962, on the basis of conversations with Lloyd Morrisett, Richard Atkinson and I submitted a proposal to the Carnegie Corporation of New York for the construction of a computer-based laboratory dedicated to the investigation of learning and teaching. The proposal was funded in January 1963 and the laboratory began operation in the latter part of that year as computing equipment that was ordered earlier in the year arrived and was installed. The laboratory was initially under the direction of an executive committee consisting of Atkinson, Estes, and me. In addition, John McCarthy of the Department of Computer Science at Stanford played an important role in the design and activation of the laboratory. In fact, the first computer facilities were shared with McCarthy and his group.

From a research standpoint, one of my own strong motivations for becoming involved in computer-assisted instruction was the opportunity it presented of studying subject-matter learning in the schools under conditions approximating those that we ordinarily expect in a psychological laboratory. The history of the first five years of this effort, through 1968, has been described in great detail – probably too much detail for most readers – in two books (1968a, 1972a) and in a large number of articles. I shall restrict myself here to a few general comments.

To some extent those initial hopes have been realized of obtaining school-learning data of the sort one expects to get in the laboratory. Massive analyses of data on elementary-school mathematics have been presented in my own publications, including the two books listed above, and a comparable body of publications has issued from the work of

Atkinson and his colleagues on initial reading. My own experience has been that even a subject as relatively simple as elementary-school mathematics is of unbounded complexity in terms of understanding the underlying psychological theory of learning and performance. Over the past several years I have found myself moving away from the kind of framework that is provided by stimulus sampling theory and that has been so attractive to me for so many years. The new ideas are more cognitive in character and organized around the concept of procedures or programs as exemplified, for instance, in a simple register machine, that is, a simple idealized computer with a certain number of registers and a small, fixed number of instructions (1973c). I think that the ideas of stimulus sampling theory still have importance in terms of learning, even in the context of such procedures or programs, but certainly there is a shift in conceptual interest characteristic not only of my own work but also of that of a great many psychologists originally devoted to learning.

One of my initial interests in computer-assisted instruction was the teaching of logic at the elementary-school level and subsequently at the college level. Once complexity of this level is reached, psychological theory is in a more difficult spot in terms of providing appropriate conceptual tools for the analysis of student behavior. Currently my work in computer-assisted instruction is almost entirely devoted to university-level courses, and we are struggling to understand how to analyze data from the sorts of proofs or logical derivations students give in the first logic course or in the course in axiomatic set theory that follows it.

Although there are many questions about the psychology of learning and performance in elementary-school mathematics that I do not understand, still I feel that I have a relatively deep conceptual grasp of what is going on and how to think about what students do in acquiring elementary mathematical skills. This is not at all the case for skills of logical inference or mathematical inference, as exemplified in the two college-level courses I have mentioned. We are still floundering about for the right psychological framework in which to investigate the complete behavior of students in these computer-based courses.

There are other psychological and educational aspects of the work in computer-assisted instruction that have attracted a good deal of my attention and that I think are worth mentioning. Perhaps the most important is the extent to which I have been drawn into the problems of evaluation of student performance. I have ended up, in association with my colleagues, in trying to conceive and test a number of different models of evaluation, especially for the evaluation of performance in the basic skills of mathematics and reading in the elementary school. Again I will not try to survey the various papers we have published except to mention the work that I think is probably intellectually the most interesting and which is at the present time best reported in Suppes, Fletcher, and Zanotti (1976f), in which we introduce the concept of a student trajectory. The first point of the model is to derive from qualitative assumptions a differential equation for the motion of students through the course, initially the drill-and-practice supplementary work in elementary mathematics given at computer terminals. The constants of integration of the differential equation are individual constants of integration, varying for individual students. On the basis of the estimation of the constants of integration we have been able to get remarkably good fits to individual trajectories through the curriculum. (A trajectory is a function of time, and the value of the function is grade placement in the course at a given time.) The development of these ideas has taken me back to ways of thinking about evaluation that are close to my earlier work in the foundations of physics.

Research on computer-assisted instruction has also provided the framework within which the large-scale empirical work on first-language learning in children has taken place. Without the sophisticated computer facilities available to me at Stanford it would not have been possible to pursue these matters in such detail and on such a scale. Even more essentially, the presence of a sophisticated computer system in the Institute for Mathematical Studies in the Social Sciences has led to the computer-based approach to the problems of language learning and performance mentioned earlier. One of our objectives for the future is to have a much more natural interaction between student and computer program in the computer-based courses we are concerned with. Out of these efforts I believe we shall also come to a deeper understanding of not only how computer programs can best handle language but also how we do, in fact, handle it. (Part of this search for naturalness has led to intensive study of prosodic features of spoken speech and how to reproduce them in computer hardware and software.)

I have not yet conveyed in any vivid sense the variety of conceptual and technical problems of computer-assisted instruction that I have tried to deal with in collaboration with my colleagues since 1963. This is not the place to undertake a systematic review of these problems, most of which have been dealt with extensively in other publications. I do, however, want to convey the view that the best work is yet to be done and will require solution of formidable intellectual problems. The central task is one well described by Socrates long ago in Plato's dialogue *Phaedrus*. Toward the end of this dialogue, Socrates emphasizes that the written word is but a pale image of the spoken; the highest form of intellectual discourse is to be found neither in written works or prepared speeches but in the give and take of spoken arguments that are based on knowledge of the truth. Until we have been able to reach the standard set by Socrates, we will not have solved the deepest problems in the instructional use of computers. How far we shall be able to go in having computer programs and accompanying hardware that permit free and easy spoken interaction between the learner and the instructional program is not possible to forecast with any reasonable confidence, for we are too far from yet having solved simple problems of language recognition and understanding.

At the present time we are only able to teach well skills of mathematics and language, but much can be done, and it is my conviction that unless we tackle the problems we can currently handle we will not move on to deeper solutions in the future. Because I am able to teach all my own undergraduate courses in a thoroughly computer-based environment, I now have, at the time of writing this essay, the largest teaching load, in terms of number of courses, of any faculty member at Stanford. During each term I offer ordinarily two undergraduate courses, one in logic and one in axiomatic set theory, both of which are wholly taught at computer terminals. In addition, I offer either one or two graduate seminars. As I have argued elsewhere on several occasions, I foresee that computer technology will be one of the few means by which we can continue to offer highly technical and specialized courses that ordinarily draw low enrollment, because of the budgetary pressures that exist at all American universities and that will continue unremittingly throughout the remainder of this century. Before I am done I hope to add other computer-based courses in relatively specialized areas, such as the foundations of probability and the foundations of measurement. The enrollment in one of these courses will ordinarily consist of no more than five students. I shall be able to offer them only because I can offer them simultaneously. My vision for the teaching of philosophy is that we should use the new technology of computers to return to the standard of dialogue and intimate discourse that has such a long and honored tradition in philosophy. Using the technology appropriately for prior preparation, students should come to seminars ready to talk and argue. Lectures should become as passé as the recitation methods of earlier times already have.

In 1967, when computer-assisted instruction was still a very new educational technology, I organized with Richard Atkinson and others a small company, Computer Curriculum Corporation, to produce courses in the basic skills that are the main focus of elementary-school teaching. In retrospect, it is now quite clear that we were ahead of our times and were quite lucky to survive the first five or six years. Since about 1973 the company has prospered, and I have enjoyed very much my part in that development. I find that the kind of carefully thought out and tough decisions required to keep a small business going suits my temperament well.

I have not worked in education as a philosopher. I have published only one paper in the philosophy of education and read a second one, as yet unpublished, on the aims of education, at a bicentennial symposium. Until recently I do not think I have had any interesting ideas about the philosophy of education but I am beginning to think about these matters more intensely and expect to have more to say in the future.

Philosophy and Science

From the standpoint of research I think of myself primarily as a philosopher of science, but to a degree that I think is unusual among professional philosophers I have had over the period of my career strong scientific interests. Much of this scientific activity could not in fact be justified as being of any direct philosophical interest. But I think the influence of this scientific work on my philosophy has been of immeasurable value. I sometimes like to descibe this influence in a self-praising way by claiming that I am the only genuinely empirical philosopher I know. It is surprising how little concern for scientific details is to be found in the great empirical tradition in philosophy. It has become a point with me to cite scientific data and not just scientific theories whenever it seems pertinent. I recently made an effort to find any instances in which John Dewey cited particular scientific data or theories in his voluminous writings. About the only place that I found anything of even a partially detailed character was in the early psychology textbook written in the 19th century. When it comes to data, almost the same can be said of Bertrand Russell. It is especially the case that data from the social and behavioral sciences are seldom used in any form by philosophers. In my monograph on causality (1970a) I deliberately introduced detailed data from psychological experiments to illustrate some subtle points about causality. In a recent paper on distributive justice (1977a) I went so far as to calculate Gini coefficients for the distribution of salaries at the various professorial ranks at Stanford and several other universities.

Set-theoretical methods.

One of the positions in the philosophy of science for which I am known is my attitude toward formalization. In various papers I have baptized this attitude with the slogan "to axiomatize a scientific theory is to define a set-theoretical predicate." A large number of my papers have used such methods, and I continue to consider them important. I should make clear that I am under no illusion that in any sense this method originated with me. My distinctive contribution has been to push for these methods in dealing with empirical scientific theories; the methods themselves have been widely used and developed in pure mathematics in this century. To a large extent, my arguments for set-theoretical methods are meant to be a constructive criticism of the philosophical tendency to restrict formal methods of analysis to what can be done conveniently within first-order logic.

I do not think of set-theoretical methods as providing any absolute kind of clarity or certainty of results independent of this particular point in the history of such matters. They constitute a powerful instrument that permits us to communicate in a reasonably objective way the structure of important and complicated theories. In a broad spirit they represent nothing really new; the axiomatic viewpoint that underlies them was developed to a sophisticated degree in Hellenistic times. Explicit use of such methods provides a satisfactory analysis of many questions that were in the past left vaguer than they need to be. A good example would be their use in the theory of measurement to establish appropriate isomorphic relations between qualitative empirical structures and numerical structures.

The many recent results in the foundations of set theory showing the independence of the continuum hypothesis and related assertions are reminiscent of what happened in geometry with the proof of the independence of the parallel postulate. But, as Kreisel has repeatedly urged, the parallel postulate is independent in second-order formulations of geometry having a strong continuity axiom, whereas the continuum hypothesis is not independent in second-order formulations of set theory. The great variety of recent results in the foundations of set theory have not really affected the usefulness of set-theoretical methods in the analysis of problems in the philosophy of science, and I am certain such methods will continue to be valuable for many years to come.

At one time I might have been upset by the prospect of moving away from set-theoretical methods to other approaches, for example, the kind of deeply computational viewpoint characteristic of contemporary computer science, but now I see such developments as inevitable and indeed as healthy signs of change. It seems likely that the theory of computation will be much more fundamental to psychology, for example, than any development of set-theoretical methods.

Schematic character of knowledge
In 1974, I gave the Hägerström lectures in Uppsala, Sweden, entitled *Probabilistic Metaphysics* (1974a). In those lectures I took as my starting point Kant's criticism of the old theology; my purpose was to criticize various basic tenets of what I termed the new theology. The five most important are these:

1. The future is uniquely determined by the past.
2. Every event has its sufficient determinate cause.
3. Knowledge must be grounded in certainty.
4. Scientific knowledge can in principle be made complete.
5. The grounds of rational belief and action can be made complete.

It is not appropriate here to develop in detail my arguments against determinism, certainty, and completeness, but it is my conviction that an important function of contemporary philosophy is to understand and to formulate as a coherent world view the highly schematic character of modern science and the highly tentative character of the knowledge that is its aim. The tension created by a pluralistic attitude toward knowledge and skepticism about achieving certainty is not, in my judgment, removable. Explicit recognition of this tension is one aspect of recent historically oriented work in the philosophy of science that I like.

It seems evident (to me) that philosophy has no special methods separate from those of science and ordinary life and has no special approaches to problems of inquiry. What makes a problem philosophical is not some peculiar intrinsic feature of the problem but its place as a fundamental problem in a given discipline or in some cases the paradoxical qualities it focuses on and brings to the surface. I am sometimes thought of as a primarily formalist philosopher of science, but I want to stress that at least as much of my scientific activity has been spent on detailed data analysis as it has on the construction of formal theories. My attitudes toward induction and the foundations of statistics, for example, have been conditioned by the extensive work in applied statistics I have done as part of other research efforts in psychology and in education.

I pointed out earlier that I thought my work in the foundations of physics was not as significant as the work in psychology because of the absence of an original scientific component. It is one of my regrets that I have not been able to do more in physics, expecially in terms of empirical data. I have together with my students pursued certain questions of data in physics with some persistence and great pleasure. If I had the time and energy to write my own ideal book on the philosophical foundations of quantum mechanics, it would present a rigorous and detailed analysis of the relevant data as well as of the theory.

I was especially pleased to receive in 1972 the Distinguished Scientific Award of the American Psychological Association in recognition of my activities as a psychologist. This dual role of philosopher and scientist would not suit everyone's taste but in my own case it has been a happy one for the vitality of my intellectual life.

III. Personal Reflections

My entire academic career has been spent at Stanford, so I have divided this section into three periods: the first five years at Stanford, the next ten, and the last twelve. What I intend is to make some more general and more personal remarks in this part of the essay and especially to comment, beyond the remarks made earlier, on some of the people who have had an influence on me.

I came to Stanford in 1950 immediately upon receiving my PhD from Columbia and I have remained here without interruption. I have had the usual sabbaticals and I have traveled a great deal, perhaps more than most of my academic colleagues, but still I have remained relatively fixed at Stanford and undoubtedly will do so throughout the remainder of my career.

1950–1955

I have already commented on the influence that McKinsey and Tarski had on me during my first years at Stanford. From another direction, as I have already mentioned, I was strongly influenced by working with David Blackwell and M. A. Girshick on their book, *Theory of Games and*

Statistical Decisions (1954). Working with them I learned a lot about both mathematical statistics and decision theory that was very useful to me later. I also began at this time working with Herman Rubin in the Department of Statistics, and I learned a great deal from Rubin, who has perhaps the quickest mathematical mind I have ever had the pleasure to interact with in any extended way. His error rate is reasonably high by ordinary standards, but the speed and depth of his reactions to a problem posed are incomparably good. During this period I also learned a great deal from my colleague in philosophy, Donald Davidson, and began with him the joint work in decision theory I mentioned earlier. In many ways we nicely complemented each other, for he comes at philosophical problems from a different direction and from a different background than I do, but our common agreement on matters of importance was more than sufficient to give us a good basis for collaboration.

I remember these early years at Stanford with great pleasure. I was working hard and intensely and absorbing a great deal about a great many different things. On the other hand, it is useful to say something about how slow one can be in taking in new ideas. I learned much from Blackwell and Girshick and also from Rubin about the foundations of statistics, but as I look back on the splendid opportunity that was available to me in working with the three of them it does not seem to me that I got the kind of grip on the subject that I feel I have acquired since that time. I cannot help but feel that an opportunity was wasted and that a delay of years was imposed by my failure to reach a deeper understanding at that time. I think one of the difficulties with my earlier work is that I did not sufficiently appreciate the necessity of getting a strong intuitive or conceptual feeling for a subject. I probably tended to operate in too formal a manner, at least so it seems to me now in retrospect. All the same, some of my best papers were written in this period, and I do not want to sound overly negative about all that I had the opportunity to learn and do in those early years.

1956–1965

I have already mentioned the important influence of Estes during the year 1955–1956 at the Center for Advanced Study in the Behavioral Sciences. The continuation of the work in learning with applications to multiperson interactions and to mathematical concept formation in children was intellectually a major part of my life during the ten years ending in 1965. The work with Estes continued; we spent many summers together. We planned a monograph as the outgrowth of our work but for various reasons did not complete it. We did write the two long technical reports that were eventually published in shortened form as papers. But the extent of Estes's influence on my thinking during this period is underestimated by referring simply to the publication of two papers.

In the summer of 1957 there was a Social Science Research Council workshop, or rather collection of workshops, at Stanford. An outgrowth of the workshop on learning was the volume *Studies in Mathematical Learning Theory* (1959), edited by R. R. Bush and W. K. Estes, in which I published several papers, including the first paper with Estes. Perhaps the most important intellectual event for me that summer was the encounter with Duncan Luce and the famous 'red cover' report that later was published by Luce as his classical book *Individual Choice Behavior* (1959). He and I had great arguments about the exact interpretation of his axioms. I initially thought he had wrongly formulated his central choice axiom but he succeeded in persuading me otherwise, and out of those first encounters has grown a strong personal friendship and a large amount of collaborative work.

Although during this time I published two logic textbooks, *Introduction to Logic* (1957a) and *Axiomatic Set Theory* (1960a), in this ten-year period more than any other time in my career most of my effort was devoted to psychological research rather than to work in philosophy. I have already mentioned a good many of the individual psychologists I had the pleasure of working with in these years.

Another important influence on me was interaction with Dana Scott over several years, beginning with the period when he was an undergraduate at Berkeley and carrying through intermittently until he joined the faculty at Stanford some years later. Among mathematical logicians I have known, Scott is unusual in possessing a natural taste for philosophical problems and great interest in their analysis. We wrote only one paper together (1958b), but our conversations about a range of intellectual matters have extended over many years. Scott has the kind of clarity typical of logicians put at an early enough age in the Tarski mold. In some ways I am definitely less compulsive about clarity than I was in the days when I was working with McKinsey and later with Scott. Whatever one may say about the psychological healthiness of reducing compulsiveness of this kind, I am not at all sure it has been a good thing intellectually. It is perhaps an inevitable aspect of my widening intellectual interests since the late fifties.

50

In the last several years of this period, one of the strongest influences on my own work was the succession of able graduate students who wrote doctoral dissertations under my guidance and with whom I often collaborated. I mention (in chronological order) especially Helena Kraemer, Jean Donio, Barry Arnold, M. Frank Norman, and Paul Holland, all of whom took degrees with me in the Department of Statistics at Stanford and all of whom were concerned with mathematical or statistical problems in the foundations of learning theory. (Since 1960 I have had a joint appointment in the Departments of Philosophy and Statistics.) During the same period Michael Levine worked on a dissertation in psychology, which he completed in a formal sense a year or two later. Both Michael Levine and Frank Norman were as graduate students great sticklers for mathematical precision and correctness of formulation of theorems and proofs. I remember well the pleasure they took in correcting any mistakes I made in my graduate course on mathematical learning theory.

By the end of this period my attention was moving to the kinds of psychological questions, many of them applied, that arose in connection with computer-assisted instruction, and, on the other hand, I began to return to a more intense consideration of purely methodological problems in the philosophy of science. This does not mean that my interest in psychological research ended but rather that the 'learning theory' period running from 1955 to 1963 was reaching a natural end.

At the end of this period Duncan Luce and I undertook to write a long chapter on preference, utility, and subjective probability for Volume III of the *Handbook of Mathematical Psychology*. Writing this long article introduced me to Luce's awesome habits of work. Very few people I know are able to meet deadlines for completing a piece of work on time; practically no one is able to complete an agreed-to assignment in advance of the deadline. Luce is one of the few that can; but it is not simply the meeting of the deadline that is impressive, it is his clear and relentless pursuit of the details of a particular theory or argument. I learned a great deal from him in writing this long survey article and have continued to do so. As the impact of his book *Individual Choice Behavior* has shown, he has a superb gift for simple formulation of quite general concepts and laws of behavior.

One important event for my own work and life that took place during this period was the founding, together with Kenneth Arrow, of the Institute for Mathematical Studies in the Social Sciences at Stanford. Stanford was then administered in a sufficiently informal way that it is not easy to peg the exact date on which the Institute was formed. It was a natural outgrowth of the Applied Mathematics and Statistics Laboratory, which had been put together in the late forties by Albert H. Bowker, now Chancellor at the University of California at Berkeley, to provide an organizational framework and an intellectual home for a wide range of work in applied mathematics and statistics. My own research began there in the summers, starting with the apprenticeship to Blackwell and Girshick mentioned earlier. The forming of the Institute followed in the late fifties. I have continued to direct the Institute since 1959, and it has been a pleasant and constructive home for most of my research efforts since that date.

It was also during this period that I had my one serious flirtation with university administration. I was a half-time Associate Dean of the School of Humanities and Sciences at Stanford for three years and during the last term, the fall of 1961, Acting Dean. During this period I had several opportunities to assume full-time administrative positions at Stanford and some offers to do so elsewhere. I enjoyed the administrative work during this period and think that I have some flair for it, but certainly one of the wisest decisions I have personally ever made was to move away from administration and back into a regular position of teaching and research.

During this period I would probably have left Stanford except for the continued support of Bowker, first when he was Chairman of the Department of Statistics and Director of the Applied Mathematics and Statistics Laboratory, and later when he was Graduate Dean. He more than anybody else was responsible for creating for me an intellectual atmosphere at Stanford and a context for constructive research that have been so attractive that for many years I have not thought seriously about leaving.

1966–1978

To continue this theme of administration as I move into the final period of these personal reflections, I have found that the large-scale computer activities on which we embarked in 1963 have turned out to be a sizable administrative problem in their own right. At the peak of our activities in 1967–1968 we had almost 200 persons, including staff, research associates and graduate students, involved in the Institute. The activity is much smaller now and I am thankful for that, but it continues to be a relatively complex affair and demands, as it has demanded since 1963, a fair share of my time. I do not regret the time spent, for my temperament is such that I would be restless in a purely sendentary life of paper-and-pencil research. The complex problems of running a computer operation on the frontiers of the technology currently available have provided just the right kind of stimulation to keep me contented and not inclined to seek administrative outlets of a more extensive nature, except those already mentioned at Computer Curriculum Corporation.

The efforts in computer-assisted instruction during these last ten years have been in association with a very large number of people, too many to mention here. My numerous joint publications in this area provide partial evidence of the extent of this collaboration, but I should also mention the many extremely able young programmers and engineers with whom I have worked and who have contributed so much to our efforts. At first I did not rightly appreciate the important role that able technical people can play and indeed must play in any successful research effort involving complex hardware and software. I had in the past heard such stories from my physics friends, but this was my first opportunity to learn the lesson firsthand. It is humbling to direct a complex activity in which you know that you yourself are not competent in most of the aspects of the operation. Large-scale research and development work has this character; I am not entirely happy with it. Increasingly in parts of my own research I have enjoyed working alone, but this is certainly not true of the work in computer-assisted instruction as it is not true of my experimental work in psychology.

Also, there are certain kinds of extended efforts that I would simply not be capable of carrying through on my own. I have in mind especially the effort I have engaged in jointly with David Krantz, Duncan Luce, and Amos Tversky in the writing of our two-volume treatise, *Foundations of Measurement*. This has been my longest collaborative effort, and I am pleased to say that we are still all speaking to each other.

Friendships that extend over many years have not been a topic I have emphasized in this essay, but a number have been important to me. One sad fact is that after staying at Stanford so many years I find that all of the persons with whom I formed relatively close personal ties in the 1950s have now departed. This includes Albert Bowker, now at Berkeley, Donald Davidson, now at the University of Chicago, William Estes, now at Rockefeller University, and Richard Atkinson, currently Director of the National Science Foundation. There are, of course, a number of individuals on the campus, especially colleagues in Philosophy and in the Institute for Mathematical Studies in the Social Sciences, that I work with and enjoy interacting with, but most of them are a good deal younger and are not friends of many years standing. Jaakko Hintikka has been my part-time colleague at Stanford for many years. We have edited several books together and given a number of joint seminars that have been rewarding and pleasurable. On several occasions, Julius Moravcsik also participated in these seminars and I have benefited from my discussions with him about the philosophy of language. A third colleague in philosophy who has been at Stanford for many years but increasingly on a full-time basis is Georg Kreisel, and in the last few years we have developed the habit of talking extensively with each other about a wide range of topics. I value the regular round of talks with Kreisel and look forward to their continuing in the years ahead. Although Kreisel primarily works in the foundations of mathematics, he has a long-standing interest in the foundations of physics. He is especially good at giving broad general criticisms of the first drafts of manuscripts on almost any subject about which I write, and I try to do the same for him.

I close with some brief remarks about my personal life. I was married to my first wife, Joanne Farmer, in 1946, and together we had three children, John, Deborah, and Patricia, who at the beginning of 1978 are 17, 20, and 26 years of age; Joanne and I were divorced in 1969. In 1970, I married Joan Sieber and we were divorced in 1973.

Since 1956 I have lived on the Stanford campus, and since 1961 in the house that I now occupy. It is a large, comfortable house, built in 1924, and is located in the old residential section, San Juan Hill, on a spacious lot. I feel completely anchored to Stanford and the Bay Area. It is unlikely that I will ever move anywhere else. All in all, I feel fortunate to have had the kind of life I have had for the past twenty-seven years at Stanford. Another twenty of the same sort is more than is reasonable to ask for, but I plan to enjoy as many as I can.

Stanford,
March, 1978.

Note

1. There is a certain amount of overlap in the content of this self-profile and an autobiography I wrote earlier (1978a), focused on my interest in psychology. I am indebted to Georg Kreisel for a number of useful criticisms. I also wish to thank Lofti Zodeh for the photograph which forms the frontispiece of this volume.

References

Blackwell, D., and Girshick, M. A. (1954) *Theory of Games and Statistical Decisions*, Wiley, New York.

Brown, R. (1973) *A First Language*, Harvard University Press, Cambridge, Mass.

Bush, R. R., and Estes, W. K. (Eds.) (1959) *Studies in Mathematical Learning Theory*, Stanford University Press, Stanford, Calif.

Estes, W. K. (1950) 'Toward a Statistical Theory of Learning', *Psychological Review* **57**, 94–107.

Hamburger, H., and Wexler, K. (1975) 'A Mathematical Theory of Learning Transformational Grammars', *Journal of Mathematical Psychology* **12**, 137–177.

Hull, C. L. (1943) *Principles of Behavior*, Appleton-Century-Crofts, New York.

Hull, C. L., Hovland, C. I., Ross, R.T., Hall, M., Perkins, D. T., and Fitch, F.B. (1940) *Mathematico-deductive Theory of Rote Learning*, Yale University Press, New Haven, Conn.

Kahneman, D., and Tversky, A. (1972) 'Subjective Probability: A Judgment of Representativeness', *Cognitive Psychology* **3**, 430–454.

Knuth, D. E. (1968) 'Semantics of Context-free Languages', *Mathematical Systems Theory* **2**, 127–131.

Koopman, B. O. (1940a) 'The Axioms and Algebra of Intuitive Probability', *Annals of Mathematics* **41**, 269–292.

Koopman, B. O. (1940b) 'The Bases of Probability', *Bulletin of the American Mathematical Society* **46**, 763–774. Reprinted in *Studies in Subjective Probability* (ed. by H. E. Kyburg and H. E. Smokler). Wiley, New York, 1964.

Kucera, H., and Francis, W. N. (1967) *Computational Analysis of Present-day American English*, Brown University Press, Providence, R. I.

Luce, R. D. (1959) *Individual Choice Behavior: A Theoretical Analysis*, Wiley, New York.

Mackey, G. W. (1963) *Mathematical Foundations of Quantum Mechanics*, Benjamin, New York.

Noll, W. (1964) 'Euclidean Geometry and Minkowskian Chronometry', *American Mathematical Monthly* **71**, 129–144.

Robb, A. A. (1936) *Geometry of Space and Time*, Cambridge University Press, Cambridge.

Savage, L. J. (1954) *The Foundations of Statistics*, Wiley, New York.

Sen, A. K. (1970) *Collective Choice and Social Welfare*, Holden Day, San Francisco.

Smith, R. L., Jr. (1972) 'The Syntax and Semantics of ERICA', Technical Report 185, Institute for Mathematical Studies in the Social Sciences, Psychology and Education Series, Stanford University.

Tarski, A. (1935) 'Der Wahrheitsbegriff in den formalisierten Sprachen', *Studia Philosophica* **1**, 261–405.

Tversky, A., and Kahneman, D. (1971a) 'Availability: A Heuristic for Judging Frequency and Probability', *ORI Research Bulletin* **11** (6).

Tversky, A., and Kahneman, D. (1971b) 'Belief in the Law of Small Numbers', *Psychological Bulletin* **76**(2) 105–110.

Whitehead, A. N., and Russell, B. (1913) *Principia Mathematica* (Vol. 3), Cambridge University Press, Cambridge.

Woods, J., and Walton, D. (1977) 'Post hoc, ergo propter hoc', *Review of Metaphysics* **30**, 569–593.

Zeeman, E. C. (1964) 'Causality Implies the Lorentz Group', *Journal of Mathematical Physics* **5**, 490–493.

PART TWO

CARLOS-ULISES MOULINES & JOSEPH D. SNEED

SUPPES' PHILOSOPHY OF PHYSICS

I. Introduction

Patrick Suppes has contributed to the philosophy of physics in a variety
of ways: directly in work on physical geometry, the axiomatic foundations
of classical and relativistic particle mechanics, and the foundations of
quantum mechanics; less directly in work on extensive measurement and
the general nature of empirical theories. At first glance, these contributions
appear diverse and essentially independent of each other. They appear
neither to be manifestations of an explicit, coherent approach to the philosophy of physics nor contributions to a systematic program of research
in the philosophy of physics. We believe this first impression is misleading.
In fact, there is a coherent approach to the philosophy of physics underlying these contributions. Though many of these contributions are important for what they say about specific, traditional problems in the philosophy of physics (e.g., the epistemological status of the concept of mass
in classical physics), we feel that their full significance cannot be appre-
ciated until they are viewed in the context of Suppes' more global views
about the nature of physical science and empirical science in general.
Thus our strategy in this paper is first to say something about Suppes'
general view of the structure of empirical science, second to see how this
general view leads to a 'research program' in the philosophy of physics
and finally to examine in detail some of Suppes' own contributions to this
research program.

II. Suppes' Philosophy of Science

Some may find it surprising that we attribute a *philosophy* of empirical

Bogdan, R.J. (Ed.) 'Patrick Suppes' 59–91.
Copyright © 1979 by D. Reidel Publishing Company, Dordrecht, Holland.

science to Suppes. His name is not among those – Carnap, Popper, Hempel; perhaps also Kuhn, Feyerabend and others – whom the general intellectual public views as representing major contemporary 'theories' about the nature of empirical science. Suppes has neither published a bulky general work on the philosophy of science nor made sweeping general pronouncements about the nature of empirical science. On the contrary, his philosophical work consists mainly (though surely not exclusively) of painstaking, detailed and highly technical analysis of concrete, specific scientific concepts and theories.

Indeed we find this focus on the concrete and specific indicative of one of the central features of Suppes' philosophy of science. For Suppes, the philosophy of science is not an *a priori* enterprise. A general, synoptic view of some branch of science (to say nothing of the *whole* of science) can only be afforded *after* most of the detailed analysis and reconstruction of its conceptual structure is completed. Philosophy of science in this style requires that *its* practitioners know as much, if not more, about the specific sciences they treat as the practitioners of these sciences themselves. Suppes' contributions to the philosophy of physics have intrinsic interest. But perhaps more important, they provide examples of a level of detail, rigor and precision in formulating problems in the philosophy of science that was uncommon in the early '50's (and regrettably not much more common today). In the work of Suppes, the philosophy of physics approaches the standards of rigor and precision that have become commonplace in the philosophy of mathematics. His commitment to "philosophical rigor commensurate with the rigor of the subject matter" is a cornerstone of Suppes' philosophical approach and may prove to be the most influential feature of his work in the philosophy of physics.

Even if it were true that the main significance of Suppes' work lies in the intrinsic interest of the specific problems he treats and the methodological examples they provide, it would be precipitous to conclude that there is no general view of the nature of empirical science underlying this work. Indeed one finds abundant evidence to the contrary. Scattered throughout Suppes' writings are numerous revealing, more or less explicit, remarks from which a systematic philosophy of science can be plausibly reconstructed. This reconstruction is the burden of the first part of our essay.

It is not difficult to discover the broad outlines of Suppes' research program in the philosophy of science. He states them quite explicitly, as early as 1954, in [24]. The program outlined there has been rather systematically pursued by Suppes, his students and co-workers for more than twenty years.

According to Suppes, philosophers of science have three main problem areas to deal with:

- reconstruction of given scientific theories;
- construction of realistic theories of measurement;
- the foundations of probability.

The first two problem areas (at least) are intimately interconnected. Understanding how Suppes views this connection is essential to understanding his work in non-stochastic physics. Suppes' work in the foundations of quantum mechanics seems most naturally viewed as belonging to the third problem area. Accordingly, we shall begin by considering separately Suppes' research program in the first two areas, its implications for the philosophy of physics and some examples of his contributions that fall into this category. We will then return to his contributions to the foundations of quantum mechanics.

Suppes is obviously not alone in thinking that reconstruction of empirical theories is a central task of the philosophy of science. Carnap and most other recent philosophers of science have shared this view. Suppes, however, differs from other philosophers in his conception of how this reconstruction is to be carried out. To see this difference clearly, one must first describe the more or less commonly shared view of the nature and motivation for reconstruction of empirical theories.

Unlike theories of pure mathematics, empirical theories are not easy to identify and distinguish from one another. It is not always clear what concepts and principles belong to one theory rather than another; which of these concepts are primitive and which are defined; which principles are derived from others. Further, it is not always clear how different theories are related to each other *and* to their applications – the features of the world they tell us about. Even in the physical sciences – usually regarded as paradigms of rigor – practicing scientists rarely express themselves professionally in ways that provide clear answers to questions like this. Yet, presumably, these are things one must know to answer even the most naive questions about an empirical theory; what does the theory say about the world? – what are the reasons for believing what it says is true?

Such ambiguity and fuzziness may be quite harmless in the literature of ongoing empirical sciences. Most philosopheres of science charitably assume that practicing scientists could – if they would just take the trouble – ultimately clear up these questions. Their working hypothesis is that empirical science is not irredeemably confused. The task of the reconstructive philosopher of science is to be clear where 'ordinary people' are not – to make coherent sense out of what practising empirical scientists say and do professionally. He must first identify empirical theories precisely, make explicit the logical relations among different theories and finally say how the theories relate to the 'outside world' they tell us about. Roughly a theory first must be identified and analysed in isolation; then its connections with other things must be illuminated.

A bit more precisely, one can formulate the aims of reconstructing emprical theories as:

> — clarifying the *internal structure* of an empirical theory;
> — providing a *semantics* for an empirical theory (clarifying its relation to something 'outside' itself).

The *semantical* task may be understood in two different ways. The semantics of a given theory T can be clarified by determining how T relates to *other theories* T_1, T_2, . . . which may have some kind of 'prior' epistemological status. This is in principle a feasible undertaking once these single theories have been identified and clarified – although the details in specific cases may be quite complicated. On the other hand, one may think that the semantics of T is not completely settled until some connection between T and some *entities that are not theories* (e.g., sense experiences, physical reality, actions or whatever) have also been reconstructed.

The second view appears now to be less popular among philosophers of science than it was twenty years ago even though the alternative that 'everything is theory' appears to lead to a sophisticated form of subjective idealism as unpalatable as the more common varieties. Despite their differences, *both* approaches to the semantical task for a *specific* theory may be expected to travel part of the way along the same road. Even if we require (or anticipate) that there is a non-theoretical 'outside' that is the ultimate semantical ground for T, this connection will not, in most cases, be straightforward. There will usually be a rather complicated network of mediating theories T_1, T_2, . . . between T and the non-theoretical 'outside.' The idealist and realist could productively work together in elucidating the logical connections among these mediating theories leaving their metaphysics temporarily in abeyance.

There is nothing specifically Suppesian about this formulation of the reconstructive aim of philosophy of science. It is the specific approach that

Suppes takes both to the problem of clarifying the internal structure of empirical theory and providing it with a semantics that differentiates his views from the mainstream of recent philosophy of science. Roughly, Suppes believes that the internal structure of an empirical theory is most illuminatingly revealed by axiomatization of the theory in set-theoretic terms. Once cast in this form, a semantics for the theory is provided by relating the given theory to other theories cast in the same form and ultimately grounding the semantics of the *quantitative* concepts in epistemologically prior theories of *qualitative* concepts through a realistic theory of fundamental measurement. This is to be contrasted with the mainstream view that the internal structure of a theory is to be revealed by an axiomatic theory in a formal language (usually first-order logic) and the semantics to be settled through providing a (perhaps partial) interpretation of the formal language (sometimes called coordinating definitions).

In the following sections we will discuss the 'Suppes Program' in more detail focusing on its implications for the philosophy of physics. For two reasons, the major part of our discussion will deal with the method of set-theoretic axiomatization. First, Suppes' contribution to the theory of measurement is treated at length in another article in this volume. Second, successful examples of carrying out the Suppes Program in physical sciences consist of set-theoretic axiomatizations of rather complicated "real-life" theories and the laying bare of relations among theories cast in this form. We know of no successful provision of the semantics for an interesting physical theory in the manner of the Suppes Program. However, our failure to emphasize the semantic aspect of the Suppes Program should not be taken to indicate that we do not believe it to be as important as clarifying of a theory's internal structure. Quite the contrary. It would be difficult to see why a set-theoretic axiomatization of an empirical theory would be of any interest in the absence of *some* way to provide it with a semantics. A fair assessment of the Suppes Program requires us to remember that it *has* a semantic part. We can of course question whether this part of the program is adequate.

III. Suppes' Program in the Philosophy of Physics

The Internal Structure of Physical Theories

Suppes' approach to clarifying the internal structure of an empirical theory might be described as 'formalistic.' This would be correct if by 'formalistic' one meant only that the approach employs formal, axiomatic systems. However, this description is rather uninformative in that it says nothing about what kind of formal axiomatic systems are employed and for what purposes they are used. Moreover, the description is somewhat misleading in that it suggests that the Suppes approach is not essentially different from that of Carnap and his followers (see for example [13]).

The 'formalism' of Suppes differs from that of the Carnap school in two important respects. First, it is less synoptic in its scope and second, it is not tied to the method of axiomatization within a formal language. The 'strict' formalism of the Carnap school is 'synoptic' in that the aim of reconstructive philosophy of science is seen as a comprehensive reconstruction of all scientific knowledge exhibiting its grounding in some epistemically unassailable claims. Piecemeal reconstructions of *parts* of empirical science at a relatively high level of abstraction from perceptual data have not appeared to interest the Carnapians. Rather, they appear to have been primarily concerned since the publication of the *Aufbau* [4] with philosophical issues arising out of their own methodology. Their attitude seems to have been: "Just wait until we get our tools sharpened; then we'll get to work systematically on real emprical theories." In contrast, Suppes and his co-workers, together with others following their examples, have attempted to apply formal methods to clarifying the internal structure and relations among full-blown, highly abstract physical theories such as classical particle mechanics in the Newtonian [14] as well as the Lagrangian and Hamiltonian [10] formulations, special relativistic particle mechanics [26], classical rigid body mechanics [1], classical equilibrium thermodynamics [17], dealing with such questions as the epistemological status of 'mass' and 'force' in classical mechanics [14], the precise formulations of classical and relativistic invariance principles [15], [16], [19], [26] and the reduction relation between classical rigid body and particle mechanics [1].

It is, however, in the second respect that Suppes' 'formalism' differs most obviously from that of the Carnapians and indeed the mainstream of recent philosophy of science. A central tenet of this tradition is that the logical structure of empirical theories can be described using an axiomatic theory in some formal language. (Here 'axiomatic theory' is used in the sense of Tarski [40], and the formal language in question is usually taken to be first-order predicate logic). Many have apparently taken it to be a corollary of this view that *no* interesting questions about the logical structure of empirical theories can be answered *until* this structure is described by an axiomatic theory in a formal language. In contrast, Suppes has demonstrated that it is possible to formulate precise, interesting questions about real physical theories without the apparatus of a formal language. Suppes achieves this by employing the apparatus of informal (non-axiomatic, or naive) set-theory. Using set-theory instead of axicmatic theories in a formal language may be regarded as a weaker, but nevertheless expedient and adequate degree of formalization. The Bourbaki program has demonstrated the power and fruitfulness of informal set-theory as a universal language of mathematics. Suppes proposes to use informal set-theory as a universal language for empirical science as well.

The axiomatizations of physical theories Suppes provides using the apparatus of informal set-theory are 'abstract' in the sense of Hilbert. That is, the primitive concepts are regarded as 'implicitly' defined by the axioms in which they appear. No claim is made, as it is in the case of Euclid's axiomatization of geometry, that the axioms are, in some sense, self-evidently true. The question is rather whether they are 'true of' some particular physical objects and specific physical properties they have. The axiom system characterizes a class of 'models.' Roughly, it allows us to say that some physical systems – applications of the theory in question – *are in* this class of models.

In appearance, at least, Suppes-type axiomatizations of physical theories are much closer to those of working physicists – e.g., Newton's own formulation of classical particle mechanics and more recent efforts like Hamel's [6], or Carathéodory's axiomatization of thermodynamics [5] – than an axiomatization within a formal language would be. These axiomatizations fail, to differing degrees depending upon the specific example, to meet modern standards of logical rigor. Primitive concepts and axioms are sometimes not clearly identified; questions of independence of primitives and axioms are not carefully raised; the epistemological status of the axioms is often fuzzy; 'physical intuition' is sometimes employed as an inference rule in obtaining theorems. Yet is is not implausible to regard these early attempts to introduce axiomatic methods into physics as simply crude attempts to do what we now know how to do more precisely – characterize the class of models for the theory. Suppes himself comments on this 'model theoretic' viewpoint in [27].

There does not appear to be any opposition in principle between employing axiomatic theories in a formal language and informal set-theoretic axiomatizations to exhibit the internal structure of physical theories – some rather polemical statements of Suppes to the contrary notwithstanding.[1] The issue is a purely practical one: what is the most expedient way to exhibit enough of the logical structure of the theory to formulate and answer precisely the questions about the theory that concern us? It is reasonably clear that the construction of axiomatic theories in a formal language is more cumbersome and inconvenient than the free and informal use of set-theory and mathematics. One of the major merits of Suppes' work is to have demonstrated by example that informal set-theoretic axiomatization is – at least for some kinds of questions about physical theories – a fruitful alternative to axiomatization in a formal language. The obsession with constructing formal axiomatic systems appears to account for much of the remoteness of current philosophy of science from the philosophical problems in physical science. Suppes' work liberates us from this obsession by demonstrating that departure from the method of formal axiomatization does not entail a lapse into obscurantism.

To understand precisely what is at issue here it is necessary to say something more about why axiomatization of physical theories in a formal language is impractical.

First, non-trivial physical theories are formulated within portions of mathematical language which, in spite of being reasonably well defined, are not easy to formalize in first-order logic, and indeed *have not yet* been formalized in any formal language. Outstanding examples of those portions are: partial differential equations, matrix theory, tensor analysis. Before dealing with even such a simple physical theory as classical particle mechanics, we should have to assume that an enormous part of mathematics has already been formally axiomatized – which is obviously not the case; so we should have to do it ourselves or *wait*.

Second, physical theories are not constructed as isolated structures. They usually assume a lot of other theories – mathematical as well as physical, or even 'qualitative' theories. Their concepts and laws only make sense assuming that other concepts and laws of previous theories have already been adequately described. This is also true for purely mathematical theories, but not in the same degree and complexity as for physical theories. Consequently, should we characterize any physical theory, let us say, a theory of thermodynamics, as a formal axiomatic system, the whole cluster of presupposed theories (e.g., theories of mechanics, of physical geometry, of analysis, algebra, etc.) should already be at hand as formal axiomatic systems.

This issue is more problematic than it seems. It is not only a question of nasty work to be done. A deep methodological problem is involved too. We have already noted that relations between different physical theories are much more complicated than in the case of mathematical theories. This is especially true for presupposition-relations. It is many in cases not altogether clear which theory presupposes another. Such relations can only be cleared up *after* the different theories have been identified as single structures. But the strict formalistic methodology requires to know the relations first, and then to construct step by step the whole array of single theories as formal systems. There is a kind of pragmatic (not logical) vicious circle here; a circle which paralyzed the formal language approach in the case of complex physical theories.

Finally, there is some reason to think (see [22]) that even the set-theoretic axiomatizations provided by Suppes are only a first step in clarifying the internal structure of physical theories. Roughly, they characterize the conceptual core of the theory that is used to make specific empirical claims about the theory's intended applications. Even if we could capture the class of models of these axiom systems by an axiomatic system in some formal language, we would still have a piece to go in capturing, within the formal language, what the theory says about the world.

Despite these practical difficulties, there still appear to be questions about the internal structure of physical theories that cannot be handled by informal set-theoretic axiomatizations. Most obvious are classical metalogical questions such as completeness and decidability. But these questions do not appear to be particularly interesting in the case of physical theories. Most non-trivial physical theories appear to be both incomplete and undecidable. Suppes himself [36], has called attention to the possibilty that non-extensional or modal concepts may be required exhibiting the structure of some empirical theories. Indeed the device of "constraints" on theoretical function that the present authors found essential to the reconstruction of classical particle mechanics ([22], Chapter VI) or classical equilibrium thermodynamics [17] is, from the point of view of a formal language approach, an example of such a modal concept. It remains to be seen whether non-extensional formal languages can be profitably employed to deal with modalities in physical theories.

Another limitation on the set-theoretic approach becomes apparent when a distinction between theoretical and non-theoretical concepts is drawn (see ([22], Chapter I). This is the question of the so-called 'Ramsey eliminability' of the theoretical concepts in favor of the non-theoretical concepts. The theoretical, non-theoretical distinction relative to a given theory can be drawn within the set-theoretical formalism and the semantical role of the theoretical concepts described. Yet the question of whether that semantical role can be filled by the non-theoretical concepts, though it can be intuitively approached, cannot be answered satisfactorily within the set-theoretic formalism. (See [22], pp. 131–33 and [38].) Precisely how axiomatization within a formal language can resolve this philosophically important question for physical theories like classical particle mechanics and thermodynamics remains an open question at this time.

The Semantics of Physical Theories

Let us turn now to Suppes' views about how the internal structure of physical theories as revealed by a set-theoretic axiomatization is to be related to something outside the theory – how the structure is to be interpreted.

It is important to remember here that the entities Suppes offers us as characterizing the internal structure of physical theories are abstract axiomatic systems. In most interesting cases these structures will not be categorical. They will have many non-isomorphic models. More important, they will typically have many models that obviously have nothing to do with intended applications of the physical theory whose internal structure they describe. Generally and roughly, to provide a semantics for the theory in question is to describe the concrete, real physical systems that are claimed by the theory to be models for this structure.

More specifically, Suppes appears to believe that the semantics of a physical theory is ultimately fixed by singling out sets of concrete physical objects and qualitative relations among them whose extension is determined by observations, operations or experiments. Most interesting physical theories involve *quantitative* concepts (e.g., mass functions). Sometimes these may be interpreted simply by stipulating that one is to take as the values of the quantitative concept numbers obtained by calculation from quantitative concepts appearing in *other* physical theories (e.g., one may calculate the moment of inertia of a rigid body from the position of the particles comprising it and their masses). Reduction and/or *derived* measurement theories describe these connections. But ultimately there will come a point where some quantitative concepts are linked to qualitative concepts. This link is described by a fundamental measurement theory for the quantitative concept in question. For Suppes, fundamental measurement theories play a role analogous to co-ordinating definitions in early operationalism or meaning postulates in later logical empiricism (see [7]). On this view, theories of fundamental measurement are associated with every quantitative physical theory – though perhaps only through an intricate chain of derived measurement theories. These fundamental measurement theories are usually ignored by physicists. In the standard expositions of physical theories they are not even formulated in loose terms. A task of the philosopher in reconstructing the theory is to make explicit the theories of derived and fundamental measurement that are 'implicit' in the standard expositions of the theory. In doing this, the philosopher characterizes the intended models for the set-theoretic axiomatization of the theory – provides a semantics for the theory.

Theories of fundamental measurement used in this way must satisfy some intuitive adequacy conditions. These theories must be *realistic* in the sense that it is plausible to think of physicists actually having at hand the objects in their domains and actually being able to carry out enough operations or experiments on these objects to determine the extensions of the relations. During the second half of the 19th and the early part of the 20th century some philosophers and physicists (see for example [9] and [3]) made serious attempts to formulate precisely fundamental measurement theories for basic physical concepts such as length, time, mass, etc. These attempts were more or less successful but shared a common failing of being 'unrealistic'. Roughly, they treated measurement theories as highly idealized structures dealing with entities as abstract as the physical theories themselves. They required us to suppose that measuring rods of ever increasing length could be constructed or that locomotives could be placed on the pans of an analytical balance. While such idealizations may be permissible and even necessary at the higher levels of physical theory, they are unsatisfactory at the most fundamental semantical level. If we are to move from the very abstract level of physical theory down to the earth of the laboratory, then idealizations must stop somewhere. On this view, idealization should stop at the level of fundamental measurement.

It must be emphasized that the job of constructing realistic theories of fundamental measurement – once their philosophical importance has been recognized – is not a trivial one. Suppes' own work in the theory of measurement discussed elsewhere in this volume provides ample testimony to the technical difficulties involved in carrying out this program. We will not discuss these matters further here.

It appears to be Suppes' view that *all* quantitative concepts appearing in the set-theoretic axiomatization of a physical theory must be interpreted by going outside the theory in question – either by reduction, derived or fundamental measurement. The possibility that some of these concepts –

those that are 'theoretical' with respect to the given theory – could remain uninterpreted and yet be intelligibly (through a Ramsey-sentence-like device) used to say something about the remaining non-theoretical concepts which *are* interpreted in these ways is not mentioned in his writings. The present authors have shown elsewhere that this is, in fact, a plausible way to treat the concepts of mass and force in classical particle mechanics ([22], Ch. VI) and concepts such as entropy and thermodynamic temperature in classical equilibrium thermodynamics ([17]). We do not regard these results as in any way undermining the main thrust of the Suppes program. Rather, we believe they lend plausibility to the claim that physical theory ultimately rests on realistic fundamental measurement by showing how to deal with quantitative concepts that would be difficult (if not impossible) to relate to such measurement either directly or through a chain of reduction or derived measurement. Whether Suppes' program can in fact be carried through for the remaining non-theoretical concepts in these physical theories and others remains an open question at this time.

IV. The Reconstruction of Mechanics

It is convenient to regard a substantial part of the work of Suppes and his collaborators as piecemeal contributions to the broad enterprise of reconstructing the entire science of mechanics – identifying and describing precisely various mechanical theories and the relations among them. The work we have in mind is the axiomatizations of classical particle mechanics [14], relativistic kinematics [26], and rigid body mechanics [1] together with treatments of invariance principles in classical [15], [16], [19] and relativistic particle mechanics [26] and the reduction of rigid body mechanics to particle mechanics [1]. The most efficient way to comment on this reconstructive program in a limited space is to look in some detail at one part of it. We will focus our attention on the most easily accessible part – the treatment of classical particle mechanics. The full Suppes program for this fragment of mechanics consists of exhibiting the internal structure of classical particle mechanics and describing its semantics. The internal structure of classical particle mechanics is described in the set-theoretic axiomatization provided by McKinsey, Sugar and Suppes (hereafter referred to as the MSS axiomatization) [14]. The program (as yet uncompleted) of providing a semantics has been discussed by both

Suppes and his critics. We will consider in turn both these aspects of the program for classical particle mechanics.

The Internal Structure of Classical Particle Mechanics

The MSS axiomatization of classical particle mechanics takes particles and numerical valued position, mass and force functions on particles as primitive in defining a set-theoretic predicate ". . . is a system of classical particle mechanics." This, roughly speaking, identifies the class of things that *are* systems of particle mechanics. It sets the stage for further analytical work, proving theorems about systems of classical particle mechanics, defining interesting special cases where "special force laws hold" and investigating questions of independence of the primitive concepts.

That this work represents real progress can best be seen by comparing it with previous attempts to axiomatize classical particle mechanics. The best such attempts are Hamel's [6], Hermes' [8] and Simon's [20] axiomatizations. Hamel's axiomatization, although insightful, belongs to the informal working physicist's kind. Hermes' and Simon's work is more germane to the needs of the philosopher of science; it is more formal. However, from our point of view, it has an important shortcoming: it is philosophically biased. Both Hermes and Simon ascribe to a rather straightforward operationalism. For mechanics this means that they try to give a purely kinematical basis to the theory by defining the dynamical concepts in terms of the kinematical ones (i.e., to define mass and force in terms of position and time).

Several objections can be raised to this kind of approach:

First, it is not altogether clear why we should axiomatize mechanics by definitionally reducing its dynamical to its kinematical portion. That is, it is simply not clear that operationalism is the right view of theories. In any case, operationalistic (or otherwise) reductions are more profitably discussed *after* different physical theories have been identified.

Second, the theory axiomatized from an operationalistic point of view is not the same as the one usually called 'classical particle mechanics'. It is a more restrictive theory. Not all common applications of classical particle mechanics can be regarded as models of this operationalistic version. In the case of Hermes, the restriction is very strong. The models allowed by the theory are inelastic collisions only. Simon's axiomatization is not so restrictive, but it still cannot account for all generally acknowledged applications of classical particle mechanics. All of Simon's systems of particles must be dynamically isolated, that is, they must be models of momentum-conserving mechanics, and not just classical particle mechanics. Many intended applications of classical particle mechanics are certainly not isolated systems. Besides, Simon adds a curious axiom to the usual axioms of an isolated system (conservation of linear momentum and angular momentum): that the system be *holomorphic* (that is, it should not contain any isolated subsystem). This is, of course, still more restrictive and it means a radical departure from the theory as it is usually expounded.

Third, in order to get their operationalistic version of the theory, both Hermes and Simon introduce certain 'physical hypotheses', whose logical status is rather dubious – leaving aside the question of their physical plausibility. For example, Hermes asserts that "all pairs of particles have collided sometime" ([8] p, 287). Simon's operational determination of mass depends on choosing a unique system of reference. Therefore, Simon resorts to a reformulation of Mach's principle. The system of the fixed stars *is* dynamically isolated (physical hypothesis). Consequently, it *should* be taken as the universal system of reference (methodological principle). Moreover, the operationalistic definition of mass by kinematical means does not imply by itself that the thus determined mass-values are always positive. This is, again, a 'physical hypothesis' to be added.

It is not altogether clear what status such physical hypotheses and methodological principles have within an axiomatic system. The question is: should they be taken as axioms of the theory or should they not? To put it in other terms: in order to *identify* the theory, is it necessary to state those special hypotheses? It seems that neither Hermes nor Simon are willing to take their physical hypotheses as axioms of the theory (and, of course, even less as definitions). It should also be clear that such hypotheses are not intended as semantical principles similar to Carnap's meaning postulates. They are statements about some portion of the world (terrestrial balls or remote stars).

The main trouble with Hermes' and Simon's axiomatizations is that they try to deal simultaneously with two different kinds of questions about a given theory. They try to reconstruct its logical structure and at the same time to clear up semantical questions about the operational meaning of the concepts involved and about the empirical applicability of the theory. From a methodological point of view, this is confusing.

On the other hand, Hermes and Simon had a purpose in intimately connecting both kinds of questions. In some sense, they showed that a physical theory cannot be formally reconstructed in the same way as a purely mathematical theory. This is an important insight. We shall return to this point below.

The MSS axiomatization is free from difficulties of this kind. Its sole aim is to describe formally the internal structure of classical particle mechanics. The structure of the theory is determined by the conditions its five primitives (particles, time, position, mass and component force) must fulfill plus the single fundamental law (Newton's Second Law) which has to be satisfied in all applications of the theory. All further mechanical laws are conceived as restrictions of this basic core introduced to deal with special applications. No unique model of the theory is assumed (as in the case of Simon). Anything can count as an intended model, so long as it satisfies the set-theoretical predicate defining classical particle mechanics.

To show the adequacy of the axiomatization, some theorems, which are significant for philosophical and/or physical reasons, are derived; for example: the mechanical version of determinism, the equivalence of a system of many particles with a system of a single particle located at the center of mass of the system, and the possibility of embedding every system of classical particle mechanics in a system of Newtonian particle mechanics (i.e., a system satisfying, in addition, Newton's Third Law). It is also important to note that a metatheoretical result about this theory (the mutual independence of position, mass, and component force) is precisely formulated and proved for the first time.

Can we say that the Suppes Program for exhibiting the internal structure of classical particle mechanics has been successfully carried out? In spite of the important results just mentioned, we think this part of the program remains incomplete in several important respects. The internal structure of classical particle mechanics appears to be somewhat more complex than the MSS axiomatization reveals. Roughly speaking, describing the structure revealed by the MSS axiomatization is a necessary first step in describing the more complex structure. But it is not the whole story. Space limitations preclude a detailed defense of this claim here. (See however [22] Chapter VI.) We will simply list three features of classical particle mechanics that we believe to be important which are not revealed by the MSS axiomatization.

First, there appears to be an important difference between the role of the kinematical and dynamical primitive concepts in the theory. If this difference is not somehow reflected in the internal structure of the theory, it is difficult to provide a plausible semantics for the structure. This point is discussed in more detail below.

Second, though the Suppes approach to classical particle mechanics frees us from the prejudice (implicit in the formal language approach) that the formalized theory must have just one big intended interpretation, Suppes does not recognize that there are additional important structural features of the theory lodged in relations among *different* models (intended applications) of the theory. In the case at hand, unicity of mass ratios and extensivity of mass with respect to particle concatenation as well as certain features of special force laws appear to be most naturally treated as relations among different models (intended applications) of classical particle mechanics. Roughly, the MSS axiomatization captures the structure of *single* models (applications) of classical particle mechanics. It reveals nothing about relations among these models (applications) that are equally significant features of this theory's internal structure.

Finally, though the MSS axiomatization provides us with the means of precisely stating various special force laws (e.g., Hooke's law or the law of gravitation) the structure of an *array* of such laws is not exhibited. Very roughly speaking, how the applications of classical particle mechanics in which *different* special force laws are stipulated all 'hang together' to comprise the 'theory' is not revealed. Even less apparent is how one deals with the development of classical particle mechanics over time as new special force laws are discovered and applied to new applications. Roughly, one wants to say that one-and-the-same 'theory' is developing over time. The identity criteria for classical particle mechanics suggested by the MSS axiomatization do not seem adequate to this question.

The Semantics of Classical Particle Mechanics

The foregoing criticisms should not be misunderstood. They should not be taken as evidence that Suppes' work on axiomatization is unimportant. We are only suggesting that the MSS axiomatization can only be taken as the first step to clarifying the internal structure of classical particle mechanics. But it should be clear that we consider this accomplishment an absolutely essential first step.

We take care to avoid identifying ourselves with philosophers who tend to minimize the importance of such a first step to clarifying the internal structure of a physical theory. They suppose the 'real' task of the philosopher of science is only to clarify the *meaning* of scientific concepts and theories. A good example for this kind of view is the quite negative commentary Truesdell (the communicator) made about the MSS axiomatization when it was published for the first time:

The communicator is in complete disagreement with the view of classical mechanics expressed in this article. ...he does not believe the present work achieves any progress whatever toward the precision of the concept of force, which always has been and remains still the central conceptual problem, and indeed the only one not essentially trivial, in the foundations of classical mechanics ([15] p. 253).

Truesdell was troubled by the fact that the proposed axiomatization of classical particle mechanics did not handle the 'conceptual problem' of the *meaning* of force, while restricting itself to the 'trivial' task of laying down a couple of axioms. Truesdell wanted a semantical clarification of force which, of course, cannot be supplied when the aim is solely to reconstruct the formal structure of the theory.

From a different philosophical standpoint, Simon offered a similar kind of criticism of the MSS axiomatization. He defended his own axiomatization of Newtonian mechanics against its rival by implying that the MSS axiomatization was a 'merely formal' undertaking, while his own work examined the 'more important' semantical issues:

The authors of CPM (i.e., the MSS axiomatization) state that: "Our sole aim has been to present an old subject in a mathematically rigorous way." My aim in NM (i.e., Simon's axiomatization) was to present an old subject in a mathematically rigorous and *operationally meaningful* way . . . *The viewpoint taken in NM is that in the axiomatization of a piece of physical theory we are concerned not only with the formal and analytic aspects of the axiom system, but equally with the semantical relations between the system and the pheonomena it purports to denote* (Simon's italics, [20] pp. 340–341.)

A kind of direct answer to such criticisms could be the following: "Well, there is no particular difficulty about the semantics of the concepts involved in an axiomatized physical theory. Just build an interpretation of the primitive non-logical constants appearing in the axioms into an empirical domain in the standard way known from formal semantics. In the case of the MSS axiomatization of classical particle mechanics, P would be interpreted as a finite set of physical objects, T as an interval of real numbers, and the three mechanical functions as sets of tuples containing physical objects and numbers. This is all there is to the semantics of classical particle mechanics."

This is, of course, the kind of answer one would expect from a logician. It is a very clear answer. But it is not the kind of answer to satisfy Truesdell or Simon. Nor, indeed, is it the one Suppes would give them. When discussing the semantics of physical theories people expect more than just an interpretation function into a given domain. The semantics of physical theories (to abbreviate: 'physical semantics') is felt to be something more complex than the semantics of formal systems (formal semantics). It is not that formal semantics is wrong for physical theories; but it seems that there are important questions to be asked about physical theories that can be labelled 'semantical questions' (i.e., questions about meaning) and that cannot be appropriately solved (and, indeed, not even formulated) within formal semantics. The trouble is: what is this surplus of semantics? Why is it that the logician's answer is seen as adequate for purely formal systems and not so for physical theories?

A first tentative answer to these questions may be given along the following lines. In order to properly *understand* physical concepts, the construction of an interpretation function is not enough. Physical understanding cannot be completely covered by just settling the reference of physical concepts.

This is, of course, a very vague and general answer. Indeed, it is almost no answer at all. Since we can ask now: "How do we provide physical understanding?" However, even this formulation of the question is of some help. It helps to distinguish different proposals for providing physical understanding.

Some philosophers maintain that, in order to understand the highly abstract concepts of theoretical physics like real vector valued position and force functions one has to connect them somehow to more familiar everyday concepts already well-understood. In particular, they should be connected to the language of laboratory operations and observations expressed in simple *qualitative* terms. Such operations and observations would be the ultimate semantical ground of theoretical physical science. Let us call this approach 'operationalism' in a very broad sense. We think Suppes sympathizes with this general setting. However, there are many different approaches within general operationalism and Suppes would certainly not agree with all of them. There is, for example, the strict operationalistic tendency towards *defining* all theoretical concepts of physics through laboratory operations or through elementary concepts of space and time. In the case of mechanics, this means reducing dynamics to kinematics by definition. This is an important tradition in the philosophy of mechanics from Mach to Simon. Another is Carnap's program for connecting theoretical to observational concepts by explicitly establishing, not strict definitions, but so-called meaning postulates.

Suppes belongs to neither of these traditions. He is well-aware of their difficulties and over-simplifying character. His operationalism is of a more sophisticated sort. It is enlightening to look at his reaction to Truescell's criticism about the concept of force. He is not willing to admit that the MSS axiomatization is wrong or trivial, but he readily admits that something more is required to obtain a complete picture of classical particle mechanics:

What is missing and what is needed in the analysis of forces is a kind of explicit analysis in terms of elementary primitives. Clearly the primitive notions that McKinsey, Sugar and I used were complicated and already put into the axioms a substantial mathematical apparatus. The axioms were not simple in the way that primitive concepts and axioms of geometry are simple. What is needed is an analysis of the concept of force in the style of Tarski's classic article, *What is Elementary Geometry*? ([35] p. 467).

He then goes on to advocate, as an example of the kind of completion needed, the treatment given in a paper of Krantz' to the concept of force: a rather simple mini-theory is built, where (static) force is analyzed in terms of some elementary qualitative operations.

This approach to the matter can be rightly considered as a kind of operationalism. But it is important to see that it is different from strict or Carnapian operationalism. There is no proposal of *defining* the theoretical concept of force or of linking it to qualitative concepts through meaning postulates. Rather, two different theories are considered as independent structures: the theory of classical particle mechanics, where force appears on the same footing with position, etc., and a qualitative theory about certain operations on sets of spatial configurations. To explicate the concept of force means to link (but not to reduce definitionally) one theory to the other one. This is an *inter*-theoretical relationship (and not an *intra*-theoretical one as in the case of operational defintitions or meaning postulates). Indeed, the relationship envisioned is generally one-many. For every quantitative concept of the higher-level theory, at least one (but perhaps more) corresponding elementary qualitative theory must be built.

The specific form of the link between every quantitative concept of the higher-level theory and its corresponding qualitative theory is given by a *representation theorem*. Roughly speaking, this is a theorem stating that the existence and uniqueness of a quantitative concept satisfying some conditions stated in the higher-level theory can be derived from the realization of the axioms of the qualitative theory in a given domain.

The task of building whole arrays of elementary qualitative theories associated with given scientific theories and of proving representation theorems for them is the core of the semantic task. Suppes believes that accomplishing this task provides the appropriate answer to the semantical questions which bothered us. To understand a physical concept is to know exactly what the elementary measurement theories associated with it are. Such theories constitute the surplus of semantics we are looking for.

Is this answer the correct one? We have some doubts. Again, we do not wish to argue that providing realistic theories of fundamental measurement is useless, only that it may be only a partial solution to the semantic problem. That is, not all specific questions of physical semantics can be settled by providing a measurement theory (fundamental or derived) for every physical concept. We briefly summarize our doubts and the kind of 'addenda' we think should qualify Suppes' semantic program.

One need not be an orthodox Wittgensteinean to recognize that some questions about meaning may be illuminated by looking at the *use* of the concepts in question. This appears rather clearly to be the case with the concept of force in classical particle mechanics. It does not require a very subtle reading of the standard expositions of classical particle mechanics to note that all the methods described therein for measuring forces (determining the values of force functions) require us to assume at least that Newton's second law holds and commonly that some other special force law holds as well. Only a little further reflection is required to notice that the *extension* of the concept of force in this theory will be determined, in part at least, by which special force laws are claimed to hold on in which intended applications of classical particle mechanics. That is, the values we actually assign to forces will depend on how we *use* laws involving forces. This suggests first that we have to accept a kind of watered-down, theory-relative 'holism'. We cannot tell the full story about the meaning of force until we see the whole array of intended applications of classical particle mechanics laid out together with the special force laws that are alleged to hold in each. Further, this suggests that the extension of the concept of force in classical particle mechanics may be expected to change as the theory develops over time to include new applications in which new special force laws are maintained affording new possibilities for determining force-values.

This suggests (but certainly does not prove) that the meaning of the concept of force in classical particle mechanics cannot be completely captured by a relation between this concept and a distinct, 'underlying' or 'epistemologically prior' fundamental measurement theory for force. For if we could do this, we should expect to see (implicitly at least) traces of such a theory in expositions of classical particle mechanics. We *should* expect to find physicists (implicitly at least) appealing to such a theory in arguing for the acceptability of specific procedures for determining force values. Moreover, we *should not* expect to find physicists speaking of discovering new methods of determining forces as the theory is extended to new applications. What was an acceptable method of determining force values would have been settled once-and-for-all.

This suggestion of the inadequacy of fundamental measurement as an account of the meaning of force in classical particle mechanics acquires additional plausibility when it is embedded in an *alternative* account of the semantics for this concept. Such an account is provided in [22] (Chapter VI). Roughly, this account maintains that forces (and masses as well) are employed in a kind of modified Ramsey-sentence to say something about a *range* of kinematically described intended applications. Forces (and masses) employed to satisfy this Ramsey-sentence in *different* applications are mutually dependent. The specific nature of this dependence ('constraints' on the force function) is an essential feature of the concept of 'force' in classical particle mechanics. This dependence allows us to carry information about which specific values of the force function are required to satisfy the Ramsey-sentence in some applications where these values are uniquely determined (up to scale transformations) to others where they may not be. This feature provides an account of what physicists are doing when they speak of 'measuring forces'.

Even if this kind of account of the role of force in classical particle mechanics is completely adequate, it does not make the enterprise of constructing a fundamental measurement theory for force completely uninteresting. It does, however, suggest that the role of a fundamental measurement theory for force in classical particle mechanics would be quite different than that apparently envisioned for it by Suppes. To see what role it could play, we must say something about how the range of intended applications for classical particle mechanics might be determined.

If Kuhn [12] is right and if the formal reconstructions of his ideas given in [22] and [23] are accurate, then the whole array of intended applications may be 'anchored' in some *paradigmatic* sub-class which always remains a part of the theory's intended applications and through some 'resemblance' relation determines (in part at least) what else can be in it. The determination of this set of paradigmatic applications *need not* have anything to do with fundamental measurement, but it could. In the case in point, it is not implausible to think that pre-Newtonian theories of statics determine (but do not comprise) a *part* of the paradigm applications of classical particle mechanics. Roughly, these theories of statics must reduce to a special case of particle mechanics *and* reduce in such a way that static forces correspond to dynamic forces. *If* one could provide a theory of fundamental measurement for *static* forces one might then say that this theory of fundamental measurement played a role in describing the paradigm applications of classical particle mechanics. Yet there are still pretty clearly paradigm applications of classical particle mechanics (e.g. to celestial mechanics) in which the forces apparently cannot be regarded as grounded in a fundamental measurement theory.

A Ramsey sentence account of the role of a concept like force, perhaps coupled with a paradigmatically determined range of intended applications, suggests that the two ways of explicating the meaning of concepts like force could require more than grounding them in a fundamental measurement theory. A third possibility is suggested when we consider *inter*-theoretical relations like equivalence and reduction. These relations are quite important for 'physical semantics'. One cannot fully understand the physical concepts appearing in one theory without knowing how that theory is related to other distinct theories. It is reasonably clear that the concept of moment of inertia in rigid body mechanics can only be fully understood when it is seen precisely how this concept is related to particle mechanical mass through a reduction relation. Conversely, understanding this reduction relation adds something to our understanding of the concept of mass. We can now use applications of rigid body mechanics to determine values of particle mechanical mass.

It might seem natural to maintain that the meaning of 'moment of inertia' in rigid body mechanics is fully explained by exhibiting this reduction relation and that this is essentially a theory of derived measurement for moment of inertia. But this account appears inadequate when we notice that there are applications of rigid body mechanics in which we can calculate moments of inertia directly from angular velocities (assuming, of course, that the system obeys the laws of rigid body mechanics) without appeal to particle mechanics. More significant is that the reduction relation provides us with methods of determining particle mechanical mass that we would not have in its absence. Indeed, a plausible reconstruction of particle mechanical mass determinations using an equal-arm balance involves taking the balance system as a model for rigid body mechanics and exploiting the reduction relation to take what is really a moment of inertia determination into a mass ratio determination. This suggest that the meaning of the mass concept in particle mechanics changes when we 'discover' rigid body mechanics *and* how to reduce it to particle mechanics. This in turn, suggests another reason why fundamental measurement cannot be the whole story for the semantics of the mass concept in classical particle mechanics.

In the case of the equal arm balance method of determining particle mechanical masses, it is plausible to think that a corresponding theory of fundamental measurement could be constructed. Yet, this theory alone would not reveal the inter-theoretic relations that are essential to regarding the qualitative operations described in the theory of fundamental measurement as being ones that have anything to do with particle mechanical mass. The theory of fundamental measurement would not tell the whole story. Other cases where inter-theoretic relations are exploited to determine the values of particle mechanical functions do not have 'written on the face of them' the purely qualitative character the static equilibrium of the equal arm balance affords.

In summary, we conclude that the Suppes program for providing a semantics for physical theories by relating the quantitative concepts appearing in them to theories of fundamental measurement is incomplete in the following respects:

> – the meaning of quantitative concepts which are theoretical relative to the theory in question *may be* fully determined without reference to *any* other theory.
> – inter-theoretical relations like reduction, linking theoretical concepts relative to one theory to those in another, may further restrict the meaning of the theoretical concepts in *both* theories without going outside the theory pair in question.

However, at least in the case of classical particle mechanics, it does appear plausible to expect that the semantics for the non-theoretical, kinematical concepts will ultimately be provided by relating them to a theory of fundamental measurement. Despite nearly a century of work on this problem, a fully satisfactory account of how quantitative kinematics (metric geometry) may be related to *physically realistic* qualitative kinematics remains to be provided.

Suppes himself has commented on this lacuna [32]. For a recent attack on this problem from a somewhat non-traditional point of view, see [2].

V. The Foundations of Quantum Mechanics

Suppes' work in the foundations of quantum mechanics appears to have a somewhat different thrust than his other work in the philosophy of physics. Suppes has not offered us anything that could be viewed as a logical reconstruction of all (or even part) of quantum mechanics. Nor has he systematically addressed the question of how one might provide a physical interpretation or physical semantics for such a logical reconstruction.

He has, however, criticized some well known efforts at logical reconstruction in a way that indicates he believes these to be important *and* open questions. He regards the von Neumann axiomatization as inadequate because it characterizes axiomatically only the Hilbert space leaving as informal exposition the derivation of probability measures from the Hilbert space. More significantly perhaps, he criticizes the Mackey axiomatization, which *does* deal axiomatically with the probability measures, for failing to say how features of the axiomatic reconstruction are to be interpreted physically:

. . . Mackey's axiomatization is not complete, for to get us a system adequate to analyze detailed physical examples, further axioms are needed to set up the proper correspondence between observables and operators. To solve particular problems it is by no means sufficient to know only that such a one-one correspondence exists; the correspondence must be given constructively by additional axioms ([28] p. 388).

This suggests, at least, that Suppes views a full reconstruction of quantum mechanics – like other physical theories – as requiring not simply a characterization of its internal logical-mathematical structure, but also a physical semantics.

Suppes' own work, however, does not explicitly and systematically address these questions. Rather, the major underlying thrust of this work is to draw out the implications of regarding quantum mechanics as a stochastic theory on a par with other stochastic theories in physics and stochastic theories in other empirical sciences. Suppes regards "probability theory and modern mathematical statistics as the universal methodology of all empirical science. . . the methodological cornerstone of science." ([29] p. 319) From this point of view, all applications of probability theory in empirical science should have roughly the same structural features. The same probabilistic concepts should be employed and the same questions formulated with these concepts meaningful, if not always answerable, in all applications.

Suppes maintains that the most philosophically problematic aspects of quantum mechanics are not the hoary questions of indeterminacy and wave-particle duality, but rather the apparently aberrant use of probability concepts. At a rather general level Suppes has frequently deplored the relative lack of sophistication with which probability concepts are employed by quantum physicists and philosphers commenting on quantum mechanics. Typical are these remarks:

It is doubtful that any simple way can be found of avoiding the perplexing and paradoxical problems that arise in quantum mechanics, when probability notions are [not] developed with anything even faintly approaching the thoroughness with which they are used in other disciplines. For those familiar with the applications of probability and mathematical statistics in mathematical psychology or mathematical economics, it is surprising indeed to read the treatments of probability even in the most respected texts of quantum mechanics. . . . What is surprising is that the level of treatment both in terms of mathematical clarity and in terms of mathematical depth is surprisingly low. Probability concepts have a strange and awkward appearance in quantum mechanics, as if they had been brought within the framework of the theory only as an afterthought and with apology for their inclusion ([29] pp. 334–5).

When Popper talks about quantum mechanics as a statistical theory, he is talking, it seems to me, with that surprise evinced by those who look at quantum mechanics from the standpoint of classical physics – surprise that the theory brings within its purview certain statistical relations and denies at the theoretical level the determinism so characteristic of classical physics. Looked at from the standpoint of standard statistical theories, the surprise about quantum mechanics is rather different. . . . The surprise is that natural questions are neither asked or discussed. Popper's own neglect of these standard questions of covariation or correlation is a reflection that he has not really taken seriously as yet the rethinking of quantum mechanics as a statistical theory. What Heisenberg, for example, has had to say about these matters would make the hair of any right-thinking statistician stand on end ([34] p. 770).

Suppes supports these general claims by detailed analysis of some of them as aberrant features of quantum mechanical applications of probability theory.

Turning to this more specific level, Suppes finds the key to a detailed

understanding of the philosophically problematic feature of time-inde-
pendent quantum mechanics in the following facts about quantum mechanical probabilities. According to the generally accepted Copenhagen
interpretation of the mathematical formalism of quantum mechanics,
certain mathematical operations performed on vectors in a Hilbert space
representing the state of a physical system and Hermitian operators in
the space representing physical observables of the system yield real valued
functions that may be interpreted as unconditioned, marginal probability distributions over the possible outcomes of measurements of the
physical observable. Apparently Wigner in 1932 [39] first noted that there
was a natural way to generalize this recipe which might plausibly be expected to generate joint probability distributions over possible outcomes
of observations of two or more physical observables of a system. Wigner
found to his surprise that the natural generalization did not always work.
For physical observables associated with non-commuting operators in the
Hilbert space, the recipe sometimes generated functions that could not
be interpreted as joint probability distributions at all – much less joint
distributions compatible with the marginals generated by the standard
recipe. Later in 1967 Nelson [18] showed essentially that no recipe (natural
or perverse) could exist that would always yield joint distributions compatible with the marginals generated by the standard recipe.

Suppes finds these features of quantum mechanical probabilities to be
highly atypical.

The strangeness of these results from a methodological standpoint is difficult to overemphasize. . . . the applications of probability theory range over all domains of science, . . . The mathematical techniques of probability theory, as well as the conceptual
foundations have received an enormous amount of attention from mathematicians, statisticians, and philosophers. In the several domains with which I am familiar or which I
have at least cursorily inspected I have not been able to find a single example having the
conceptual status of these results about the non-existence of a joint distribution in quantum mechanics ([29] p. 333).

He suggests that focusing attention on these, from the standpoint of general
probabilistic and statistical methodology, highly aberrant features of quantum mechanics will illuminate other problematic features of this theory.

For example, Suppes maintains that the non-existence of joint distributions for non-commuting observables provides more direct insight into
what quantum mechanics tells us about the impossibility of simultaneous
measurements than does the much more commonly mentioned Heisenberg uncertainty relation. The uncertainty relation tells us that the product

of the variances of quantum mechanical probability distributions for non-commuting observables will always be greater than some fixed number. That is, when the variance of one distribution is small, the variance of the other must be large. This fact is a straightforward consequence of the mathematical formalism of quantum mechanics. It is commonly interpreted to mean that, according to quantum mechanics, values of non-commuting observables cannot be measured simultaneously with arbitrary precision. Suppes argues that merely from this fact about the joint distributions, nothing whatsoever follows about what single measurement operations can be carried out with what degree of precision. He cites examples from stochastic theories in psychology (for example, [29] pp. 323 ff.) where a similar relation between variances of different observables obtains for 'identically prepared' systems without prompting us to conclude that the theory tells us that simultaneous single measurements of these observables with equal precision are impossible.

Suppes believes the correct understanding of the implications of quantum mechanics is that simultaneous measurement of non-commuting observables is not possible at all. This he believes to follow from the non-existence of joint distributions for non-commuting observables.

The real point is that the uncertainty relation does not represent a genuine statistical relation at all, for there does not in general exist a joint probability distribution of the momentum and position random variables. The real claim to be made is that when a proper joint distribution of momentum and position does not exist, then these two properties are not simultaneously measurable at all. ([28] p. 385) . . . There is no underlying sample space which may be used to represent the simultaneous measurements, exact or inexact.

What Suppes apparently means here is that it is difficult to see how it is possible to formulate quantum mechanics in the manner of standard probabilistic theories in which all random variables are conceived as being defined over a single underlying sample space. This is true so long as one sticks with the standard interpretations of quantum mechanical distribution as unconditioned marginals. The impossibility of providing a single underlying sample space Suppes interprets here as meaning that simultaneous measurement is not possible at all.

The absence of joint distributions for non-commuting observables also provides, according to Suppes, the most plausible argument for employing nonclassical logic in quantum mechanics. His argument is this:

(A)   the logic appropriate to empirical applications of probability theory is the logic of propositions to which probabilities are assigned in that application.

(B)   the appropriate logic should be such that every proposition in it is assigned a probability by the application of probability theory.

(C)   the quantum mechanical formalism cannot be consistently interpreted as assigning probabilities to conjunctions of all propositions to which it assigns probabilities.

(D)   therefore, the logic appropriate to applications of quantum mechanics should not be closed under conjunction.

(E)   classical logic is closed under conjunction.

(F)   therefore the appropriate logic should not be classical logic.

Premise (C) is simply a reformulation of the no-joint-density result. Among other things, this argument makes quite explicit that recommending the use of non-classical logics to describe applications of quantum mechanics does not entail, without further assumptions, a recommendation that classical logic be replaced by something else in *all* contexts. Premise (A) mentions only logics appropriate to specific contexts.

In our view, the most questionalbe premise in this argument is (B). Essentially, Suppes says that to get a smoothly running mathematical theory of probability it is expedient to restrict the domain of probability functions so that we can always be sure that the results of certain calculations we make with them are well-defined.

> . . . the arguments for insisting that a probability may be assigned to every event are already a part of classical probability theory. It is only for this reason that one considers an algebra or, σ-algebra, of sets as the basis for classical probability theory. If it were permitted to have events to which probabilities could not be attached, then we could always take as the appropriate algebra the set of all sub-sets of the basic sample space. The doctrine that the algebra of events must have the property asserted in the second premise is too deeply embedded in classical probability to need additional argument here. One may say that the whole point of making explicit the algebra of events is just to make explicit those sets to which probabilities may be assigned. It would make no sense to have an algebra of events that was not the entire family of sub-sets of the given sample space and yet not be able to assign a probability to each event in the algebra ([30] p. 15).

Certainly, the restriction of the domain of probability functions to a σ-algebra is sound mathematical practice. No applications of probability theory appear to require assigning probabilities to the sub-sets outside this algebra and the mathematics is easier when we ignore them.

But it does not follow from this that we should always ignore the propositions to which empirical applications of probability theory fail to assign probabilities. There is no straightforward way in which an empirical theory that tells us the values of *some*, but not all, of the probabilities on a given algebra of events (propositions) must be inconsistent. It may be true that in most or all standard empirical applications of probability theory the underlying sample space is chosen so that the application of the theory assigns probabilities to all events in it. But Suppes does not show us that this *must be* so, nor even offer a plausible explanation of why it *is* so. So long as it were possible to consistently 'fill-in' the missing probabilities in some way, there appears to be no compelling reason to 'erase' the propositions to which the application of probability theory does not assign probabilities. But the real problem with quantum mechanics in its usual interpretation is not just that it does not assign probabilities to some propositions, but rather that probabilities *cannot* be assigned to these neglected propositions that are consistent with other probabilities already assigned. In this case, adopting a logic in which the troublesome propositions simply do not appear is an attractive move. But another move might be to *expand* the set of propositions over which probabilities are defined in a manner that retains the classical character of the logic of these propositions, permits consistent assignment of probabilities to all propositions and retains the probabilities given by the empirical application on a restricted sub-set of these propositions. Suppes' premise (B) rules out this move but his rationale for doing so does not appear compelling.

Suppes' more technical work in constructing non-classical logics appropriate to applications of quantum mechanics departs somewhat from the mainstream of mathematical work in this area in that Suppes is somewhat more concerned than the mathematicians with what the physical interpretation of the logic might be.

...many of the proposals made in the literature are hard for me to fathom from an empirical or experimental standpoint. It is a simple enough matter formally to define orthocomplemented modular lattices and relate them to the structure of subspaces that arise in quantum mechanics, but exactly how this logic corresponds to the set of empirical propositions or events is ordinarily not elaborated in any detail ([33] p. 334]).

The quantum mechanical logics that Suppes constructs do not reproduce the lattice of sub-spaces of a Hilbert space, but do have a kind of intuitive plausibility based on considerations of the impossibility of simultaneous observations that is lacking with other attempts. Despite his own pleas for concreteness, Suppes does not show us in detail how the probability theory based on his quantum logic could be used in physical applications. It would be quite interesting to see how the treatment of some standard application of quantum mechanics – say the hydrogen spectrum or the Stern-Gerlach effect – would look treated with the standards of rigor customary in mathematical statistics *and* some non-classical probability theory.

In his more recent work Suppes (collaborating with M. Zanotti) has turned his attention to time dependent quantum mechanics [37]. But the basic idea remains the same. They ask, "How does time-dependent quantum mechanics compare with other applications of the theory of stochastic processes?" Here again the answer is that the quantum mechanical description of a stochastic process is 'incomplete' in ways that more orthodox applications are not. This incompleteness is essentially independent of the no-joint-density feature of steady state quantum mechanics.

The Suppes-Zanotti proposal for dealing with this 'incompleteness' is rather interesting in the light of Suppes' earlier argument for employing nonclassical logics in applications of steady state quantum mechanics. They conjecture that time-dependent quantum mechanics can be embedded in a stochastically complete theory that is mathematically and empirically consistent with the existing theory or at least empirically consistent. Further they suggest that such an embedding has at least heuristic value.

It might be objected that quantum mechanics should remain in a state of stochastic incompleteness because there is no evidence that a stochastically complete theory of the sort we have developed here . . . will lead to any new observable phenomena, and thus the stochastic completeness is not only wasted but in a sense misleading. We think that this narrow positivistic view should be rejected. The stochastic theory of quantum phenomena gives a very easily understandable picture of the phenomena, especially, as we have emphasized here, their dynamical aspects ([37] p. 324).

Suppes and Zanotti explicitly maintain that their proposal for completing time dependent quantum mechanics does not vitiate the claim that non-classical logic is appropriate to these theories but maintain as well that:

. . . if it were to turn out in the long run that the classical theory of stochastic processes proved to be the appropriate framework for developing the theory of quantum phenomena in a conceptually natural way, the general significance of quantum logic would almost certainly be reduced ([37] p. 325).

It is difficult to see how Suppes could consistently reject proposals to complete steady state quantum mechanics in a way that avoided the need for a non-classical logic.

In summary, the most important feature of Suppes' work in the foundations of quantum mechanics appears to be that he has a coherent point of view about how quantum mechanics ought to be formulated and applied. It ought to look like any other empirical application of the mathematics of probability and statistics. Philosophical problems arise just where we find departures from standard statistical methodology. Solutions to these problems should be suggested by looking at other applications of statistics and probability. Some traditional problems with quantum mechanics do seem to be clarified by this point of view. But it remains to be seen whether it will lead to a satisfactory logical reconstruction of quantum mechanics. From this point of view the most important open questions in the foundations of quantum mechanics appear to be specific and detailed questions of how applications of quantum mechanics look when formulated as standard applications of statistical methodology. Such simple questions as "What is the sample space appropriate to the application of quantum mechanics to explain the hydrogen spectrum?" need to be considered. Until we do this, we cannot begin to provide a logical reconstruction of quantum mechanics. We still do not know precisely what the set-theoretic structure of its applications looks like.

Universidad Nacional Autonoma de Mexico
University of California at Santa Cruz

Notes

[1]In [31] (p. 218) he says: "A simple standard formalization of most theories in the empirical sciences is not possible." (By "standard formalization" Suppes means formalization in first-order logic.) But the purist formalizer could rightly reply that: (a) in many cases, standard formalization is not logically impossible, but 'only' quite difficult in practice; and (b) he is by no means restricted to first-order logic, since one can build formal systems within higher-order languages.

References

[1] Adams, E. W.: 1959, 'The Foundations of Rigid Body Mechanics and the Derivation of Its Laws from Those of Particle Mechanics', in *The Axiomatic Method* (ed. by Henkin, Suppes, Tarski), North-Holland, Amsterdam, pp. 250–265.
[2] Balzer, W.: 1976, *Empirische Geometrie und Raum-Zeit-Theorie in Mengentheoretischer Darstellung*, Doctoral Dissertation, Universität München.
[3] Campbell, N. R.: 1928, *An Account of the Principles of Measurement and Calculation*, Longmans, Green, London and New York.

[4] Carnap, R.: 1928, *Der Logische Aufban der Welt*, Berlin, Schlachtensee.
[5] Caratheodory, C.: 1909, 'Untersuchungen uben die Grundlagen der Thermodynamik', *Math. Ann.* 67.
[6] Hamel, G.: 1901, 'Die Axiome der Mechanik', *Handbuch der Physik* 5, pp. 1–42.
[7] Hempel, C. G.: 1952, *Fundamentals of Concept Formation in Empirical Science*. The University of Chicago Press.
[8] Hermes, H.: 1959, 'Zur Axiomatisierung der Mechanik', in *The Axiomatic Method* (ed. by Henkin, Suppes, Tarski), North-Holland, Amsterdam, pp. 282–290.
[9] Hoelder, O.: 1952, 'Die Axiome der Quantität und die Lehre von Mass', *Berichte über die Verhandlungen der Königlichen Sachsischen Gesellschaft der Wissenschaft zu Leipzig, Mathematische-Physische Klasse* 53, 1–64.
[10] Jamison, B. N.: 1956, *An Axiomatic Treatment of Langrange's Equations*, M. S. thesis, Stanford University, Stanford, California.
[11] Krantz, D. H., R. D. Luce, P. Suppes, A. Tversky: 1971, *Foundations of Measurement*, vol. I. Academic Press, New York and London.
[12] Kuhn, T. S.: 1962, *The Structure of Scientific Revolutions*. The University of Chicago Press, Chicago.
[13] Kyburg, H.: 1968, *Philosophy of Science: a Formal Approach*. New York, Macmillan.
[14] McKinsey, J. C. C., A. C. Sugar, P. Suppes: 1953, 'Axiomatic Foundations of Classical Particle Mechanics', *Journal of Rational Mechanics and Analysis*, 2, 253–272.
[15] McKinsey, J. C. C., P. Suppes: 1953, 'Transformations of Systems of Classical Particle Mechanics', *Journal of Rational Mechanics and Analysis*, 2, 273–289.
[16] McKinsey, J. C. C., P. Suppes: 1955, 'On the Notion of Invariance in Classical Mechanics', *British Journal for the Philosophy of Science* V, 290–302.
[17] Moulines, C. U.: 1975, 'A Logical Reconstruction of Classical Equilibrium Thermodynamics', *Erkenntnis*, 9, 101–130.
[18] Nelson, E.: 1967, *Dynamical Theories of Brownian Motion*. Princeton University Press, Princeton.
[19] Rubin, H., P. Suppes: 1954, 'Transformations of Systems of Relativistic Particle Mechanics', *Pacific Journal of Mathematics*, 4, 563–601.
[20] Simon, H.: 1947, 'The Axioms of Newtonian Mechanics', *Philosophical Magazine*, XXXVI, 888–905.
[21] Simon, H.: 1954, 'The Axiomatization of Classical Mechanics', *Philosophy of Science*, XXI, 340–343.
[22] Sneed, J. D.: 1971, *The Logical Structure of Mathematical Physics*, Reidel, Dordrecht, Holland.
[23] Stegmuller, W.: 1973, *Theorie und Erfahrung, 2. Halbband* (*Theorienstrukturen und Theoriendynamik*), Springer, Berlin-Heidelberg-New York. (English translation by W. Wohlhutter titled *The Structure and Dynamics of Theories*.)
[24] Suppes, P.: 1954, 'Some Remarks on Problems and Methods in the Philosophy of Science', *Philosophy of Science*, 21, 242–248.
[25] Suppes, P.: 1957, *Introduction to Logic*. Van Nostrand, New York.
[26] Suppes, P.: 1959, 'Axioms for Relativistic Kinematics with or without Parity', in *The Axiomatic Method* (ed. by Henkin, Suppes, Tarski), North-Holland, Amsterdam, pp. 291–307.

[27] Suppes, P.: 1960, 'A Compansion of the Meaning and Use of Models in Mathematics and the Empirical Sciences', *Synthese*, **12**, 287–301.

[28] Suppes, P.: 1961, 'Probability Concepts in Quantum Mechanics', *Phil. of Sci.*, **28**, 278–289.

[29] Suppes, P.: 1963, 'The Role of Probability in Quantum Mechanics', in B. Baumrin (ed.) *Philosophy of Science, The Delaware Seminar*, vol. 2, 1962–63, New York, Wiley and Sons, pp. 319–337.

[30] Suppes, P.: 1966, 'The Probabilistic Argument for a Non-Classical Logic of Quantum Mechanics', *Philosophy of Science*, **33**, 14–27.

[31] Suppes, P.: 1970, *Set-theoretical Structures in Science*, (mimeo reprint) Stanford University, Stanford, California.

[32] Suppes, P.: 1973, 'Some Open Problems in the Philosophy of Space and Time', *Synthese* **24** (1972), 298–316. Reprinted in P. Suppes (ed.) *Space, Time and Geometry*, Dordrecht: Reidel, pp. 383–401.

[33] Suppes, P.: 1973, 'Logics Appropriate to Empirical Theories' in C. A. Hooker (ed.) *The Logico-Algebraic Approach to Quantum Mechanics*, Dordrecht: Reidel, pp. 329–340.

[34] Suppes, P.: 1974, 'Popper's Analysis of Probability in Quantum Mechanics' in P. A. Schilpp (ed.), *The Philosophy of Karl Popper* (vol. 2) La Salle, Ill.: Open Court, pp. 760–774.

[35] Suppes, P.: 1974, 'The Axiomatic Method in the Empirical Sciences', in *Proc. Tarski Symposium, Proc. Symposium in Pure Mathematics*, 25 (ed. L. Henkin et al.). AMS, Providence, R.I.

[36] Suppes, P.: 1974, 'The Essential but Implicit Role of Modal Concepts in Science', in *PSA 1972* (ed. K. F. Schaffner, and R. S. Cohen). Reidel, Dordrecht, Holland.

[37] Suppes, P. and Zanotti M., 'Stochastic Incompleteness in Quantum Mechanics', *Synthese*, **29**, 311–330.

[38] Swijtink, Z. G.: 1976, 'Eliminability in a Cardinal', *Studia Logica*, XXXV, 71–89.

[39] Wigner, E. P.: 1932, 'On the Quantum Correction for Thermodynamic Equilibrium', *Phys. Rev.*, 749–759.

[40] Tarski, A.: 1965, *Introduction to Logic and to the Methodology of Deductive Sciences* (tr. by O. Helman), New York, Oxford University Press.

R. DUNCAN LUCE

SUPPES' CONTRIBUTIONS TO THE
THEORY OF MEASUREMENT

A Philosophy of Measurement

More than any other living person, Suppes has affected contemporary
presentations of theories of measurement. They bear the imprint of his
views as to the appropriate axiomatic formulation of the intended empirical information and the nature of the theorems to be proved. I do not
mean to imply that before him scientists were unaware of what needed to
be done, but rather that he has stated the requirements more generally
and more forcefully than others had. In essence, he formulated more
clearly than anyone before him the common features of existing measurement theories – primarily those of Helmholtz (1887), Hölder (1901),
Campbell (1920, 1928), Wiener (1921), von Neumann and Morgenstern
(1947), and Savage (1954), as well as his own contributions of the 1950's –
and he emphasized various relevant logical distinctions. Of course, philosophers of physics had earlier discussed the nature of measurement,
especially important being the works of Bridgman (1922), Campbell (1920,
1928), and Cohen and Nagel (1934), but none had achieved a fully satisfactory mathematical treatment.

The first systematic statement of his views is found in the Suppes and
Zinnes (1963) expository chapter in the *Handbook of Mathematical Psychology*, and it pervades the jointly authored volume *Foundations of Measurement* (Krantz, Luce, Suppes, and Tversky, Vol. I, 1971, Vol. II, in preparation). That it has been accepted by others is evidenced both by the
nature of the articles that have appeared in the 1960's and 70's and by
other expository works such as Pfanzagl's *Theory of Measurement* (1968).

The key elements of Suppes' approach to measurement can be briefly
coded by these words: relational structures, representation and unique-

ness theorems, invariance and meaningfulness, logical status of axioms, and finiteness.

Relational Structures

It used to be somewhat vague in discussions of measurement exactly what were the empirical objects and observations to which numbers would be assigned, exactly what part of the number system would be employed, and exactly which numerical operations were representing which empirical operations. To a degree, these choices were clarified by discussion and example, but they were never so clear as in the ruthlessly formal, set-theoretic approach demanded by Suppes of himself, his students, and his collaborators (as one of the latter, I know whereof I speak). For Suppes, a qualitative structure is always a relational structure, i. e., of the form

$$\mathscr{A} = \langle A, S_1, \ldots, S_n \rangle,$$

where A is a set and each S_i, $i = 1, \ldots, n$, is a relation of some order k_i on A. (In practice k_i mostly is either 2, 3, or 4, corresponding to binary relations such as orderings, ternary relations such as operations, and quaternary relations of orderings of differences.) Because of the intended interpretation of an empirical structure, namely as something to be measured in terms of a concept of greater than, it is always the case that one of the relations – conventionally, S_1 – is some sort of an ordering relation and is usually written $\gtrsim$. Most often it is a weak order – connected and transitive – but sometimes something weaker is involved – quasiorder, interval order, semiorder, etc. In practice, of course, the set A must be identified with concrete objects or events, but so far as the theories are concerned A is treated as an abstract set and whatever structure it has empirically is embodied in the relations defined over A and the axioms they satisfy.

Equally well, the domain of numerical measures is interpreted as a numerical relational system

$$\mathscr{R} = \langle R, T_1, \ldots, T_n \rangle,$$

where R is a subset of the real numbers (or possibly something somewhat richer, such as a set of nonstandard reals) and the T_i are each relations of the same order, k_i, as the corresponding S_i. Again, because of the intended interpretation, T_1 is very special: it is $\geqslant$ or some modification thereof.

Representation and Uniqueness Theorems

The goal of the measurement theorist is to formulate constraints – axioms

– on the relations of the empirical structures fulfilling two requirements. First, each axiom should either be an (approximately) true empirical statement – a law of the most primitive sort – or it should be a technical constraint of one sort or another which we choose to accept for convenience. Second, the collection of axioms should be sufficient (and necessary if at all possible) for the existence of a homomorphism from the empirical relational structure to the numerical one. To be quite explicit, one requires axioms sufficient to prove the existence of a function ϕ from A into the set of numbers R such that for all $i = 1, \ldots, n$ and all k_i-tuples of elements $a_1, \ldots, a_{k_i}$ from A,

$$S_i(a_1, \ldots, a_{k_i}) \quad \text{iff} \quad T_i[\phi(a_1), \ldots, \phi(a_{k_i})].$$

Such a theorem is called a *representation theorem*, and the homomorphism ϕ is frequently called a *scale of measurement*.

Accompanying the representation theorem is another one, called a *uniqueness theorem*, which describes the family of all homomorphisms from the empirical structure to numerical structures. It can be divided into two parts, one of which is usually suppressed. The visible one assumes that the numerical relational structure is fixed, and it describes how to generate from one homomorphism all homomorphisms into that structure. Put another way, the uniqueness theorem describes the endomorphisms of the relational structure. Often it is easiest to summarize it by stating the number of values of the homomorphism that can be specified in advance so as to render the homomorphism unique: a unit for mass; a unit and a zero for non-absolute temperature or utility; etc.

Early on Stevens (1946, 1951) emphasized these groups of endomorphisms, and he classed measurement as ordinal, interval, or ratio according as the set of endomorphisms includes all strictly increasing functions, or the positive linear ones, or just multiplication by positive constants. He was never very explicit exactly as to where these constraints on measurement scales came from, and he did not seem to accept fully its dependence on an axiomatic theory of measurement. For example, he insisted that the scale obtained by his empirical method of magnitude estimation was a ratio scale, but he never provided any detailed justification for that claim. By contrast, Suppes is very clear that such concepts of uniqueness rest explicitly on a detailed theory of measurement.

The (usually) unstated uniqueness theorem concerns alternative numerical relational structures. For example, the measurement of length and mass is almost always into $\langle Re^+, \geqslant, + \rangle$, where Re^+ is the set of positive reals. But by taking the exponential of that homomorphism, it is evident that the measurement could be into $\langle Re^+, \geqslant, \cdot \rangle$. Mostly, we do not worry about this sort of nonuniqueness because it is agreed that it is purely a matter of convention which one we choose. So we have accepted the convention of using + when it comes to combining within an attribute and · when it comes to combining between attributes, as for example momentum which is conventionally treated as the product of velocity and mass. Obviously, these conventions could have been different. In any event, it is a relatively trivial exercise to characterize all conceivable alternative numerical structures, and so there is not much interest in doing so (see p. 99–102 and 273 of Krantz *et al.*).

Invariance and Meaningfulness

When Stevens first focussed attention on the notion of scale type – the set of endomorphisms of the numerical representation – he pointed out an important connection between that set and the sorts of statistical statements that remain invariant under these transformations. There ensued a heated debate in both the psychological and, to a lesser degree, statistical literatures about the correctness of his proscriptions concerning statistical practice. To this day, the issues do not seem fully resolved, even among those very familiar both with measurement and statistics. For example, Suppes and I have never reached agreement about what limitations scale types impose on the use of statistical tests.

In the 1950's Suppes pointed out that what Stevens had said about the invariance of certain statistics was but a special case of a more general question, namely, which statements that one might formulate in terms of a measurement representation correspond to something meaningful in the empirical structure. For example, it is clear that it is not meaningful to assert that the mass of a particular object is 5, whereas it is quite meaningful to say that the ratio of one mass to another is 5.

Suppes' (1959) first approach to the problem was in terms of formal languages, but so far as I know that attack has not been pursued further by him or anyone else. An alternative, and much more comprehensible, set-theoretic approach was later suggested by Suppes and developed by Robinson (1963) and applied by Adams, Fagot, and Robinson (1965) to the statistical problems posed by Stevens. A summary of this work was given by Suppes and Zinnes (1963). The idea is that a statement formulated entirely in terms of measures and logical connectives is meaningful if and only if it is invariant under the endomorphisms of the numerical relational structure. A precise formulation of the word 'statement' either requires invoking formal languages, as in the 1959 paper, or treating a statement as defining a relation on the set R.

Of course, the notion of invariance under transformations plays an important role in many formulations of physics. A number of Suppes' papers concern the concept in various branches of mechanics. It also is a key idea in dimensional analysis, where it is required that physical laws be invariant under certain classes of transformations called similarities. Recently, I have shown (Luce, 1978) that within the richer context of measurement structures tied together, as in physics, by distribution laws, the concept of dimensional invariance is exactly the same as that of meaningfulness, namely, invariance of empirical relations under the automorphisms of the qualitative dimensional structure.

Logical Status of Axioms

Little has yet been said about the constraints imposed on the empirical relations S_i except that S_1 is always some species of ordering, $\gtrsim$. Obviously, other axiomatic properties must hold among the relations, and Suppes was one of the first to point out some logical distinctions among them.

First, there are the universal axioms that are logical consequences of the representation together with properties of the real numbers. One is that S_1 must be a weak ordering if T_1 is $\geqslant$. Another is that if S_2 is a ternary relation corresponding to a binary operation, say $\circ$, and if T_2 corresponds to $+$, then $\circ$ must satisfy the monotonicity property, for all a, b, c in A,

$$a \gtrsim b \text{ if and only if } a \circ c \gtrsim b \circ c.$$

Such axioms as these are called *necessary*.

Any axiom that is not necessary must, therefore, restrict the class of possible structures from the most general class having the representation. Suppes called these axioms *structural*, and that term is widely used. Usually the structural axioms involve some sort of existence statement. One example is the solvability axioms that assert the existence of a solution to an empirical equation. For example, in a structure $\langle A, \gtrsim, \circ \rangle$, we often assume that for all a, b in A with $a > b$, there exists c in A such that $a \sim b \circ c$, where $\sim$ denotes both $\gtrsim$ and $\lesssim$. Sometimes the existential nature of the axiom is masked and combined with another type of axiom into some form of topological continuity.

A second classification is into first and second order axioms. Because the representation is usually some sort of ordinary numerical structure the cardinality of the empirical structure must in some way be restricted. The usual restrictions are either finiteness or the existence of a countable order-dense subset or some version of the Archimedian property, the assertion that positive numerical intervals are comparable. Such axioms are second order ones, and either one is included or the representation has to be modified. Recent studies (Narens, 1974a; Skala, 1975) have shown that it suffices to deal with versions of non-standard reals (Robinson, 1966).

A third sort of question about the axioms is their consistency and independence. In principle, one could ask about their categoricity, but measurement structures are in practice never categorical. Consistency is usually evident since the intended numerical representation is a model of the axioms. Independence is of course established in the usual way by exhibiting models that satisfy all but the axiom in question. For example, Suppes in his first publication (1951) took pains to give a system of axioms for extensive measurement which are independent. (He also improved on Hölder's system by weakening the structural axioms, but his system has long since been superseded by better ones.) Often, however, as for example in axiomatizations of Boolean algebras, the most economical set of independent axioms is less transparent than a slightly more redundant set of axioms, and so some degree of overlap among the axioms is permitted, including sometimes dependent axioms. (For example, in a theory of extensive structures it is a lot easier to include commutativity of ∘ rather than to deduce it.)

Finiteness

Most of the axiom systems found in the literature of measurement force the set A of the empirical relational structure to be infinite. At the same time, these axiom systems involve a finite number of relations and a finite (usually quite small) number of axioms characterizing these relations. Although such structures often seem like plausible idealizations of reality, from two points of view they are not descriptive. First, most theories of the universe say there are only finitely many objects and so any infinite structure must not be an accurate description. Second, any set of data we deal with must be finite, and perhaps the theory of measurement should be developed only for data structures. Suppes has strongly argued, both in person and by example, that we should develop finite measurement systems for, at least, the latter reason. As we shall see, he seems implicitly to have rejected the former reason. I should point out that many theorists, and I among them, have never been persuaded that the theories should be confined to the data one happens to have collected, and success in approximating the finite universe by infinite theories is adequate justification for using the infinite theories.

Basically three tacks have been followed in developing theories for finite structures. The first is to suppose that the finite set A is selected in some *a priori* way, as in a factorial experimental design, and then the data are simply the empirical inequalities that are observed. The difficulty of this approach was made clear in the very fundamental paper of Scott and Suppes (1958) in which it was established that such structures cannot be characterized by any fixed set of first order axioms. Scott (1964) and independently Tversky (1964) pursued that tack using a kind of axiom schema that increases the number of axioms with the size of A. If I have understood Suppes' reaction correctly, the logician in him was repelled by this approach. So another avenue had to be followed.

His second approach supposed somewhat implicitly that the finite data set can be selected from an unaxiomatized empirical universe in such a way that certain very special structural relations hold. Put another way, it is assumed that certain equations can be solved and the elements involved are just those solutions. In practice, the elements selected are those that end up being equally spaced in the representation or, put another way, that the integers constitute a suitable representation or, put still another way, the structure axiomatized is what is called a standard sequence in the more general theories. A systematic presentation of a number of these axiomatizations is Suppes (1972a).

They have the great virtue of being rather simple to state and the representation theorems are quite easy to prove, so for many teaching situations they are useful. Nevertheless, they are very incomplete theories. One would like the general theory to include as subsystems any set of data one might, for whatever reason, choose to collect, but one should not necessarily expect to be able to construct a representation of every subsystem. Recently Suppes has shown a way to do this for subjective probability if one is willing to accept approximate measurement for all but the standard sequence. I describe this in some detail below.

Decision Theory and Probability

Although Suppes' first paper concerned the theory of extensive measurement, all of his subsequent work on specific theories of measurement has had to do with rational decision making: subjective expected utility theory, empirical testing of these theories, and axiomatic probability.

Subjective Expected Utility Theory

During the 1950's, a number of economists, statisticians, and philosophers were trying to understand better and to generalize the theory of rational decision making that had been sparked by von Neumann and Morgenstern (1944, 1947, 1953); special attention was given to the axiomatization of expected utility. The most important development was pioneered by Savage (1954). Under plausible axioms, his very rich decision structure (all functions from finite partitions of the states of nature into events with their range a set of consequences) was adequate, first, to derive a unique subjective probability measure over the states of nature and then, using that, to construct a utility function for which subjective expected utility preserved the ordering of decisions. The latter construction parallelled closely that of the original von Neumann and Morgenstern development.

The objections to Savage's approach are by now well known – many of the most telling criticisms were first made by Suppes (1956, 1960). Perhaps the most important ones are, first, the postulation and heavy use of constant acts, i.e., functions with a single consequence, which in most contexts seem highly unrealistic, and second, the structural assumption of arbitrarily fine partitions of the states of nature into equally-likely events, which also usually is highly artificial. Thus, a strong motive for additional work during this period was to overcome these major difficulties. With the exception of Davidson, McKinsey, and Suppes (1955), which provided an alternative formulation of the von Neumann-Morgenstern model, Suppes' work at this time concentrated on working out an alternative idea which had originally been suggested by Ramsey (1931).

Let aEb denote a gamble in which a is the consequence if the event E occurs and b otherwise. Suppose that E^* is an event for which the decision maker is indifferent between aE^*b and bE^*a for all a and b, then it is easy to see that if the subjective expected utility property holds, this event must have subjective probability $1/2$. Moreover, for all consequences a, b, c, d,

$$aE^*b \gtrsim cE^*d \quad \text{iff} \quad u(a) + u(b) \geqslant u(c) + u(d)$$
$$\text{iff} \quad u(a) - u(c) \geqslant u(d) - u(b).$$

Thus, if such an event be found, the whole problem of utility construction is reduced to the question of when do orderings of gambles based on this event have a representation in terms of utility differences. So, in sharp contrast to Savage, Suppes began by constructing the utility function and only after that did he get deeply involved with the subjective probability function.

Suppes and Winet (1955) provided an axiomatization of a (quaternary) relation over $A \times A$ for which a relatively unique representation in terms of utility differences obtains; for later (and simpler) versions of this theory, see Chapter 4 of Krantz et al. Davidson and Suppes (1956) generalized this so as to construct both a utility function u and a subjective probability function P over events such that the following restricted subjective expected utility property holds: for all consequences a, b, c, d and all events E,

$$aEb \gtrsim cEd \quad \text{iff} \quad u(a)P(E) + u(b)P(\bar{E}) \geqslant u(c)P(E) + u(d)P(\bar{E}).$$

And, by invoking the existence of constant decisions, which did not please him at all, Suppes (1956) gave an axiomatization of the general subjective expected utility property.

As a theoretical program to replace the Savage structure, this effort was only partially successful. Suppes was able to get away from the infinite states of nature, but in the final analysis he was not able to bypass the constant acts. Moreover, the Ramsey context was as narrow as the original von Neumann-Morgenstern one. Not until Krantz and I (1971) (see also Chapter 8 of Krantz et al.) developed a theory of conditional expected utility did an alternative exist to Savage which is at the same level of generality, does not invoke infinite states of nature, and does not require constant acts to construct a utility function over acts. [However, for criticisms of that structure, see Balch and Fishburn (1974) and a reply by Krantz and Luce (1974), and Spohn (1977)].

Experiments on Subjective Expected Utility

Unlike many theorists, Suppes has always insisted that a scientific theory be put to empirical test. In particular, his work on decision models was interactive with an experimental program. At the time, the only empirical work in the area was that of Mosteller and Nogee (1951) who had experimented on the von Neumann and Morgenstern model. Together with the experimental psychologist Sidney Siegel, Davidson and Suppes (1957) reported a number of careful studies based on the Ramsey paradigm. In particular they first found a chance event with subjective probability $1/2$

– a die with one nonsense triad on three faces and another on the remaining three. Next they selected two sums of money and arbitrarily fixed their utility, and then they successively searched for other sums that were equally spaced in utility. A variety of cross checks were possible. This is not the place to detail these studies, except to note that they were very carefully conducted, they were extensive, and they ran afoul of the pervasive problem of error and inconsistency. The latter had been evident in the Mosteller–Nogee experiment, and it has remained a major stumbling block in evaluating all algebraic measurement theories.

At the time, Suppes attempted to deal with it by introducing an error threshold and using methods of linear programming to solve the resulting set of data inequalities. That had its faults – perhaps the most severe being that the sure-thing principle need not hold – and so a modified model and new experiment were reported in Suppes and Walsh (1959). In a closely related paper, Royden, Suppes, and Walsh (1959) studied the utility for gambling. Valiant though these experimental efforts were, they did not lead to a clear decision as to the adequacy of the expected-utility property and I do not believe that others were persuaded that this was a suitable way to handle error and inconsistency.

The problem of error has remained formidable, though recently some positive steps have been taken. One of these is the work of Falmagne (1976), and the other is the approximate probability model of Suppes discussed in the next section.

In closing this section, let me remark that the whole issue of testing decision theories remains quite murky. Suppes' approach represents one attack: fit the representation to the data as well as possible and then evaluate that fit. Of course, the questions are how best to estimate the huge number of parameters (functions) and how to evaluate the goodness of fit, neither of which has been satisfactorily answered. Moreover, assuming the model is shown to be unsatisfactory, what then? Do we simply reject the rationality axioms that lead to the subjective expected-utility representation, or do we try to modify them? An alternative approach is to study selectively various qualitative properties implied by the subjective expected-utility representation in order to discover in as much detail as possible the nature of the descriptive breakdown of the model. I tend to favor that approach, although I would be less than candid not to admit that so far it has only focussed attention on failures of the extended sure-thing principle without informing us about acceptable substitutes and different representations. Of course, many economists and statisticians argue for the (non-structural) axioms on grounds of rationality, and certainly they are compelling canons of rational behavior. For those people there is no need to study the failures empirically. Rather, as with logic, one attempts to teach rational behavior without particularly caring to describe exactly a student's failures.

Axiomatic Probability

Throughout the time I have known him, Suppes has thought much about the foundations of probability. His interest has taken at least three distinct routes. First, he has emphasized the pervasiveness of stochastic processes in the sciences, especially the social and behavioral ones, and he has spent considerable effort on Markov models for learning. Second, he has repeatedly emphasized (Suppes, 1961, 1963, 1966, 1974a) the anomaly that the single most important theory of physics, quantum mechanics, embodies a version of probability inconsistent with the widely accepted axiomatization of Kolmogorov (1933) which seems to be perfectly adequate for all of the rest of science. Third, from the Bayesian point of view, embodied in various rational theories of decision making, there is the interesting foundational question of finding a satisfactory axiomatization of qualitative (or comparative) probability that possesses a more-or-less unique numerical representation over a plausible algebra of events. This has proved to be a good deal more difficult than might, *a priori*, have been expected.

It is not relevant for me to discuss here his first interest and I have relatively little to say about the second one; I shall however discuss the latter more fully, as it is central to measurement.

Suppes (1966) took up the question of how to modify the Kolmogorov axiom system so as to make it agree with quantum mechanics. His suggestion, if adequate, is certainly simple: just restrict the definition of an algebra of sets to be closed not under all finite unions of events, but just disjoint ones. However, the fact that nearly 10 years later he is again struggling with the problem suggests that he is not satisfied with that solution. For example, on p. 771 of Suppes (1974a) we find

. . . . [Q]uantum mechanics is not a standard statistical theory – it is a peculiar, mystifying, and as yet, poorly understood radical departure from the standard methodology of probability and statistics. There is as yet no uniform agreement on how the probabilistic aspects or statistical aspects of quantum mechanics should be formulated. But it is widely agreed that there are unusual problems that must be dealt with and that do not arise in standard statistical theories . . .

The difficulty is that when the standard formalism of quantum mechanics is used the joint distribution of noncommuting random variables turns out not to be a proper joint distribution in the classical sense of probability.

These comments were made in a paper critical of K. R. Popper's study of these matters. Among other things, Popper (1959) proposed, without giving a careful mathematical analysis, a propensity interpretation of probability. Suppes (1973) suggested that axioms, much like those in Krantz *et al.* (p. 222), for qualitative conditional probability may provide a suitable axiomatization of propensity. Within that context, he is able to provide a qualitative axiom characterizing an event whose occurrence is independent of the past (e.g., radioactive decay), and to formulate a qualitative axiom for randomness.

Interesting though this may be, so far as I can see the deep issue of probability in quantum mechanics remains as problematical as ever.

Turning to the role of probability in theories of rational decision making, recall that Suppes was highly critical of the qualitative axiomatizations of Savage and de Finetti, because the structural axioms forced an infinity of events and were otherwise unrealistic. An alternative approach involving only finitely many events, due to Scott (1964) and Tversky (1964) is also unsatisfactory because of the "... combinatorial explosion that occurs in verifying the axioms when the number of events is large" (p. 166, Suppes, 1974b). So simply imposing finiteness by itself is not enough. A third problem is that of error and imprecision. His experimental work made it clear that the usual precision of measurement theories is unrealistic. Indeed, almost all real life uses of probability notions lack precision.

It is this practical sense of leaving things vague and qualitative that needs to be dealt with and made explicit. In my judgment to insist that we assign sharp probability values to all of our beliefs is a mistake and a kind of Bayesian intellectual imperialism. I do not think this corresponds to our actual ways of thinking, and we have been seduced by the simplicity and beauty of some of the Bayesian models. On the other hand, a strong tendency exists on the part of practicing statisticians to narrow excessively the domain of statistical inference, and to end up with the view that making a sound statistical inference is so difficult that only rarely can we do so, and usually only in the most carefully designed and controlled experiments. (p. 447, Suppes, 1976).

His first new approach to the problem of axiomatizing qualitative probability very neatly combines the idea that there should be a finite set of events that are equally spaced and resolved very precisely with the idea that there are many other events which are irregularly spaced in probability and, indeed, are known only approximately. A little more precisely, the structure assumed is $\langle X, \mathscr{E}, \mathscr{S}, \gtrsim \rangle$, where X is a set (sample space), $\mathscr{E}$ and $\mathscr{S}$ are both algebras of subsets of X, and $\gtrsim$ is a binary relation on $\mathscr{E}$. Intuitively, $\mathscr{E}$ corresponds to all of the events to which probabilities in some form or another will be assigned, and $\mathscr{S}$ is the set of events to which precise assignments are made. It is assumed that $\langle X, \mathscr{E}, \gtrsim \rangle$ satisfies the usual deFinetti axioms – $\gtrsim$ is a monotonic weak ordering, $A \gtrsim \phi$ for A in $\mathscr{E}$; and $X > \phi$ – and that $\mathscr{S}$ is a finite subset of $\mathscr{E}$ with the two properties:

(i)   if S is in $\mathscr{S}$ and $S \neq \phi$, then $S > \phi$.

(ii)   if S, T are in $\mathscr{S}$ and $S \gtrsim T$, then there is a V in $\mathscr{S}$ such that $S \sim T \cup V$.

He has shown that there is a unique probability measure P on $\mathscr{S}$ that preserves the order $\gtrsim$ and that assigns the same probability to every minimal event of $\mathscr{S}$. For any element A of $\mathscr{E}$, one assigns upper and lower probabilities P^* and P_* as follows: if A is in $\mathscr{S}$, then $P^*(A) = P_*(A) = P(A)$; if not, then one finds S and S' in $\mathscr{S}$ such that $S \gtrsim A \gtrsim S'$ and $S \sim S' \cup V$, where V is in $\mathscr{S}$ and is minimal, and sets $P^*(A) = P(S)$ and $P_*(A) = P(S')$. These upper and lower probabilities can be shown to satisfy a number of properties previously proposed by Good (1962) and Smith (1961), and that $P^*(A) - P_*(A) \leq 1/n$, where n is the number of minimal elements in $\mathscr{S}$. Furthermore, if we define the relation $* >$ on $\mathscr{E}$ by:

$$A * > B \text{ iff there exists } S \text{ in } \mathscr{S} \text{ with } A \gtrsim S \gtrsim B,$$

then it can be shown that $* >$ is a semiorder on $\mathscr{E}$ and

$$\text{if } A * > B, \text{ then } P_*(A) \geq P^*(B),$$
$$\text{if } P_*(A) \geq P^*(B), \text{ then } A \gtrsim B.$$

This is derived in Suppes (1974b) and summarized in Suppes (1975, 1976). In addition, in Suppes (1975) these results are used to generate a comparable theory of approximate expected utility.

In my opinion, this is a most interesting development which has widespread potential for the whole theory of measurement. It captures quite neatly the idea that in measurement there is a precisely measured finite standard series which in turn is used to provide approximate measurement of other things of interest.

His second new approach, found in Suppes and Zanotti (1976), involves a quite different tack, namely to enlarge the scope of the problem. Often in mathematics this proves a more effective route than trying to axiomatize just the structures of interest. In this case we replace $\mathscr{E}$ by a closely related family of random variables as follows. For any A in $\mathscr{E}$, its indicator function A^c is defined as:

$$A^c(a) = \begin{cases} 1 \text{ if } a \text{ is in } A \\ 0 \text{ if } a \text{ is not in } A. \end{cases}$$

Of course, $A^c + B^c$ is a function, but in general it is not an indicator function. Denote by $\mathscr{E}^*$ the algebra of *extended indicator functions* defined to be the smallest semigroup under function addition that includes all of the indicator functions of $\mathscr{E}$. The elements of $\mathscr{E}^*$ are obviously a subclass of all the random variables defined on X. The theorem proved is this: A necessary and sufficient condition for $\langle X, \mathscr{E}, \succsim \rangle$ to have a unique, order preserving probability representation is that it is possible to extend $\succsim$ to an ordering $\succsim *$ on the algebra $\mathscr{E}^*$ of extended indicator functions such that $\langle \mathscr{E}^*, \succsim *, + \rangle$ satisfies the conditions of a positive closed extensive structure (Krantz *et al.*, 1971, p. 73). It is not yet clear how useful this criterion will prove to be.

Concluding Remarks

Suppes' major contributions to the theory of measurement have been, in my opinion, four.

First, he laid bare, more clearly than anyone before him, the exact nature of a theory of measurement. He has been very exacting about stating what is empirical and what is mathematical, the types of axioms that are involved and the degree to which the structural ones can be avoided, and the limitations on meaningful numerical statements. To a degree this is didactic and expository, but it is my impression that the field has moved ahead more rapidly and surely because of his demand for logical clarity.

Second, he has focussed very sharply the distinction between finite and infinite structures. His original hope of finding finite systems of universal axioms was dashed by his fundamental paper with Scott (1958) and was not saved by Scott's (1964) axiom schema. Following that he persisted in pushing finite, equally-spaced structures (finite systems with extremely strong structural axioms), which I have never thought were very satisfactory until his recent work in approximate measurement of probability. An alternative tack, pursued by Narens (1974b), is to see the way in which increasingly large finite structures converge to infinite ones.

Third, he has and continues to contribute to the theory of qualitative probability and subjective expected utility. His first work in the mid 1950's involved cogent criticism of Savage's approach and the attempt to work out and to test empirically a substitute based on utility difference measurement. Although this, by itself, did not resolve the issues, it was surely an important intermediate step. Recently, he has developed a theory of approximate probability measurement involving a finite subsystem that is exactly measured; I find this work exciting and with a potential for wide generalization.

Finally, and by no means least, Suppes has been an important expositor of theories of measurement. His chapter with Zinnes (1963) was the first systematic statement of his outlook on measurement. Later I was involved in three expositions with him (Luce and Suppes, 1965, 1974, and Krantz *et al.,* 1971). Other papers of a largely expository character are Suppes (1960, 1961b, 1967, and 1972b). Often incorporated in these papers is a concern with history. Perhaps the purest example of this is Suppes (1971) in which he goes back to Archimedes' account of measurement and shows that much of it appears sensible if put into the framework of modern conjoint measurement theory.

Harvard University

References

Adams, E. W., R. F. Fagot, and R. E. Robinson: 1965, 'A theory of appropriate statistics', *Psychometrika*, **30**, 99–127.
Balch, M., and P. C. Fishburn: 1974, 'Subjective expected utility for conditional primitives', in M. S. Balch *et al.* (eds.), *Essays on Economic Behavior under Uncertainty*, North-Holland, Amsterdam, 1974, pp. 57–69.
Bridgman, P.: 1922, 1931, *Dimensional Analysis*, Yale University Press, New Haven.
Campbell, N. R.: 1920, *Physics: the Elements*, Cambridge University Press, Cambridge. Reprinted as *Foundations of Science: the Philosophy of Theory and Experiment*, Dover, New York, 1957.
Campbell, N. R.: 1928, *An Account of the Principles of Measurement and Calculation*, Longmans, Green, London.
Cohen, M. R. and E. Nagel: 1934, *An Introduction to Logic and Scientific Method*, Harcourt, Brace, New York.
Davidson, D., J. C. C. McKinsey, and P. Suppes: 1955, 'Outlines of a formal theory of value, I', *Philosophy of Science*, **22**, 140–160.
Davidson, D. and P. Suppes: 1956, 'A finitistic axiomatization of subjective probability and utility', *Econometrica*, **24**, 264–275.
Davidson, D., P. Suppes, and S. Siegel: 1957, *Decision Making: an Experimental Approach*, Stanford University Press, Stanford.

Falmagne, J.-C.: 1976, 'Random conjoint measurement and loudness', *Psychological Review*, **83**, 65–79.

Good, I.J.: 1962, 'Subjective probability as the measure of a non-measurable set', in E. Nagel *et al* (eds.), *Logic Methodology and Philosophy of Science: Proceedings of the 1960 International Congress*, Stanford University Press, Stanford, 1962, pp. 319–329.

von Helmholtz, H.: 1887, 'Zählen und Messen Erkenntnis – theoretisch Betrachtet', *Philosophische Aufsätze Edvard Zeller Gewidmet*, Leipzig. English translation by C. L. Bryan, *Counting and Measuring*, van Nostrand, Princeton, 1930.

Hölder, O.: 1901, 'Die Axiome der Quantität und die Lehre vom Mass', *Ber. Verh. Kgl. Sächsis. Ges. Wiss. Leipzig, Math.-Phys. Classe*, **53**, 1–64.

Kolmogorov, A. N.: 1933, *Grundbegriffe der Wahrscheinlichkeitsrechnung*, Springer, Berlin. English translation by N. Morrison, *Foundations of the Theory of Probability*, Chelsea, New York, 1956.

Krantz, D. H. and R. D. Luce: 1974, 'The interpretation of conditional expected-utility theories', in M. S. Balch *et al.* (eds.), *Essays on Economic Behavior under Uncertainty*, North-Holland, Amsterdam, pp. 70–73.

Krantz, D. H., R. D. Luce, P. Suppes, and A. Tversky: 1971, *The Foundations of Measurement*, I, Academic Press, New York.

Luce, R. D.: 1978, 'Dimensionally invariant numerical laws correspond to meaningful qualitative relations', *Philosophy of Science*, **45**, 1–16.

Luce, R. D. and D. H. Krantz: 1971, 'Conditional expected utility', *Econometrica*, **39**, 253–271.

Luce, R. D. and P. Suppes: 1965, 'Preference, utility, and subjective probability', in R. D. Luce *et al.* (eds.), *Handbook of Mathematical Psychology*, III, Wiley, New York, 1965, pp. 249–410.

Luce, R. D. and P. Suppes: 1974, 'Measurement, theory of', *Encyclopedia Britannica*, 739–745.

Mosteller, F. and P. Nogee: 1951, 'An experimental measurement of utility', *Journal of Political Economy*, **59**, 371–404.

Narens, L.: 1974a, 'Measurement without Archimedean axioms', *Philosophy of Science*, **41**, 374–393.

Narens, L.: 1974b, 'Minimal conditions for additive conjoint measurement and qualitative probability', *Journal of Mathematical Psychology*, **11**, 404–430.

von Neumann, J. and O. Morgenstern: 1944, 1947, 1953, *Theory of Games and Economic Behavior*, Princeton University Press, Princeton.

Pfanzagl, J.: 1968, *Theory of Measurement*, Wiley, New York.

Popper, K. R.: 1959, 'The propensity interpretation of probability', *The British Journal for the Philosophy of Science*, **10**, 25–42.

Ramsey, F. P.: 1931, 'Truth and probability', in F. P. Ramsey, *The Foundations of Mathematics and Other Logical Essays*, Harcourt, Brace, New York, 1931, pp. 156–198.

Robinson, A.: 1966, *Non-standard Analysis*, North-Holland, Amsterdam.

Robinson, R. E.: 1963, 'A set-theoretical approach to empirical meaningfulness of empirical statements', *Technical Report* 55, Institute for Mathematical Studies in the Social Sciences, Stanford.

Royden, H. L., P. Suppes, and K. Walsh: 1959, 'A model for the experimental measurement of the utility of gambling', *Behavioral Science*, **4**, 11–18.

Savage, L. J.: 1954, *The Foundations of Statistics*, Wiley, New York.

Scott, D.: 1964, 'Measurement models and linear inequalities', *Journal of Mathematical Psychology*, **1**, 233–247.

Scott, D. and P. Suppes: 1958, 'Foundational aspects of theories of measurement', *The Journal of Symbolic Logic*, **23**, 113–128.

Skala, H. J.: 1975, *Non-Archimedean Utility Theory*, Reidel, Dordrecht, Holland.

Smith, C. A. B.: 1961, 'Consistency in statistical inference and decision', *Journal of the Royal Statistical Society, Series B*, **23**, 1–25.

Spohn, W.: 1977, 'Where Luce and Krantz Do Really Generalize Savage's Decision Model', *Erkenntnis*, **11**, 113–134.

Stevens, S. S.: 1946, 'On the theory of scales of measurement', *Science*, **103**, 677–680.

Stevens, S. S.: 1951, 'Mathematics, measurement and psychophysics', in S. S. Stevens (ed.), *Handbook of Experimental Psychology*, Wiley, New York, 1951, 1–49.

Suppes, P.: 1951, 'A set of independent axioms for extensive quantities', *Portugaliae Mathematica*, **10**, 163–172.

Suppes, P.: 1956, 'The role of subjective probability and utility in decision-making', *Proceedings of the Third Berkeley Symposium on Mathematical Statistics and Probability, 1954–1955*, **5**, 61–73.

Suppes, P.: 1959, 'Measurement, empirical meaningfulness, and three-valued logic', in C. W. Churchman and P. Ratoosh (eds.), *Measurement: Definitions and Theories*, Wiley, New York, 1959, pp. 129–143.

Suppes, P.: 1960, 'Some open problems in the foundations of subjective probability', in R. E. Machol (ed.), *Information and Decision Processes*, McGraw-Hill, New York, 1960, pp. 162–169.

Suppes, P.: 1961a, 'Probability concepts in quantum mechanics', *Philosophy of Science*, **28**, 378–389.

Suppes, P.: 1961b, 'The philosophical relevance of decision theory', *The Journal of Philosophy* **21**, 605–614.

Suppes, P.: 1963, 'The role of probability in quantum mechanics', in B. Baumrin (ed.), *Philosophy of Science, the Delaware Seminar*, Vol. 2, Wiley, New York, 1963, pp. 319–337.

Suppes, P.: 1966, 'The probabilistic argument for a non-classical logic of quantum mechanics', *Philosophy of Science*, **33**, 14–21.

Suppes, P.: 1967, 'Decision theory', in P. Edwards (ed.), *The Encyclopedia of Philosophy*, MacMillan and Free Press, New York, 1967, pp. 310–314.

Suppes, P.: 1971, 'Archimedes's anticipation of conjoint measurement,' *XIII International Congress of the History of Science*, "Nauka" Publishing House, Central Department of Oriental Literature, Moscow, 1–17.

Suppes, P.: 1972a, 'Finite equal-interval measurement structures', *Theoria*, **38**, 45–63.

Suppes, P.: 1972b, 'Measurement: problems of theory and application', in *Mathematics in the Social Sciences*, Australian Government Publishing Service, Canberra, 1972, pp. 613–622.

Suppes, P.: 1973, 'New foundations of objective probability: axioms for propensities', in P. Suppes *et al.* (eds.), *Logic, Methodology and Philosophy of Science IV: Proceedings of the Fourth International Congress for Logic, Methodology and Philosophy of Science, Bucharest, 1971*, North-Holland, Amsterdam, 1973, pp. 515–529.

Suppes, P.: 1974a, 'Popper's analysis of probability in quantum mechanics', in P. A.

Schilipp (ed.), *The Philosophy of Karl Popper*, Vol. 2, Open Court, LaSalle, Ill., 1974, pp. 760–774.

Suppes, P.: 1974b, 'The measurement of belief', *The Journal of the Royal Statistical Society Series B (Methodology)*, **36**, 160–191.

Suppes, P.: 1975, 'Approximate probability and expectation of gambles', *Erkenntnis*, **9**, 153–161.

Suppes, P.: 1976, 'Testing theories and the foundations of statistics', in Harper and Hooker (eds)., *Foundations of Probability Theory, Statistical Inference, and Statistical Theories of Science*, II, Reidel, Dordrecht, 1976, pp. 437–455.

Suppes, P. and K. Walsh: 1959, 'A non-linear model for the experimental measurement of utility', *Behavioral Science*, **4**, 204–211.

Suppes, P. and M. Winet: 1955, 'An axiomatization of utility based on the notion of utility differences', *Management Science*, **1**, 259–270.

Suppes, P. and Zanotti, M.: 1976, 'Necessary and sufficient conditions for existence of a unique measure strictly agreeing with a qualitative probability ordering', *Journal of Philosophical Logic*, **5**, 431–438.

Suppes, P. and J. L. Zinnes: 1963, 'Basic measurement theory', in R. D. Luce *et al.* (eds.), *Handbook of Mathematical Psychology*, I, Wiley, New York, 1963, pp. 1–76.

Tversky, A.: 1964, 'Finite additive structures', *Technical Report MMPP* **64–6**, University of Michigan, Michigan Mathematical Psychology Program.

Wiener, N.: 1921, 'A new theory of measurement: a study in the logic of mathematics', *Proceedings of the London Mathematical Society*, **19**, 181–205.

ROGER D. ROSENKRANTZ

SUPPES ON PROBABILITY, UTILITY, AND DECISION THEORY

1. Introduction

This chapter surveys Patrick Suppes' work on probability, utility, inference, causality and decision theory. Much of this work has been handily
collected in [1], Part II, and wherever possible, I shall confine my references
to that one source. The topics in question are closely intertwined, both
with each other and with Suppes' interests in measurement and learning
theory. Where connections with those other topics might otherwise go
unremarked, I shall not hesitate to point them out. Underlying all of
Suppes' work in this area is a concern to frame a *realistic* theory of rational
decision and information processing, a theory sufficiently detailed 'to
generate the drawings for a machine . . . that can form concepts and
make inductions' ([1], p. 86).

2. Axiomatic Foundations of Utility and Probability

A major thrust of Suppes' work in this area has been to formulate experimentally testable theories. To be sure, his axioms are offered in a somewhat normative spirit, but they are intended to facilitate empirical assessment of the degree to which actual behavior conforms. At the same time,
theories of rational decision making should be applicable; they should not
require an inordinate amount of calculation or be overly restrictive. In
this vein, Suppes distinguishes *rationality axioms*, which "should be satisfied by any rational, reflective man", from *structural axioms*, which "impose limitations on the kind of situations to which our analysis may be
applied" ([1], p. 95). E.g., the 'sure-thing principle', which directs one to
choose an action which is best under every state of nature, is a rationality

Bogdan, R.J. (Ed.) 'Patrick Suppes' 111–129.
Copyright © 1979 by D. Reidel Publishing Company, Dordrecht, Holland.

axiom; an axiom asserting that consequences are equally spaced in utility is a structural axiom. As Suppes is well aware, the distinction cannot always be maintained. As he remarks of a system of his: "Without A.11, the Archimedean axiom, A.7 would need to be considered a structure axiom, but in the presence of A.11, I regard it as a rationality axiom". That is, one axiom may help define a class of situations in which conformity to another axiom is a requirement of mere rationality.

Suppes developed an empirical approach to decision theory (in collaboration with Donald Davidson and Sidney Siegel) in [2]. It is based on the idea sketched by F. P. Ramsey in [3]. One finds an 'ethically neutral' chance event E^* to which the agent assigns probability 1/2 ('ethically neutral' means that the agent is indifferent whether E^* occurs or not). Using his preference ranking over gambles and the assumption that he acts so as to maximize expected utility, one calibrates the agent's utility scale. To see how this is done, consider two options x and y (say, two amounts of money) with xPy (x preferred to y). The zero and unit of the utility scale can be chosen arbitrarily, and so we assign x utility one and y utility minus one. Now if the agent is indifferent between a third option, z, and a one-half gamble or mixture of x and y (i.e., one where he receives x if E^* occurs and y if E^* does not occur), then z is the midpoint between x and y on his utility scale, and we set $U(z) = 0$. By presenting a sufficient number of such choices, the agent's utility scale can be calibrated to any desired degree of fineness.

Having determined the utility function, using only E^* to generate the necessary gambles, the agent's (subjective) probability measure can now be determined. It is necessary to assume that his measure P satisfies no more than the weak condition that $P(\bar{E}) = 1 - P(E)$, writing $\bar{E}$ for the complement of the event E. For suppose that he is indifferent between (a) receiving x if E and y if $\bar{E}$, and (b) receiving z if E and w if $\bar{E}$. Given that he acts so as to maximize expected utility, we have:

$$P(E)U(x) + P(\bar{E})U(y) = P(E)U(z) + P(\bar{E})U(w)$$

whence, using $P(\bar{E}) = 1 - P(E)$ and solving for $P(E)$, we obtain:

$$(2.1) \qquad P(E) = \frac{U(w) - U(y)}{[U(w) - U(y)] + [U(x) - U(z)]}$$

where x, y, z, w are chosen so that the denominator is non-zero. Since the utilities in question are known, (2.1) determines the agent's probability measure (over all events of the given algebra of events). So much is due to

Ramsey. Notice that his method, unlike that of von Neumann and Morgenstern, requires no objective probabilities and, moreover, allows the agent's probabilities to be extricated from his utilities. The contribution of Suppes and his colleagues was to ferret out the empirical assumptions implicit in the Ramsey method and test them.

Small amounts of money were used to calibrate the utility scales of the experimental subjects, starting with the arbitrary assignments $U(6 ¢) = 1$ and $U(-4 ¢) = -1$. Write $x, y = (E)z, w$ when the agent is indifferent between receiving (a) x if E occurs and y if not, and (b) z if E occurs and w if not. The following empirical assumptions underlie the Ramsey method.

H0. xPy iff $x > y$ (more money is preferred to less).

H1. There exists a chance event E^* with $x, y = (E^*)y, x$ for all x, y.

H2. Let $a > b$. Then there are unique amounts c, d, f, g of money such that a, b, c, d, f, g are equally spaced in utility in the order f, c, a, b, d, g. (This means that $b, c = (E^*)a, a$, etc. .)

H3. For all monetary amounts x, y, z and every event E, if there is an amount w for which $x, y = (E)z, w$, then w is unique. (Having found this w, we can compute $P(E)$.)

H4. Let U be the utility function determined by H2. For all monetary amounts $x, y, z, w, x', y', z', w'$, with $U(y) \neq U(w)$, if $x, y = (E)z, w$ and $[U(x) - U(z)]/[U(y) - U(w)] = [U(x') - U(z')]/[U(y') - U(w')]$, then $x', y' = (E)z', w'$. (I.e., the subjective probability of E, given by (2.1), does not depend on the particular outcomes with which E is matched.)

These hypotheses (together with some additional but innocuous assumptions) imply axioms for utility and probability sufficient for interval measurement of utility (over a finite set of alternatives) and a unique, but not necessarily additive, probability measure satisfying the weaker conditions $P(E) + P(\bar{E}) = 1$ and $P(E) \leq P(F)$ when $E \subseteq F$. I omit the detailed proofs in order to focus on the experimental procedure for testing H0–H4.

It proved unexpectedly difficult to find an 'ethically neutral' E^* satisfying H1. In using ordinary coins and dice, subjects always showed a preference for one of the outcomes, even though the objective probabilities of both outcomes were equal. A special die had to be constructed with the nonsense syllables 'ZOJ' and 'ZEJ' each engraved on three of the six faces. (It had previously been shown that these syllables have essentially zero associational value.) 'ZOJ', then, could play the role of E^* in H1. Subjects were asked to choose between gambles using this E^* (which served for all subjects) and chose a given member of a pair invariably. Consequently, an approximate verification of H1 had to be devised. A subject was held to assign E^* (subjective) probability $1/2$ iff he satisfied

$$(2.2) \qquad x, y \leq (E^*)y, x + 1 \qquad \text{and} \qquad x - 1, y \leq (E^*)y, x$$

for several monetary pairs x, y where $\leq$ is the relation 'less preferred or indifferent to'. For the time being, I shall ignore the need to use approximations like (2.2) in discussing the experimental validation of the remaining hypotheses.

For H0, we merely check whether subjects satisfy $x, y \leq (E^*)z, y$ when $x < z$ or $x, y \leq (E^*)x, z$ when $y < z$. All subjects were found to satisfy H0. The key hypothesis is H2, which affirms the existence of a utility function for the finite set of monetary amounts employed. The test of H2 amounts to checking whether the agent's preferences over (pure and mixed) options are consistent. Since it is assumed throughout that his probability of E^* is $1/2$ and that he acts so as to maximize expected utility, any inconsistencies that show up are evidence that he lacks a well-defined utility function.

The strategy followed is to set $U(a) = -1$ and $U(b) = 1$, where $a = -4\,¢$ and $b = 6\,¢$. By offering options of the form 'x if E^* occurs, b if not' or 'a for sure', one can locate a c such that $c, b = (E^*)a, a$, and this latter indifference means that a is midway between c and b on the subject's utility scale. Hence, $U(c) + U(b) = 2U(a)$, and $U(c) = -3$ follows. Next, we seek a d such that $c, d = (E^*)a, b$, then, given this d, an f such that $f, d = (E^*)c, b$, and, finally, a g such that $f, g = (E^*)c, d$. We should then have $U(c) = -3$, $U(d) = 3$, $U(f) = -5$, $U(g) = 5$. Given that the agent has a well-defined utility function over the considered range of alternatives, additional comparisons, which serve as consistency checks, are implied. Referring to Figure 1, we see, for example, that we should have f, $b = (E^*)c$, a and $c, g = (E^*)a, d$, and so forth. Thus, the x for which x, $b = (E^*)c$, a should be f, the x for which $c, x = (E^*)a, d$ should be g, etc.. Failure of even one such consistency check was taken to falsify H2.

$$\overset{f}{\bullet} \qquad \overset{c}{\bullet} \qquad \overset{a}{\bullet} \qquad \overset{b}{\bullet} \qquad \overset{d}{\bullet} \qquad \overset{g}{\bullet}$$

Fig. 1.

To connect this theory with observable choice behavior, we need approximate versions of the given indifferences. First, given a, b, we seek c^*

such that b, $c^* \preceq b$, $c^* + 1$, where $\preceq$ abbreviates $\leq (E^*)$. Given $U(a) = -1$, $U(b) = 1$ and setting $c^{**} = c^* + 1$, we have $1 + U(c^*) \leq -2 \leq 1 + U(c^{**})$, and from this we conclude the existence of non-negative quantities ε_1, ε_2 satisfying: $U(c^*) + \varepsilon_1 = -3$ and $U(c^{**}) - \varepsilon_2 = -3$. Hence, c^* and c^{**} are, respectively, a lower and an upper bound on the exact amount c for which $U(c) = -3$. (Both c^* and c^{**} are, of course, integral amounts of money.)

Next, using c^*, we find d^{**} such that b, $a \preceq d^{**}$, c^* and $d^{**} - 1$, $c \preceq b$, a. Substituting for $U(c^*)$, $U(d^{**} - 1) \leq 3 + \varepsilon_1 \leq U(d^{**})$, whence there exists a δ_2' such that $U(d^{**}) - \delta_2' = 3 + \varepsilon_1$, or, setting $\delta_2 = \varepsilon_1 + \delta_2'$, $U(d^{**}) - \delta_2 = 3$ and $\varepsilon_1 \leq \delta_2$. Similarly, using c^{**}, we find d^* such that $U(d^*) + \delta_1 = 3$, with $0 \leq \varepsilon_2 \leq \delta_1$. The errors in measuring d are therefore at least equal to those in measuring c. The process of bracketing the exact values then continues, the errors tending to increase (and never decreasing). The bounds finally obtained for f and g are quite wide, and consequently, the consistency checks on H2 are not as sensitive as one might like.

The experimental design used in [2] has another slight defect, also noted by the authors themselves. To obtain c via c, $b = (E^*)a$, a necessitates comparing the 'mixed' option 'c if E^*, b if not' with the 'pure' option 'a for sure'. If the subject has a taste for gambling, c will be set too low, while if he has a distaste for gambling, c will be set too high. This distortion of his utility function will then be reflected in the values d, f, g, so that, if at the end we determine c' from f, $b = (E^*)c'$, a, we will then find $c' \neq c$. When this happens, the original choice of c must be adjusted and the entire process of determining f and g repeated. And if the c' found at the end from f, $b = (E^*)c'$, a still fails to coincide with the adjusted value of c, the process must be repeated once again. There is also a possibility that, *ceters paribus*, gambles with higher stakes be preferred (or dispreferred) to those with lower stakes, and that would also produce a distortion that could easily be mistaken for inconsistency. I will sketch here some possible remedies.

First off, consistency checks are more easily made if we do not require equally spaced alternatives using, for example, the implied symmetry of the indifference relation. Starting with two widely spaced monetary amounts, say $c = -8 ¢$ and $d = 10 ¢$, we could find a, b with $c < a < 0 < b < d$ and a, $b = (E^*)c$, d. Using a, b, we could find f, g with $f < c$, $d < g$ and f, $g = (E^*)a$, b. Then, for consistency, we should have f, $g = (E^*)c$, d and that the x satisfying a, $b = (E^*)c$, x be d, etc..

Secondly, monetary amounts equally spaced in utility can be obtained without recourse to pure options. We again start with, say, $c = -8 ¢$ and $d = 10 ¢$ and seek a, b as above and such that $U(b) - U(a) = U(d) - U(b) = U(a) - U(c)$. Using a, b. we then find f such that $f, d = (E^*)c, b$, and then g such that $f, g = (E^*)c, d$. Then f, c, a, b, d, g are the required equally spaced alternatives. The problem is to find a and b. In figure 2, I show the true a, b, and also a', b', with $b' < b$, $a < a'$, and a'', b'' with $b < b''$, $a'' < a$. (N.B., the utilities of these different amounts, not the amounts themselves, are plotted in Figure 2.)

$$\frac{f'' \ f' \quad a'' \ a' \ b' \ b'' \qquad g' \ g''}{f \ c \qquad a \quad b \quad d \quad g}$$
Fig. 2.

Now, from a', b' we determine f', g' as before, and also f'', g'' from a'', b''. We notice that the following inequalities serve to distinguish the three cases:

(a) $c, g = (E^*)a, d$

(b) $c, g' \leq a', d$

(c) $c, g'' \geq a'', d$.

Thus, if inequality (c) obtains, we have set b too high, while if (b) obtains, we have set b too low. By decreasing b'' and increasing b', we bracket the required b within ever narrower bounds until a b (and hence, an a) for which the approximate version of (a) holds is reached. Having obtained the required equally spaced options without recourse to 'pure' options, the latter can be used to ascertain what utility the subject assigns to gambling *per se*.

H2 was verified, using the original experimental procedure, for 15 of 19 subjects: their behavior was consistent with the existence of a utility function unique up to a linear transformation. Of the four exceptional subjects, two showed a marked distinclination to gamble and the other two "were extremely tense during the experiment, asked for advice, commented on their own lack of system, and seemed aware that they were making their decisions erratically" ([2], p. 66). H3 and H4 were tested using seven of the subjects for whom utility curves were derived. H3 was verified for all seven, while H4, which requires that the subjective probability of an event be independent of the outcomes with which it is matched, was verified for five of the seven. There were other results of interest.

1.   *Secular stability*: the experiment was rerun for 8 subjects after a period that varied from a few days to several weeks without appreciable change in the utility curves of 7 of the 8.

2. *Non-linearity of utility curves*: For the 15 subjects who satisfied H2, 12 had utility curves that were not linear in money.

3. *Non-actuarial utilities*: Few subjects based their choices on expected monetary payoffs, E.g., for subject 1, the x for which $-4, x = (E^*)6, 11$ was bounded between 14 ¢ and 18 ¢, while the actuarial value is $x = 21$ ¢.

4. *Conservatism of subjective probabilities*: the subjective probability of an event, E', whose objective probability is 1/4, was measured (or, rather, bounded) and, for 4 of 5 subjects, the upper bound was below 1/4. (Further disparities between subjective and objective probabilities are discussed and explained in [12], where references to the more recent literature may also be found.)

Having experimentally determined utility *vs.* money curves, one could use money to assess the utility of other commodities, by noting how much money the subject would spend to replace one commodity by another ([1], p. 116). Alternatively, one can use money to compare utility differences experimentally and axiomatize utility in terms of utility differences. This is the course Suppes follows in Chapter 8 of [1].

The idea of using money to assess utility differences (or intensities of preference) has recently been applied to collective choice by a number of economists (cf. [10]). A voter states how much he would pay to substitute a given option or candidate for his least preferred option. The dollar votes for a given option are then summed over voters, and the option with the largest dollar vote is elected. Voters who are *decisive* (i.e., whose vote changes the outcome) must pay a tax equal to what they have cost the other voters (viz., the dollar amount by which their preferred outcome exceeds that of the elected option when the dollar vote of that decisive voter is omitted). This tax makes it unprofitable for a voter to misrepresent the strength of his preferences. In effect, this proposal averts the Arrow Paradox by using intensities of preference (as represented by dollar votes) in addition to mere preference rankings of the considered options by the individual voters. I will return to this topic in section 7 below.

3. Behavioristic Foundations of Utility

Having devised an empirically testable theory of utility and probability, it was natural for Suppes to attempt a deeper theoretical explanation of the human behavior which that theory predicts (apparently, with some success). The proposed explanation (cf. [1], Chapter 9) invokes stimulus sampling theory. The theory assumes that subjects sample a single stimulus (which could be a pattern of stimuli) on each trial, that stimuli are each conditioned to a single response, and that the subject makes the response associated with the sampled stimulus. The crucial assumptions which govern conditioning are: (1) unsampled stimuli remain connected to the same responses, (2) if no reinforcement occurs on a given trial, there is a probability that the stimulus becomes conditioned to another response, and (3) if a stimulus is sampled on a trial, it remains connected to the same response with probability one or becomes conditioned to some other response with probability θ according as the response to which it was connected is reinforced or not. Finally, conditioning on the current trial is assumed independent of the trial number and the outcome of preceding trials, and the same is true of the probabilities with which stimuli are sampled. These 'independence of path' assumptions insure that the sequence of response random variables is a Markov chain for many schedules of reinforcement.

A single kind of reinforcement serves to illustrate the derivation of a utility function. Subjects choose one of two levers on each trial, where lever i has probability π_i of paying off, $i = 1, 2$ (a 'two-arm bandit'). Given assumption (2) above, there is a probability ε_i that the sampled stimulus will become conditioned to the other response when lever i fails to pay-off. Writing A_i for the event that the subject chooses lever i, $i = 1, 2$, the sequence of response random variables form a Markov process with transition matrix:

Table I

	A_1	A_2
A_1	$1 - \varepsilon_1(1 - \pi_1)$	$\varepsilon_1(1 - \pi_1)$
A_2	$\varepsilon_2(1 - \pi_2)$	$1 - \varepsilon_2(1 - \pi_2)$

To illustrate the derivation of Table I, consider transitions from A_1 to A_2. Thus, the currently sampled stimulus is connected to A_1. For that stimulus to be reconditioned requires that no reinforcement be given (lever 1 does not pay off), which occurs with probability $1 - \pi_1$, and that the stimulus be reconditioned to the other response, which occurs with probability ε_1.

Write p_{ij} for the transition probabilities, and let p_n be the probability of response A_1 on trial n. At asymptote, $p_n = p_{n+1} = p_{11}p_n + p_{21}(1 - p_n)$, whence $p_\infty = \lim p_n = p_{21}/(1 - p_{11} + p_{21})$, or, using table I,

(3.1) $p_\infty = \varepsilon_2(1 - \pi_2)/[\varepsilon_1(1 - \pi_1) + \varepsilon_2(1 - \pi_2)].$

When $\varepsilon_1 = \varepsilon_2$, this simplifies to:

(3.2) $p_\infty = (1 - \pi_2)/[(1 - \pi_1) + (1 - \pi_2)]$

Assume now that a finite set of alternatives, say, many levers, is presented to the subject, and that he must choose one member of a pair on each trial. Then if $p(a, b)$ is the probability that he chooses lever a over lever b, we have $p(a, b) = \varepsilon_b(1 - \pi_b)/[\varepsilon_a(1 - \pi_a) + \varepsilon_b(1 - \pi_b)]$ from (3.1), with an obvious extension of our earlier notation. U is called a (stochastic) utility function if it satisfies:

(3.3) $p(a, b) \geq p(c, d)$ iff $U(a) - U(b) \geq U(c) - U(d).$

Set $\rho_a = \varepsilon_a(1 - \pi_a)$, etc., Then, using the expression for $p(a, b)$ obtained from (3.1), we easily see that $p(a, b) \geq p(c, d)$ iff $\log(1/\rho_a) - \log(1/\rho_t) \geq \log(1/\rho_c) - \log(1/\rho_d)$. Consequently, (3.3) is satisfied by taking

(3.4) $U(a) = \log(1/\rho_a) = -\log \varepsilon_a(1 - \pi_a)$

which simplifies to $U(a) = -\log(1 - \pi_a)$ when $\varepsilon_a = \varepsilon_b$. From the last expression it is plain that $U(a)$ is unbounded and increasing in π_a. Indeed $p(a, b) = 1$ just in case option a has infinitely greater utility than option b under U. On the other hand, a statistician bent on maximizing his expected payoff would have $p(a, b) = 1$ at asymptote if $\pi_a > \pi_b$, even though this condition does not imply that $U(a) - U(b)$ is infinite. The theory in question does not apply, therefore, to the statistically sophisticated. (Numerous studies have shown that naive subjects do not behave like statisticians.) The uniqueness of the utility function (up to positive linear transformations) follows if we assume that it is continuous in ε_a and π_b.

Suppes goes on to show how the derivation of a utility function can be given when choice is made from any finite set of alternatives (not just a pair set). Write $p(a, A)$ for the probability that a is chosen in preference to any member of the set A. The natural extension of (3.3) is:

(3.4) $p(a, A) \geq p(b, B)$ iff $U(a) - U(A) \geq U(b) - U(B).$

The utility of a set of alternatives (where each alternative is assumed to have positive utility) is constrained to satisfy only the following weak conditions: (a) if $A \subseteq B$ then $U(A) \leq U(B)$, and (b) if $A \cap C = B \cap C = \emptyset$ and $U(A) \leq U(B)$, then $U(A \cup C) \leq U(B \cup C)$. A stimulus sampling theory analysis of the general 'n arm bandit' leads to:

$$(3.5) \qquad U(A) = \log \sum_{j \in A} 1/\rho_j, \qquad \text{where } \rho_j = \varepsilon_j(1 - \pi_j)$$

a function which is easily seen to satisfy (3.4) and conditions (a) and (b). This utility function, being logarithmic, has the classical property that the marginal utility of adding an alternative to a set is a decreasing function of the size of the set.

4. Comparative Probability

Given a comparative probability relation on an algebra of events, we seek necessary and sufficient conditions for the existence of a unique and strictly agreeing measure P, i.e., a unique P satisfying:

$$(4.1) \qquad P(A) \geq P(B) \qquad \text{iff} \qquad A \succeq B$$

where '$A \succeq B$' is read 'A is at least as probable as B.' It is assumed that $\succeq$ is a weak ordering (i.e., transitive and connected). The problem is to impose additional conditions on this ordering and obtain the desired representation theorem. A review of the many partial solutions may be found in [4], Chapters 5, 8 and [5] Chapter 1. Here it suffices to remark that no one has found conditions that are both necessary and sufficient for existence of a unique agreeing measure on an arbitrary (finite or infinite) algebra of events. Moreover, the additional conditions that have been imposed on $\succeq$ are anything but perspicuous. An interesting recent paper ([6]) by Suppes and Mario Zanotti draws from this the moral that events are the wrong things to consider. By introducing the auxiliary concept of an extended indicator function, they render the problem tractable.

Let $\mathscr{F}$ be an algebra of events on an arbitrary space X. The indicator A^c of event A is the function defined by:

$$A^c(x) = \begin{cases} 1, & \text{if } x \in A \\ 0, & \text{if } x \notin A. \end{cases}$$

The probability of A can then be defined as the expectation of its indicator:

$$(4.2) \qquad P(A) = E(A^c).$$

To obtain the probability of the union of several events in this way, we need to consider sums of indicators. But the sum of two indicators is not in general an indicator, for it takes the value 2 when both summands take the value 1. Hence, the class of indicators must be extended.

Let $\mathscr{F}^*$ be the smallest semi-group (under addition of functions) which contains all indicators of elements of $\mathscr{F}$, Thus, the members of $\mathscr{F}^*$, called *extended indicators* and denoted A^*, B^*, C^*, . . ., are integer-valued function on the space X. The weak ordering of $\mathscr{F}$ is extended to $\mathscr{F}^*$ by:

(4.3) $A^* \geq B^*$ iff $E(A^*) \geq E(B^*)$.

Finally, let $nA^* = A^* + ... + A^*$ (n summands) be the sum of A^* with itself n times. The following axioms are then necessary and sufficient for the existence of a unique and strictly agreeing probability measure cn $\mathscr{F}$ given by (4.2):

> *Axiom 1.* $\geq$ is a weak ordering of $\mathscr{F}^*$.
> *Axiom 2.* $X^c > \phi^c$ (ϕ^c is the empty event).
> *Axiom 3.* $A^* \geq \phi^c$.
> *Axiom 4.* $A^* \geq B^*$ iff $A^* + C^* \geq B^* + C^*$.
> *Axiom 5.* If $A^* > B^*$, then for every C^*, D^* in $\mathscr{F}^*$, there is an n such that $nA^* + C^* \geq nB^* + D^*$.

All of these axioms, save the last, are analogous to familiar axioms governing the weak (probability) ordering of $\mathscr{F}$, and require little comment. One noteworthy difference is that the analogue of axiom 4 for events requires that C be disjoint from both A and B. Axiom 5 is a kind of Archimedean axiom.

The proof that axioms 1–5 are both sufficient and necessary for existence of a unique measure follows almost immediately from the standard representation theorem for extensive measurement ([4], pp. 73–4). The uniqueness follows because the only axioms, viz., 2 and 3, which go beyond those needed for extensive measurement are clearly necessary for a probabilistic representation via (4.2). For we must have $P(A) \geq P(\emptyset)$ and $P(X) > P(\emptyset)$.

This elegant solution of the representation problem is completely general: no restrictions are imposed on X. This is in marked contrast to the strong structural conditions on X imposed by writers like Koopman, De Finetti and Savage (which only lead to a partial solution). Finally there is a certain naturalness to the formulation of probability in terms of expectation of indicators, and, of course, it has a well known historical precedent in the early work of Huyghens (cf. [11]). It is especially natural when applied to problems involving averages or frequencies, say, the proportion of applicants who will pass a qualifying examination. In all such cases, we are making qualitative judgments about the expected value of a sum of indicators. Having obtained a quantitative probability measure from the conditions governing extended indicators, we can use it to define the expectation of an arbitrary random variable in the usual way.

5. Learning and Conceptual Change

From a Bayesian point of view, 'learning from experience' goes by conditionalizing on new evidence. Suppes, however, is sceptical of "the ability of Bayesian ideas to deal with a large part of our cognitive experience" ([1], p. 86 and Chapter 11). In particular, he argues that conditionalization is "not adequate to that part of learning by experience which requires the learning of a new concept". Conditionalization also fails to describe how humans filter or select from the chaos of stimulation impinging on our sensory receptors or to show how rational changes of belief can be based on sensory stimulation that does not lend itself to verbal statement as evidence. More generally, he charges that humans lack the memory and computational capacities needed to utilize conditionalization in even the simplest of learning tasks. Suppes' challenge, it must be emphasized, is not to the correctness of Bayes' theorem where it can be applied, but rather to its adequacy, *qua* idealization, to deal with much of what falls under the heading of 'learning'. As always, the thrust of his criticism is in the direction of greater realism.

As an alternative to the overly simplified Bayesian account, he invites students of induction to examine the approaches to concept learning that have been developed in recent decades by mathematical psychologists. Most of these approaches can be viewed as special cases of stimulus sampling theory, which, happily, I have already had occasion to outline in the preceding section. This is doubtless a powerful and flexible theoretical blueprint, akin to the particulate scheme of inheritance. Just as the latter can approximate a continuous range of intermediate types by introducing many discrete elements (polygenes), stimulus sampling theory can yield incremental learning by positing many stimuli and ruling that a task is acquired when a majority of the sampled stimuli have been conditioned to the appropriate response. Nevertheless, it is not easy to see how this theory can be applied normatively to render concept learning more efficient (Suppes gives no clue), nor even, as Suppes admits, to shed light on feature selection or the filtering of sensory stimulation. There is also a disquieting vagueness about what counts as a stimulus element in any given application (e.g., the 'two arm bandit' problem of Section 4). But there is another sort of Bayesian reply that I would stress far more than these minor qualms.

A theory of rational inference can be viewed as an attempt to construct probability models that mimic the thought processes of an idealized processor of information. Bayes' theorem is but the simplest of such models, and its application correspondingly limited. One might hope to construct more complicated models, where they are called for, and conditionalization might continue to function in transforming an initial state of such a model or system into a new state upon receipt of additional information. E.g., following Laplace, one might model the change of belief that results from the 'testimonies' of several 'witnesses', taking due account of their independence and their individual reliabilities. I constructed such a model in my doctoral dissertation (*Informative Inference*, Stanford, 1968) and conditionalization remains its backbone. One other example of this sort, inductive generalization, is worth discussing in this context.

By a *composition* of a population, I mean a list of all occurring kinds together with the number of population elements belonging to each kind. A strict Bayesian approach to the inferential problem here would conditionalize on an initial probability distribution over all possible compositions of the population. Even for small populations, the number of possible compositions is enormous, and the amount of calculation required inordinate. Moreover, we seldom know the size of the population with any exactitude.

A more realistic approach was devised by Hintikka (cf. [7], ch. 7). A *strong generalization* or *concept* states which of K possible kinds is present in the population. Prior probabilities are assigned to concepts by imagining that the K possible kinds are assorted at random among α individuals. The larger α is chosen, the smaller the prior probability of a given concept will tend to be, and more importantly, the smaller the rate at which its probability will grow, given a finite sample whose exemplified kinds are a subset of those which the concept designates. Hence, α is a learning rate parameter.

The output of this analysis will be far less informative, of course, than that of the strict Bayesian approach. One might also wonder whether it is realistic to assume knowledge of the possible kinds present. But these objections are very minor. A far more serious (and conceptual) objection is that the choice of α, which is intended to reflect empirical beliefs about the homogeneity of the population, should be itself modifiable in the light of the sample, but it is not. Once you fix the value of Hintikka's parameter, you are stuck with it. Once again, there is a temptation to conclude that our 'learning from experience' in this context is too complicated to be adequately mirrored by a Bayesian analysis. That conclusion, though, is a bit premature.

In Chapter 4 of [14], I have evolved a different Bayesian analysis based on estimating the rate at which new (previously unsampled) kinds are appearing in successive samples of size n. A priori, we should expect this rate to be decreasing at a decreasing rate. I fit the observed rate to a family of convexly decreasing curves a single parameter of which determines the rate of decrease. The values of this parameter correspond to estimates of the number of new kinds that will turn up in the rth block or sample. Hence, the learning rate parameter of this model is readily interpretable, but, more to the point, it can be revised by conditionalization! (Thus, the modulator of our inferences regarding the number of kinds is itself modulated.) Here, then, is a more realistic, yet essentially Bayesian model of a fairly complicated learning process. I would be very interested to see how a stimulus sampling theorist would handle this bit of learning.

The moral, at any rate, seems clear. The Bayesian account of inductive inference can be more liberally construed, but given this broader construal, conditionalization may still be expected to play a fundamental role. Consequently, I am not sure that Suppes is right to dismiss Bayesian analysis as unrealistic. I do concur, however, in his emphasis on the need to extend our inferential methods to richer contexts, and preferably, to contexts in which the efficiency of learning can be objectively measured in relatively theory independent ways. The Bayesian methods of pattern recognition developed in [15] should be mentioned here, for these are relevant to the filtering or 'feature selection' which human concept learners employ.

6. Causality

Suppes develops a probabilistic theory of causality in his recent monograph [8]. He regards causality as a relation between instantaneous events. The fundamental concept is that of a *prima facie* cause. B is a *prima facie cause* of A iff the following conditions are met: (i) $P(A/B) > P(A)$, (ii) $P(B) > 0$, and (iii) B precedes A. Among the *prima facie* causes of A, many will be 'spurious' in the sense that an earlier event C can be found which also increases the probability of A. More precisely,

B (a *prima facie* cause) is a *spurious* cause of A (in sense one) iff there is an earlier event C satisfying (iv) $P(BC) > 0$, (v) $P(A/BC) = P(A/C)$, and (vi) $P(A/BC) \geq P(A/B)$. E.g., lightning is a spurious cause of thunder. A stronger sense of spuriousness is also defined, according to which the *prima facie* cause B is spurious iff there is a partition of events C_i each satisfying (iv) and (v) above. And, finally, B is an *ε-spurious case* of A iff condition (v) above is replaced by the slightly weaker (vi) $|P(A/BC) - P(A/C)| < \varepsilon$. Suppes suggests that the motions of the moons of Jupiter are ε-spurious causes of the earth's motion for very small ε. This is true if he means that Jupiter's moons have little effect on the probability of a large deflection in the earth's motion from its Keplerian orbit, but false, as I.J. Good pointed out in his review of [8] (*J. Am. Stat. Assoc.*, **67**, pp. 245–6), if Suppes means that Jupiter's moons have little effect on the probability of a minute deflection. Suppes rounds out his treatment by defining notions of direct, supplementary, sufficient and negative causation. Roughly, in direct causation, no other causally efficacious event intervenes between cause and effect; in sufficient causation, $P(A/B) = 1$, while in supplementary causation, $P(A/BC) > \max[P(A/B), P(A/C)]$, where B and C are supplementary causes of A. Inter-relations between the different concepts of causation are briefly explored.

The definitions are copiously illustrated throughout, but most illuminatingly, I think, with reference to linear (or incremental) learning theory. It is found (at asymptote) that the reinforcement of a given response is a non-spurious cause of its occurrence on the next trial. The intent of the theory is to make *only* the reinforcement schedule causally efficacious, yet Suppes finds that the occurrence of a response on a given trial is not a spurious, but only an ε-spurious, cause of its occurrence on the next trial. A virtue of Suppes' approach is the explicit relativization of causal claims to conceptual frameworks which may be either: (a) a particular theory, (b) a class of experiments, or (c) the most general framework comprising all the available information.

Suppes' rough statement of his leading idea (p. 10 of [8]) is somewhat misleading:

> Roughly speaking, the modification of Hume's analysis I propose is to say that one event is the cause of another if the appearance of the first event is followed with a high probability by the appearance of the second, and there is no third event we can use to factor out the probability relationship between the first and second events.

This suggests, contrary to his actual intent, that effects must frequently follow their causes. But a cause can be perfectly genuine without occasioning its effect at all frequently, provided the effect almost never occurs in the absence of the cause. (E.g., a small percentage of those vaccinated with penicillin develop an allergic reaction of which the penicillin is, nevertheless, the cause.) This way of putting the matter has led I.J. Good (cf. [9]) to a closely related formulation according to which B has a *tendency to cause A* iff non-occurrence of A confirms (i.e., raises the probability of) non-occurrence of B. The interested reader will want to compare Good's approach to Suppes' in detail. I conclude with one brief remark.

Copernicus and Kepler both viewed the irregularities of planetary motion, e.g., the frequencies with which the different planets retrogress, as causal effects of (or mere appearances resulting from) the earth's motion. Their reason for holding this was that the heliocentric theory could fit *only* the observed frequencies of retrogression, given the directly determinable periods of the planets, while the geocentric theory, which views the retrograde motions as belonging properly to the planet, by suitably adjusting the epicyclic periods, could fit any observed frequencies of retrogression. The intuition here is that a theory which fits a great many possibilities other than those actually observed fails to explain (or give the cause of) what did in fact occur. I think this intuition an important one, and I wonder how Suppes would accomodate it within his theory.

The final chapter of [8] discusses many pertinent philosophical issues: the direction of causality, free will and determinism, and causal mechanisms, but there is almost no discussion of final causes or teleology.

7. Justice and Collective Rationality

Let (x, i) denote what individual i receives in social state x. One such state, x, is *Pareto preferred* to another, y, iff each individual i prefers (x, i) to (y, i) and at least one of these preferences is strict. While this is a rather uncontroversial principle for ordering social or economic states, it is a rather weak principle. It yields only a partial ordering (transitive and asymmetric). Suppes ([1], ch. 10) proposed strengthening Pareto preference by the device of 'extended sympathy'.

To see how this works, consider two distinct individuals, i and j. For x to be Pareto preferred to y requires that i prefer (x, i) to (y, i), while j prefers (x, j) to (y, j), at least one of these preferences being strict. But each player can also imagine himself in the other's position (though without embracing the other's preferences). It might then happen that i prefers (x, j) to (y, i) while j prefers (x, j) to (y, j), or *vice versa*, where again, at least one of the preferences is strict. When this happens, I say that x is *Suppes preferred* to y. Hence, the Suppes preferential ordering of social states generalizes the idea of the Pareto ordering, and, like the latter, is easily shown to be a strict partial ordering. Unfortunately, as A.K. Sen pointed out ([13], pp. 149–150, 155), the Suppes ordering is incompatible with the Pareto ordering; x may be Suppes preferred to y even though y is Pareto preferred to x.

To see this, Sen invites us to imagine a Muslim, i, who relishes beef but won't eat pork, and a Hindu, j, who likes pork but won't eat beef. In state x, the Muslim receives 2 units of pork and no beef, while the Hindu receives 2 units of beef and no pork. In state y, the Muslim gets 1 unit of beef and no pork, while the Hindu gets 1 unit of pork and no beef. Clearly, y is Pareto preferred to x, but since the Muslim prefers (x, j) to (y, i), viz. 2 units of beef to 1 unit, and the Hindu prefers (x, i) to (y, j), viz. 2 units of pork to 1 unit, x is Suppes preferred to y.

Fortunately, as Sen also points out, the remedy is clear: the 'extended sympathy' must be further extended to an exchange of preferences as well as of positions. That is, we must compare the utility i attaches to (x, i), say, with the utility j attaches to (y, j). Unlike Suppes' original proposal, this one does require interpersonal comparisons of utility. But that seems a small price to pay, for Sen shows that the resulting Suppes–Sen ordering extends the Pareto ordering, and still remains a subordering of the orderings generated by aggregate utility and Rawls' maximin principle. That is, if x is Suppes–Sen preferred to y, then the aggregate utility the parties attach to x exceeds that which they attach to y, and the worst off individual under x is better off (utility-wise) than the worst off individual under y. As Sen remarks, "while it [the Suppes–Sen principle] does not yield a complete social ordering, it does squeeze as much juice as possible out of the use of 'dominance' . . . which is the common element in the maximin criterion, utilitarianism, and a number of other collective choice procedures involving interpersonal comparability".

One gets this far by invoking a powerful principle of extended sympathy which also satisfies Bentham's dictum that each man's preferences "count for one". I want to suggest how one might travel farther down this same road and obtain a complete ordering. Having invoked interpersonal comparisons, one can obtain a complete ordering, of course, via utilitarianism. But utilitarianism admits externalities, that is, the utilities one party attaches to the utilities of another. We want somehow to build in a requirement of extended sympathy or impartiality.

To help fix our ideas, imagine that the cooperating parties are members of a commune, and that they hire an economist who, by surveying the resources and skills available to them, is able to list all feasible production-consumption schedules or economic states. The description of each such state should include: (1) the labor input of each worker, (2) the associated production schedule of goods and services, (3) the resources expended in production, (4) the portions of the product to be saved and consumed, (5) the distributive share of each worker in the portion of the product designated for consumption. Each worker-voter has an equal voice in the communal economic decision making. To exclude externalities, I draw a veil of ignorance over the labor inputs and distributive shares of other workers in presenting the alternative economic states, so that each worker-voter knows only his own labor input and share of the product in a given state. Votes are equated with utilities, and the state with the largest number of utility votes is chosen.

Given the veil of ignorance, the chosen state need not be that for which aggregate utility is a maximum. Moreover, some jobs will be generally dispreferred to others, and that means that the marginal utility of fixed wage increments will decrease more slowly for workers assigned those jobs, with the result that less preferred jobs will attract higher wages. As Suppes himself suggested in a seminar, if all workers have identical skills and tastes, wages should be affixed to jobs in such a way that each worker is exactly indifferent between doing any two of the jobs at their assigned wages. The jobs could then be apportioned randomly among workers. Further development of these ideas will be found in [16]. For a different way of constraining individual preferences to be 'impersonal', cf. Harsanyi [17]. From the present perspective, the salient feature of all these approaches is that they view just distributions as arising from a collective choice process.

8. Concluding remarks

This chapter has surveyed Suppes' contributions to the many topics considered, though rather selectively. Limitations of time and space have precluded serious discussion of many of his ideas, but my regret at this omission is ameliorated somewhat by the thought that his work is still very much 'in progress', and there will no doubt be future opportunities to confront it anew. Perhaps enough has been said here to convey something of its range and significance. Suppes' quest for greater realism and greater rigor and his search for more powerful principles of rationality lend his output in this area its personal stamp. This focus of his has subtly, but quite substantially, transformed nearly every one of the topics touched on. As Bjørnson said of the great mathematician, Abel, "where he has been cannot be imagined without him."

Virginia Polytechnic Institute and State University

References

[1] P. Suppes (1969), *Studies in the Methodology and Foundations of Science*, D. Reidel, Dordrecht.

[2] D. Davidson, P. Suppes and S. Siegel (1957), *Decision Making: an Experimental Approach*, Stanford University Press, Stanford, California.

[3] F. P. Ramsey (1931), *The Foundations of Mathematics and Other Logical Essays*, Harcourt-Brace, New York.

[4] D. H. Krantz, R. D. Luce, P. Suppes, and A. Tversky (1971), *Foundations of Measurement* (vol. 1), Academic Press, New York.

[5] T. Fine (1973), *Theories of Probability*, Academic Press, New York.

[6] P. Suppes and M. Zanotti (1976), 'Necessary conditions for existence of a unique measure strictly agreeing with a qualitative probability ordering', *J. Phil. Logic*, **5**, 431–438.

[7] K. J. J. Hintikka and P. Suppes (eds.) (1966), *Aspects of Inductive Logic*, North-Holland, Amsterdam.

[8] P. Suppes (1970), *A Probabilistic Theory of Causality*, North-Holland, Amsterdam.

[9] I. J. Good (1961–1962), 'A causal calculus', *Brit. J. Phil. Sci.*, **11**, 305–18; **12**, 43–51; **13**, 88.

[10] T. N. Tideman and G. Tullock (1976), 'A new and superior process for making social choices', *J. Pol. Econ.*, **84**.

[11] I. Hacking (1975), *The Emergence of Probability*, Cambridge University Press, Cambridge.

[12] A. Tversky and D. Kahneman (1974), 'Judgment under uncertainty: heuristics and biases', *Science*, **185** (Sept.), 1124–30.

[13] A. K. Sen (1970), *Collective Choice and Social Welfare*, Holden-Day, San Francisco.

[14] R. D. Rosenkrantz (1978), *Inference, Method, and Decision*, D. Reidel, Dordrecht.

[15] C. H. Chen (1973), *Statistical Pattern Recognition*, Hayden, Rochelle Park, New Jersey.

[16] R. D. Rosenkrantz (1978), 'Distributive Justice', in C. A. Hooker, J. J. Leach and E. F. McClennen (eds.), *Foundations and Applications of Decision Theory*, D. Reidel, Dordrecht, vol. II, 91–119.

[17] J. C. Harsanyi (1955), 'Cardinal welfare, individualistic ethics, and interpersonal comparisons of utility', *J. Pol. Econ.*, **63**, 309–21.

RICHARD E. GRANDY

SUPPES' CONTRIBUTION TO LOGIC AND LINGUISTICS

Patrick Suppes' contributions in the areas of logic, linguistics and philosophy of language are marked by a characteristic methodological approach. The end is always a clear formulation of a theory that makes it accessible to empirical test; the means is a formulation within a well-understood mathematical theory. The product of his inquiries is not always, however, a definitive set of observational predictions derived from the more precisely formulated theory; often the inquiry leads to conceptual or mathematical problems that must be resolved before any testable consequences can be derived. Thus the work is best seen as a *program* directed toward making the theories in question more precise and testable. I have divided Suppes' work into three areas: the logic of empirical theories, theories of syntax, theories of semantics. In each case I have found it necessary to select from among his considerable writings those which seem most significant and representative. Each area is treated in a section below.

I. Logic of Empirical Theories

Studies in the axiomatic foundations of various theories constitute a considerable portion of Suppes' work in the philosophy of science, but these papers do not concern us here since they consist of axiomatizations within standard logical theories and hence are applications of, rather than innovations in, logic. However, in a paper 'Logics appropriate to empirical theories',[1] Suppes has pointed out "two sorts of examples of

Bogdan, R.J. (Ed.) 'Patrick Suppes' 131–147.

empirical theories for which it is natural and convenient to introduce a logic that is deviant in some respect" (p. 364). The first example is drawn from the theory of measurement and derives its importance from the prominence that invariance considerations have in modern physics. Some statements are true or false regardless of the system of measurement units used, whereas others depend on a choice of units.

For example, the statement that Venus has greater mass than Earth is true or false, independent of what unit of mass is used. Put another way, the truth value of the statement is invariant under an arbitrary positive similarity transformation of the units of mass. . . . On the other hand, the statement that the mass of Venus is greater than 10^{10} has no such invariance, for its truth or falsity will vary with the units of mass selected. (364–5).

For the purpose of formalization, Suppes considers a first order language with identity, individual constants, a two place relation $<$, two-place functions $+$ and $\cdot$, and a one-place function m. A model of such a language will be an ordered septuple $\langle R, A, <, +, \cdot, m, f \rangle$ where R is the set of real numbers, A a non-empty set, $<$ the less-than relation among reals, $+$ and $\cdot$ the corresponding functions on reals, m is a real valued function from A to R, and f is a function from the individual constants to $A \cup R$. Since three elements of the septuple remain fixed, we will generally specify a model by giving only the remaining quadruple $\langle R, A, m, f \rangle$. m corresponds to a measurement of physical quantity possessed by the objects A. With each type of measurement we can associate a group of numerical transformations that characterizes the type of measurement scale. If the quantity is hardness, then the transformations are all positive monotonic functions, if m is classical position, then the group consists of all linear transformations.

Given a model $M = \langle R, A, m, f \rangle$ and a group of transformations G we can define the set of G-transforms of M as those models $M' = \langle R, A, g(m), f \rangle$ where $g \in G$. Suppes now introduces a definition of empirical meaningfulness for formulas of the language and gives a three-valued semantics. The resulting system is a truth-functional but nonclassical logic, and this has several unappealing features. Clearly a statement such as $m(a) = k$ is not invariant and hence will be assigned neither true nor false but the third truth value u. Similarly $m(a) = k + 1$ and $m(a) \neq k$ are variant and must be assigned u. But now we are required to assign

(1) $m(a) = k \lor m(a) \neq k$ and
(2) $m(a) = k \lor m(a) = k + 1$

the same truth value if the semantics is to be truth-functional. This is rather implausible since the former will be true under any transformation and the latter will not. Suppes deals with this difficulty by defining "empirical meaningfulness" so that a statement is empirically meaningful only if every atomic part is, and an atomic formula is meaningful only if it is invariant. Thus he justifies assigning $m(a) = k \vee m(a) \neq k$ the value u by reference to the fact that it is empirically meaningless.

The notions of truth and thus of consequence depend on the characterization of empirical meaningfulness, which in turn is characterized in terms of the groups of transformations. It is unknown for most groups whether meaningfulness can be characterized axiomatically. However, it is questionable whether the approach sketched above is the most appropriate for the problem. The definition of empirical meaningfulness was motivated by the necessities of preserving truth functionality in the three valued semantics, but no basic reasons for choosing the three valued semantics were given. In fact, the outcome that (1) is assigned u is a good reason for rejecting the three valued semantics since it is invariant.

In one sense, if we give up two-valued logic, the minimal departure is to move to three valued logic. But this move requires giving up the standard characterizations of validity and consequence. A preferable alternative would be to move to a Boolean-valued logic with additional operations. The advantages of this approach are several: (1) we keep the familiar logic; (2) two statements that are neither true nor false can be assigned different values; (3) the new operations can be used to characterize the further properties of statements we wish to formalize.

Accordingly, I suggest that we reconsider the problem, beginning by extending the language by the addition of a sentence operator I. The informal interpretation of $I\phi$ is 'ϕ is invariantly true'. The semantics will be the rather natural one obtained by assignin to each sentence the set of models in which it is true, where the truth values are subsets of the set of models. More formally, we define a G-model structure to be an ordered pair consisting of a model M and the set of all models that are G-transforms of M. We can now define a valuation function V over the set of formulas not containing I by letting $V(\phi) = \{M' : \phi$ is true in $M'\}$. Further, we define $I\phi$ to be true in a model in a structure just in case ϕ is true in all models in the structure. It is easy to show that this is a truth-functional semantics with conjunction, disjunction and negation defined as intersection, union and relative complement respectively. Since the semantics is Boolean-valued, all valid formulas of standard logic will remain valid.[2]

Returning to the sentence that provoked our disagreement, we can see that if $\mathfrak{M}$ is the set of all models in a G-structure then $V(m(a) = k) \cup$ $- V(m(a) = k$ is $\mathfrak{M}$. Hence (1) is true in all models and $I(m(a) = k \vee m(a) \neq k)$ is true, whereas (2) is not invariant and so $I(m(a) = k \vee m(a) = k + 1)$ will be false. Since the definition of $I\phi$ has all of the formal features of the definition in modal systems S5 (since G always produces an equivalence class of models), we know that the schemas $I(\phi \rightarrow \psi) \rightarrow (I\phi \rightarrow I\psi)$, $I\phi \rightarrow \phi(-I - \phi \rightarrow I - I - \phi)$ are all valid and the rule: 'if ϕ is a theorem, then $I\phi$ is a theorem' is sound. Which further formulas are valid will depend on the nature of G. If, for example, we have the set of similarity transformations for G, then $I(m(a) = 2m(b))$ will be true.

At this time, I do not know whether it is possible to axiomatize the set of valid formulas for any of the common type of G structure. However, the method of recasting the problem described in the last few pages offers a significant advantage over the systematization suggested originally, for problems of axiomatization of Boolean algebras with operators is a well-understood and explored area of mathematics. Thus we have made more accessible the problems of the logic of invariance raised by Suppes. His justification for the philosophical value of three-valued logic, it appears, is not compelling, but the judgment that invariance questions pose interesting logical problems is quite correct.

II. Syntax

At least one of the goals of a contemporary grammatical theory for a natural language is to provide a formal means for generating all and only the sentences of the language. However, there are some serious methodological problems in judging when a grammatical theory is successful in this enterprise. For one thing, one must make projections from the available data in a stronger way than is usual. In any scientific theory one wishes to account not merely for past and present observations but for all future ones as well; in linguistic theory, this would mean that the grammar should include sentences that could be uttered by a speaker under suitable circumstances but might happen not ever to be, perhaps because the circumstances did not arise, e.g. 'There is a hippopotamus in the rutabaga patch'. But there are also strings of words which probably could never be uttered by a human being in spontaneous speech because they exceed the limits of memory or processing. For example, strings ten thousand words long or relatively short extensions of sentences such as

(3) *Someone someone someone someone admires admires admires admires no one.*

Strings such as (3) exhibit more complex (or iterated) forms of structures that generate clearly accptable sentences. In fact, given sufficient time, patience, concentration and pencil and paper, English speakers can understand the structure of (3). Unfortunately there is no clear principled way of drawing a line with respect to iteration such as that exhibited in (3). A sentence with two such iterations might be spoken, one with 50 would certainly not, but there is no sharp division between.

A second point that raises methodological difficulties is the process of testing individual sentences of moderate length. The process of simply waiting and listening to see whether a speaker eventually produces a given sentence S is too time-consuming to be contemplated. But if one simply presents the sentence to the speaker-listener and observes 'bizarreness' reactions or lack thereof, one has considerable difficulties in sorting out the cause or the bizarreness reactions when they occur, and on the other hand listeners often reconstrue sentences to make them grammatical or intelligible without any discernible signs of the effort involved. Finally, asking speakers directly to make judgments of grammaticality is a dubious procedure since one is attempting to discern the speakers' tacit linguistic competence and not his or her usage of the word 'grammatical'. A speaker's conscious conception of grammaticality may well be at odds with the linguistic competence exhibited.

As a way of overcoming some of these difficulties in testing grammatical theories, Suppes has proposed the use of probabilistic grammars. A generative grammar can be regarded as a set of rules for producing sentences with associated syntactic structures. A probabilistic grammar associates with each rule a probability so that, with each syntactically structured sentence, there is associated a derived probability. The goal then is to find values for the rule probabilities which make correct predictions for the probabilities of occurrence of sentences in the corpus.

Explanation of the advantages of the probabilistic approach will be facilitated if we give an (admittedly oversimplified) example from Suppes' 'Probabilistic grammar for natural languages'.[3]

	Production Rule	Probability
1.	$S \rightarrow NP + VP$	1
2.	$VP \rightarrow V_1$	$1 - a$
3.	$VP \rightarrow V_2 + NP$	a

4.	$NP \rightarrow PN$	$1 - b$
5.	$NP \rightarrow AdjP + N$	b
6.	$AdjP \rightarrow AdjP + Adj$	$1 - c$
7.	$AdjP \rightarrow Adj$	c

A sentence with the structure $PN + V_2 + Adj + N$ will be generated by applying rules (1), (3), (4), (5), and (7), so the probability of such a sentence structure is $abc(1 - b)$.

Suppes makes several points intended to avoid misunderstanding of the nature and significance of the enterprise. First, it must be noted that the grammar does not generate sentences by a left-to-right process with the probability of a constituent depending on the probability of its predecessor. The concept of a probabilistic grammar is one that in principle places no restriction on the nature of the production rules. The particular example is, of course, a context-free grammar, but there are no insuperable difficulties in attaching probabilities to the rules of a transformational grammar. (I will return to this point shortly).

The second important point is that the goal of probabilistic grammar is non-trivial. In the above case the grammar has three parameters a, b, c whose values must be chosen, but the number of sentence types is infinite (counting Adj^n as distinct from Adj^{n+1}) in principle, and twelve (counting all strings $Adj^n + N$ for $n > 2$ as similar) in practice. Given a particular corpus of utterances, one uses the method of best fit to estimate the parameters a, b and c, and one can then determine how good the fit is between the predicted probabilities of sentence types and the actual distribution of sentence types.

One advantage of the probabilistic approach is that it may enable one to solve concerns about sentences of excessive length. To illustrate, the grammar generates sentences of the form

$$Adj + Adj + \ldots Adj + Adj + N + V_1$$

with arbitrarily long finite strings of adjectives. For such a sentence with n adjectives the probability is $(1 - a)b(1 - c)^{n-1} c$. If $1 - c$ is relatively small then the probability of such strings diminishes very rapidly. This is a specific instance of the general fact that beyond a certain length longer strings are generally less likely than shorter strings. Thus the probabilistic grammar may capture one of the most obvious and pervasive features of actual language use.[4]

A further potential advantage of probabilistic grammar, which, in my opinion, Suppes does not sufficiently emphasize, is that it can provide means of discriminating between distinct grammars with the same weak generative capacity. Two grammars G_1 and G_2 have the same weak generative capacity if the set of sentences they generate are the same; two grammars have the same strong generative capacity iff they generate the same sentences *and* assign the same structural descriptions to those sentences. Two grammars that are weakly equivalent may differ considerably, and yet they will be undistinguishable on grounds of predicting which strings of the language are sentences. More subtle discriminations between such grammars on observational grounds are difficult to obtain, for there are few ways to elicit information about what structural descriptions speakers attribute to sentences.

However, given two weakly equivalent grammars we can pose the further question whether one provides a better basis for a probabilistic grammar for a given corpus. If the degree of fit which is obtained between the predicted distribution and the actual is considerably better for one grammar than the other, then we have strong empirical reasons for choosing one grammar over the other. Note that this comparison can be made even if the grammars have different numbers of rules and consequently different numbers of parameters. A grammar that has a larger number of parameters available to be fitted to the data must provide a closer fit than a grammar with few parameters if it is to be chosen as significantly better. The statistical test of goodness of fit takes into account the number of degrees of freedom (parameters) in assessing to what extent the predictions of a grammar are better than would be expected by chance. Thus probabilistic grammar also provides a means for answering in a principled way questions about whether it is better to utilize a grammar with a larger number of categories and/or rules.

It must be recognized, however, that the process of adding probabilistic parameters to weakly equivalent grammars will not necessarily provide an empirical discrimination between them. It may be that two weakly equivalent but distinct grammars will each fit the distribution data equally well. This is possible because the data themselves are not given independently of a grammar. The frequency predictions are not of the occurrence of individual sentences, but rather of structural types of sentences, and, since distinct grammars will in general assign distinct structural descriptions to sentences, the distribution of structural types is only determined relative

137

to a grammar. Hence two different grammars may lead to distinct descriptions of the data, and each grammar may provide a good probabilistic fit for the data as analyzed according to that grammar.

Unfortunately, we are not yet at the point where this theoretical nicety can arise, for we do not yet have any adequate grammar for an entire language. In an attempt to begin with a relatively simple (yet interesting) language, Suppes has applied the conception of a probabilistic grammar to children's language. For the corpus that was used and the grammar that was proposed, the fit was not very successful.[5] This negative result is compatible, of course, with at least two different possibilities. It may be that the factors that underlie the distribution of sentence types are not accessible to such simple grammatical analysis.

The second possibility is simply that the grammar is not an adequate one for the language. Children's syntax is a little understood subject and the natural inclination to posit simple versions of adult grammars to explain their construction may well be erroneous. In fact, the categories used in adult language such as noun-verb-adjective can only be applied to children's language with considerable effort and should be used with at least as much care. Typical sentences such as 'daddy apple' can be multiply ambiguous and it may well be that, at this stage of language development, semantics rather than syntactic features are the dominant factor in determining structure.

III. Semantics

Turning to questions of semantics, we find that there are two major aspects to Suppes' work. The first consists of the application of concepts from model theory which are well known to philosophers, to detailed problems of natural language. This work is intended to show how model theoretic techniques can be illuminating in the analysis of actual language use, and to open the possibilities of further use of such techniques by psychologists. I will not discuss this work any further here, since the significance lies not in any innovations in formal semantics but in the application of formal semantics to problems in psychology.[6]

More original is the attempt, primarily in 'Congruence of Meaning',[7] to outline a program for a more sophisticated and satisfactory treatment of issues concerning meaning and sameness of meaning than has previously

138

been attained. The basic idea is fairly simple; it is that we should distinguish different relations of congruence of meaning, just as geometers distinguish different relations of congruence among geometrical figures. One distinct advantage is that in putting matters in terms of sameness and difference relations we may very likely be able to sidestep questions about what (kinds of things) meanings are.

Since the analogy with geometric congruence is central to the motivation, we will review in some detail the role of congruence in geometry. The earliest and most natural congruence relation is one that obtains between two figures when "one figure, by being moved in space, can be made to coincide with the second figure so that the two figures coincide in all their parts".[8] A stronger criterion of congruence would be that two figures are congruent if one can obtain such a coincidence by linear transformations alone (with no rotation). A slightly weaker concept of congruence is obtained if we require only that two figures have the same shape but not the same size. On this criterion A and B are congruent if A can be made to totally coincide with B by movements in space and shrinking or expanding of A.

Much weaker congruence relations are also of interest.

A significant example is topological congruence. Two figures are topologically congruent when one is a homeomorphic image of the other, that is, can be obtained from the other by a one-one bicontinuous transformation. In this case, for example, a square and a triangle are topologically congruent. On the other hand, dimensionality is preserved. . . . and therefore a sphere is not homeomorphic to a circle or a pyramid to a triangle (23).

Each of these congruence relations plays a central role in some branch of geometry and gives rise to an important mathematical theory. Each can also be seen (with some stretching) as a way of making precise the informal conception of 'same shape'. There are three questions that we will want to ask about each of the congruence relations among sentences which Suppes suggests. The first is whether the definition is sufficiently precise to permit formal study; the second is whether the relation defined corresponds to some aspect of 'same in meaning'; the third is whether the definition is likely to give rise to a formal theory of any importance.

The only congruence relation among sentences which has been traditionally studied in philosophy of language is that of logical equivalence. This is, of course, a clear and theoretically important relation, but it is far too loose to capture any intuitive sense of sameness of meaning.

Carnap suggested in *Meaning and Necessity* a tighter criterion of sameness of meaning, but 'intensional isomorphism' has been generally discredited as too restrictive.

Suppes proposes four distinct definitions of congruence relations, but before discussing these in detail, we must specify the background. The definitions are given relative to a syntax and semantics which are taken as fixed. The syntax is assumed to be a context-free grammar; the semantics is a model-theoretic one that fits in an especially simple way with the grammar. The model structure assigns objects (or sets of objects or *n*-tuples of objects . . .) to (some of) the terminal symbols of the grammar. With each of the production rules of the grammar is associated a set-theoretic function that combines the semantic objects assigned to the syntactic items that are being combined. For example, if one of the production rules is

$$N \rightarrow Adj + N$$

and if all adjectives are predicative, then the semantic function associated with the rule would simply be intersection. Thus if we use this rule to generate a portion of a tree

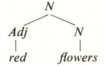

then the N node would be assigned the intersection of the sets assigned to 'red' and 'flowers'.

Suppes chooses context-free grammars and simply related model structures partly because they provide the easiest examples to discuss, partly to avoid some complications that would distract from the motivation of the definitions. He should not be misinterpreted as asserting that such simple structures will suffice for all constructions of natural languages. We will discuss later the extent to which complications of the grammar and semantics might cast some doubt on the feasibility of the project.

One further point requires discussion before presenting the definitions of congruence. Suppes defines congruence relations relative to a class of model structures, not necessarily with respect to the class of model structures of the language. The reason for this is that we may well want to keep some nonlogical elements of the language fixed in interpretation. One example would be to include arithmetic in the language and hold the interpretation of arithmetic terms fixed in all model structures. Another example would be to achieve the effect of Carnapian meaning postulates by, for example, requiring that the model structures considered all assigned 'man' the intersection of the sets assigned to 'rational' and 'animal'.

The definitions are given in approximate order of strength.[9]

Definition 1. If T_1 and T_2 are semantic trees for sentences S_1 and S_2, then S_1 is strongly $\mathfrak{M}$-congruent to S_2 if and only if the trees T_1 and T_2 can be made semantically identical with respect to each model structure of $\mathfrak{M}$, except perhaps for labelling, by identifying isomorphic trees.

The effect of this definition is illustrated by reference to a language that contains elementary portions of English, French, and Russian. On this definition, for such a language the sentences

> *The book is red.*
> *Le livre est rouge.*

are congruent, but neither of them is congruent to

> *Kniga krasnaya.*

The last sentence is not strongly congruent to the others because of the lack of copula and article.

The relation of strong congruence is extremely sensitive to variations in both syntax and semantics and hence questions about whether the relation holds between two such sentences are inextricably bound up with questions about appropriate grammars and semantics. (I assume that one ultimately wants to be able to ask and answer questions about English sentences and that the answers, though they must be with respect to a grammar and semantics, will be relative to the best grammar and semantics.) For example, Suppes mentions that the sentences

> (A) *All men are mortal*
> (B) *Every man is mortal*

are strongly congruent. It is certainly the case that in intuitive terms the two are close in meaning, but it is questionable whether they are strongly congruent. For the two sentences to have isomorphic syntactic trees it must be the case that the node of the tree corresponding to 'men' be isomorophic to that corresponding to 'man'; but if we use as seems correct, an analysis in which 'men' consists of two morphemes 'man' plus PLURAL, then the trees are not syntactically isomorphic. But if the syntactic trees are not isomorphic then the semantic trees cannot be either. Secondly, even if one accepted that the syntactic trees should be isomorphic it could still be argued that the semantic trees should differ, since the plural noun has a different semantic function from the singular. The difference between 'the men' and 'the man' seems to be a function of the semantics of the nouns and not of the definite article(s?). This does not imply that there is something wrong with the definition of congruence, just that the specific claim that on the best grammar and semantics the two original sentences are strongly congruent is questionable. Since the two sentences do appear to be very close in meaning it would be desirable to find a relation on which they are congruent. We will return to this point shortly as it proves to be quite important.

The second congruence definition is incomparable with the first in that some pairs which are congruent according to one are not according to the second and vice versa. This second definition is intended to capture the relation which holds between

> *John and Mary are here.*
> *Mary and John are here.*

and is called permutational congruence in form and meaning.

Definition 2. Let T_1 and T_2 be semantic trees for sentences S_1 and S_2. Then S_1 is permutationally $\mathfrak{M}$-congruent to S_2 in form and meaning if and only if T_1 can be obtained from T_2 by a sequence of permutations of branches for every model structure of $\mathfrak{M}$.

A third definition of congruence is weaker than this in that it only requires coincidence in meaning.

Definition 3. If T_1 and T_2 are semantic trees for S_1 and S_2, then S_1 and S_2 are permutationally-congruent with respect to meaning if and only if T_1 can be obtained from T_2 (except possibly for labeling) by a sequence of permutations of branches of subtrees for every model structure in $\mathfrak{M}$.

Like the first definition, this one ignores labelling and hence sentences of different natural languages can be congruent (assuming that they are part of the language for which the definition is given). Suppes gives as examples of sentences permutationally 𝔐-congruent with respect to meaning, the triple

> *John and Mary are here.*
>
> *Marie et Jean sont ici.*
>
> *Marie und Johann sind hier.*

and the pair

$$2 + 2 = 4 \qquad 4 = 2 + 2$$

The last and weakest of his definitions of congruence differs from logical equivalence only in allowing that a more restricted set of models may be used.

Definition 4. Two sentences are 𝔐-paraphrases of each other if and only if the roots of their trees denote the same object with respect to every model structure in 𝔐.

If we make the type of restriction discussed earlier including in the model structures 𝔐 only those in which the interpretation of arithmetic terms is standard and fixed, then sentences that are not logical paraphrases, such as

> *Mary has three apples and John has four.*
>
> *Mary has three apples and John has one more.*

are 𝔐-paraphrases. There is some plausibility to saying that this pair has a similarity of meaning, but if one takes more extreme cases of paraphrases this becomes less and less plausible. For example, it is likely (though we are not sure) that

> *David has two apples.*
>
> *There are three numbers such that if each of them is raised to the power which is the number of apples David has, then the sum of the result for the first two is equal to that for the third, and David has more than one apple.*

are 𝔐-paraphrases of each other.

I have been critical of several of the definitions of congruence, but I want it to be clear that the spirit of the criticism is that the *specific* definitions are of questionable value. This is not to cast doubt necessarily on the entire project. Let us consider then the question what improvements might be made on the definitions suggested; or rather, let us consider what would have to be done in order to improve upon them, since it is not possible in the short space available here to go into the details that would be required.

There are two directions in which improvements in the treatment of congruence might be expected. The first would be to attempt a more systematic analysis of the congruence relations. The definitions given above are rather natural ones and provide a beginning point for the inquiry, but one would ultimately want a more thorough understanding of the nature of different congruence relations and their connections. For example, it would seem natural from this point of view to give:

Definition 5. If T_1 and T_2 are semantic trees for S_1 and S_2 then S_1 and S_2 are permutationally $\mathfrak{M}$-congruent with respect to form if and only if T_1 can be obtained from T_2 (except for semantic values) by a sequence of permutations of branches of subtrees for every model structure in $\mathfrak{M}$.

This relation is not of much theoretical interest in isolation, but is important for a systematic study of congruence relations, because we can easily see that *permutational $\mathfrak{M}$-congruence with respect to form and meaning* is the relation that is the intersection of *permutational $\mathfrak{M}$-congruence with respect to form and permutational $\mathfrak{M}$-congruence with respect to meaning*. In general, then, it would be desirable to find a basic set of congruence relations such that all others of interest can be generated by various operations on the basic set.

The second direction in which we should look for an improvement in the theory of sentence congruence is grammar. The definitions given above made use of the grammar of the language only in the specification of the trees, but made no reference whatsoever to any of the details of the grammars. However, it appears from linguistic theory thus far that different elements of the grammars of natural languages play different roles. For example, the categories of noun phrase, verb phrase, adjective phrase enter into the grammar of English in significantly different ways from the categories noun, verb or adjective. Noting this fact and the previously observed similarity between "Every man is mortal" and "All men are mortal" which I have argued is not captured by Definition 1 we might attempt to give another definition of congruence. This relation we will call *nonterminal phrasal congruence* and the basic idea is that sentences which stand in this relation are identical except for terminal portions of the trees. More precisely we can define a phrasal terminal subtree in a tree to be a subtree of the tree from terminal symbol(s) up to and including one node labelled *NP*, *VP*, *AP* or *PP*. To illustrate, in the tree

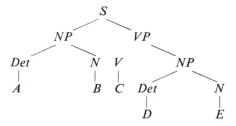

if *A* through *E* are terminal symbols, then

and

are phrasal terminal subtrees. We can now define the relation of non-terminal phrasal congruence.

Definition 6. If T_1 and T_2 are semantic trees for S_1 and S_2, then S_1 and S_2 are nonterminal phrasally congruent if and only if T_1 and T_2 are identical except for portions of phrasal terminal subtrees below the top node.

On this definition, the sentences discussed before

> *All men are mortal.*
> *Every man is mortal.*

will evidently be congruent, since they differ only below the first *NP*. The definition, by ignoring both semantic and syntactic details below a certain point in the trees, is also able to treat

> *Bachelors pay more for automobile insurance.*
> *Unmarried adult males pay more for automobile insurance.*

successfully.

We are in a position now to consider a general objection against the usefulness of congruence relations in analyzing sameness of meaning for natural languages. The use of congruence relations recognizes that there are distinct senses that are attached to the phrase 'sameness of meaning' and attempts to make each of the various senses precise. But many of the objections to the conception of 'same meaning' are not simply objections to the assumption that there is a single such relation. Rather, many such objections take the form of pointing out that sameness of meaning is a matter of degree, that sentences are more or less the same in meaning. Put in another equivalent form, the relation of 'same in meaning' is not transitive, but of course transitivity is an essential property of congruence relations.

The point can easily be illustrated by considering our last definition. The sentences

Every dedicated traveler visits every state eventually.
All dedicated travelers visit every state eventually.
All dedicated travelers visit all states eventually.
All dedicated travelers visit all states sooner or later.

are all non-terminal phrasally congruent on at least one reasonable grammar and semantics of English. But the relation of sameness or similarity of meaning is much stronger between each sentence and the successive one than it is between those which are farther apart. Each successive sentence is obtained by changing a single terminal subtree, and the examples show that sentences that differ by a single subtree are quite close in meaning, whereas those which differ by three are less close.

We cannot define a congruence relation that captures the closeness of meaning between two sentences that differ by a single change of subtree, because a congruence relation by definition must be transitive. Hence any congruence relation that holds between the successive sentences must hold between all of the sentences.

This suggests that we are probably using the wrong branch of geometry in studying sameness of meaning. If we want to capture the basic fact that sentences differ in meaning not only in different ways but also in different degrees, then we need something like a metric of meaning differences. On this approach the difference in meaning between any two sentences would be measured in terms of the number and nature of transformations required in order to transform one into another. Carrying out such a theory would require considerable conceptual analysis of transformations in order to obtain a suitable base for the definitions. One cannot simply treat all transformations alike in that some are far more complex than others, so that one would probably require a characterization of transformations in terms of a basic set of fairly simple transformations from which all others could be defined. Furthermore, the application of the theory of actual language use would require careful thought and experimentation in order to find an appropriate assignment of metric values to the basic transformations and to determine the effects of various modes of composition of transformation.[10]

University of North Carolina
at Chapel Hill

Notes

[1] In J. W. Addison, L. Henkin & A. Tarski (Eds.), *Theory of Models* (Proceedings of the 1963 international symposium at Berkeley.) Amsterdam. North-Holland, 1965, pp. 364–75. All further page references in this section are to this paper.

[2] An apparent alternative would be to use supervaluation semantics, but in fact Boolean valued logic can be used for any purpose for which one uses supervaluations. One need only define the appropriate Boolean values in terms of sets of valuations.

[3] *Synthese* 1970, **22**, 95–116. All page references are to the reprinting in D. Davidson and G. Harman (Eds.) *Semantics of Natural Language*, Dordrecht: Reidel, 1972, pp. 741–62.

[4] Of course it is an empirical question whether a probabilistic grammar of this type can capture the exact regularity. It may be that the distribution is of a different form than that associated with the above grammars. This could occur, for example, if the distribution of probabilities showed a sharp decline when embeddings exceeded a particular number.

[5] The corpus is Adam I, a transcript of a 26 month old boy obtained by Roger Brown and associates (p. 749). It was found however that good fits were obtained with first grade readers.

[6] See, for example, 'The semantics of children's language', *American Psychologist*, 1974, **29**, 103–114.

[7] *Proceedings and Addresses of the American Philosophical Association*, 1972/1973, **46**, 21–38.

[8] *Ibid*, p. 28, quoting Kiselyov.

[9] My exposition follows Suppes' quite closely, but I give definitions in a slightly different form. He gives each definition mentioning all semantic trees where I mention specific ones. A semantic tree is a syntactic tree with semantic assignments added. Strictly writing, each definition should be stated for sentences with respect to those semantic trees mentioned, but I omit this complication in the interest of brevity.

[10] I am indebted to Bob Rodman, David Rosenthal and Brian Skyrms for helpful suggestions about and criticisms of an earlier draft.

WILLIAM H. BATCHELDER & KENNETH WEXLER

SUPPES' WORK IN THE FOUNDATIONS OF PSYCHOLOGY

I. Introduction

Patrick Suppes' contributions to the foundations of psychology all concern the development of psychology as a formal science. The aim is to develop formal theories that are conceptually clear and empirically testable in the spirit of theoretical work in the physical and biological sciences.

Prior to 1950, formal theory in psychology was confined to the so-called 'harder' areas of psychology – audition, vision, psychophysics, physiological psychology – all of which enjoy an interface with physics or biology. That work has roots in the 19th century going back to such eminent scientists as Gustav Fechner, Ewald Hering, and Hermann von Helmholtz. However, their formal theories all involved the explanation of psychological phenomena in terms of phenomena in the physical or biological sciences. Psychology *qua* psychology had essentially no formal theory prior to 1950.

Suppes has been a leader in developing formal scientific theory in the so-called softer or more psychological areas of psychology such as learning, thinking, psycholinguistics, and social psychology. His approach has been non reductionistic; theories are axiomatized in terms of primitive concepts that truly belong in psychological discourse. For reasons that will become apparent, most of Suppes' early formal work concerns learning theory. Part II of this essay will concern Suppes' contributions to learning theory. The third part will take up later work in 'cognitive psychology' and the final part will involve an overview of Suppes' work. We will not discuss relevant work in measurement, decision making and education, as they are considered elsewhere in this volume.

Bogdan, R.J. (Ed.) 'Patrick Suppes' 149–186.
Copyright © 1979 by D. Reidel Publishing Company, Dordrecht, Holland.

Prior to 1950, the softer areas of experimental psychology were dominated by learning theory. Learning theory was developed by the 'system builders' such as Pavlov, Thorndike, Skinner, Guthrie, Hull, and Tolman (see Hilgard and Bower, 1966). These theorists and their colleagues contributed many ideas to psychology as well as an extensive body of experimental results; however, their work was devoid of serious formal theorizing.

The first important efforts to develop formal, testable theories in learning occurred in the early 1950s. The inputs to this development are found in the work of Estes (1950) and Bush and Mosteller (1951, 1955). The area of mathematical learning theory (MLT) emerged from this work, and Suppes played a major role in that development.

At about that time, Suppes had committed himself to a particular type of formalism which he called the *axiomatic method*. This method demands that a theory be formulated as a complex predicate in terms of set-theoretic primitives. Unlike well-known metamathematical approaches, set theory and other standard branches of mathematics are taken as given. The axioms of the theory impart substantive character to the primitives. Suppes writes (1954, p. 244):

Unfortunately a good many philosophers seem to labor under the misimpression that to axiomatize a scientific discipline, or a branch of mathematics, one needs to formalize the discipline in some well-defined artificial language. . . . Luckily we can pursue a program of axiomatization without constructing any formal languages. The viewpoint I am advocating is that the basic methods appropriate for axiomatic studies in the empirical sciences are not metamathematical (and thus syntactical and semantic), but set-theoretical. To axiomatize the theory of a particular branch of empirical science in the sense that I am advocating is to give a definition of a set-theoretic notion. . . . .

The aim of the axiomatic method is to achieve clarity both in the separation of primitive from derived notions and in the separation of purely mathematical from substantive assumptions. While the method permits one to characterize the class of models of a theory and to answer such questions as whether primitives are independent, whether axioms are consistent and independent, and when two models are isomorphic, these questions occupy a secondary importance to the primary goal of clarity itself. Issues such as the completeness of the theory or the number of axioms in a 'minimal' set are of no interest for theories formalized as set-theoretic predicates.

In early 1950, Suppes began projects to axiomatize physics, measurement, probability and decision making. These developments are discussed elsewhere in this volume. In the academic year 1955–56, Suppes was a fellow at the Center for Advanced Study in the Behavioral Sciences, where he met Estes. Out of that collaboration Suppes became interested in MLT. Unlike Suppes' other projects, MLT offered a chance to apply the axiomatic method to a newly developing area. Apart from some work of others in economics, no scientific area had been developed from the ground up via the axiomatic method.

II. Mathematical Learning Theory

Before discussing Suppes' contributions to MLT, some overview is desirable. Organisms modify their behavior over time. Many of these changes in behavior are thought to result from experience in the world. Traditional learning theory attempts to explain how experience modifies behavior.

Learning theorists developed a number of explanations of learning, most of which centered around the constructs of stimulus, response and reinforcer. A stimulus elicits or provides the occasion for a response, which in turn results in an outcome or reinforcer[1] which operates to change future response probabilities to the stimulus. Despite many complexities, this stimulus-response-outcome scheme lies at the heart of the learning theories of Thorndike, Skinner, and Hull. Independent of the ultimate conceptual adequacy of the scheme, it was the starting point for the development of formal theories of the learning process.

The formal theories imagine a hypothetical setting within which a particular organism receives as input one of a finite number of (mutually exclusive) stimulus situations $\mathscr{S} = \{S_1, \ldots, S_K\}$ on each of a series of trials (discrete points in time, $n = 1, 2, \ldots$). On each trial n, the organism makes one of a finite number of (mutually exclusive) response outputs $\mathscr{R} = \{R_1, \ldots, R_L\}$. Following the response on a trial, one of a finite number of (mutually exclusive) outcomes (reinforcers) $\mathcal{O} = \{o_1, \ldots, o_M\}$ occurs.

It is assumed that the stimulus, response and outcome events are observables on any trial; consequently, when an organism is run for N trials in such an experiment, the data can be viewed as an ordered string of three-tuples of the form:

(1) $\langle S(n), R(n)\ O(n) \rangle_{n=1}^{N}$,

where $S(n) \in \mathscr{S}$, $R(n) \in \mathscr{R}$, and $O(n) \in \mathcal{O}$ are the observable events occurring on trial n.

Suppose one has a learning task that can be described in terms of the observables in Equation 1 and that one conducts an experiment on a number of like organisms, where each is run for N trials. The data from each organism take the form of Equation 1, i.e., each organism's data can be regarded as a sample point in the *sample space*

$$(2) \qquad \mathcal{X} = \prod_{n=1}^{N} (\mathcal{S} \times \mathcal{R} \times \mathcal{O})$$

consisting of $(K \cdot L \cdot M)^N$ sample points.

A mathematical learning model can be viewed as setting up a *probability space* on $\mathcal{X}$ in the usual measure-theoretic sense of Kolmogorov. That is, the model implies the existence of an object

$$(3) \qquad \mathcal{M} = (\mathcal{X}, \mathcal{A}, P),$$

where $\mathcal{A}$ is the Borel field of *cylinder sets* of $\mathcal{X}$ and P is a probability function defined on $\mathcal{A}$ (see Loève, 1963, Chapter 3 or any advanced text on probability theory). Most learning models entail a family of probability spaces in Equation 3, that is, the model has a vector of learning parameters $\boldsymbol{\theta} = (\theta_1, \ldots, \theta_r)$, and for every possible numerical value of $\boldsymbol{\theta}$, there is a unique numerical probability function $P(\boldsymbol{\theta})$ in Equation 3.

Each organism's response string is regarded as a sample point for the model, and various *descriptive statistics*[2] of the data can be tabulated. The empirical test of the model involves the *estimation* of the parameter vector $\boldsymbol{\theta}$ and a statistical test of the *goodness-of-fit* of the model to the empirical data. One can derive predictions from the model of the descriptive statistics, and see if the predictions match the data values. Parameter estimation and goodness-of-fit are standard topics in mathematical statistics and need not concern us here. However, it is important to note that most learning models are axiomatized in terms of theoretical internal structures rather than directly in terms of Equation 3. Consequently it is usually a difficult problem to explicate the model directly in terms of its implied probability spaces. This, of course, is a standard situation in formal science.

A. Foundations of Mathematical Learning Theory

Two major theoretical frameworks dominated early efforts in MLT. The first was Estes' (1950) *stimulus sampling theory*. The second was *stochastic learning theory* or, more particularly, the linear model framework formulated by Bush and Mosteller (1951, 1955). Both frameworks were grounded in probability theory; however, neither was developed axiomatically.

In an important collaborative effort, Estes and Suppes[3] (1959, 1974) explicated the detailed underlying probability spaces of the stochastic processes entailed in both frameworks. A brief consideration of the two frameworks will clarify the consequences of this foundational work.

Stimulus sampling theory envisions that every objective stimulus situation can be represented by a population of unobservable stimulus elements each of which is connected to a particular response member of $\mathscr{R}$. On any trial, the organism is assumed to 'take a sample' of elements from the population. The response probabilities are determined by the relative proportion of elements in the sample conditioned to each response. The outcome on a trial serves the role of (possibly) changing the response connections to the stimulus elements in the sample; however, unsampled elements on a trial remain unchanged. Thus, on any trial, the 'learning state' of the organism can be thought of as a partition of the population of elements into subsets corresponding to each possible response connection.

Various possibilities for models in the stimulus sampling framework correspond to choice of: (1) the number of stimulus elements and their initial response connections, (2) the rule for sampling from the population on each trial, (3) the rule for selecting trial outcomes and their postulated effect on the response connections to sampled elements (see Atkinson and Estes, 1963, for a comprehensive discussion of these possibilities).

The linear model framework is much more easily described. On each trial $n + 1$, the probability of a particular response P_l is computed in terms of $P_{n,l}$, the previous trial probability, by a linear function of the form

$$(4) \qquad P_{n+1,l} = (1 - \theta_{l,m}) P_{n,l} + \alpha_{l,m},$$

where $1 \leq l \leq L$, $1 \leq m \leq M$ refer to $R(n)$ and $O(n)$, respectively; and $0 \leq \theta_{l,m}, \alpha_{l,m} \leq 1$. Naturally, the parameters $\theta_{l,m}$ and $\alpha_{l,m}$ are chosen to conserve probability, i.e., for all $n \geq 1$, $0 \leq P_{n,l} \leq 1$ and $\sum_{l=1}^{L} P_{n,l} = 1$.

Particular models in the framework depend on the outcome delivery rule and the postulated effects of each outcome on the response probabilities.

The important idea about a linear model is that current response probabilities are *deterministic* functions of the immediately preceding response probabilities. The function is always linear and its parameters depend only upon the *observed* events occurring on the previous trial. In contrast, the stimulus sampling framework implies that current response probabilities are *probabilistically* determined from *unobservable random processes* occurring on the previous trial. Because of these and other differences, many researchers expected the frameworks to differ considerably in their empirical implications.

The foundational work of Estes and Suppes accomplished a number of important purposes, First, the axiomatized versions of the learning models permitted straightforward derivations of a number of theoretical predictions from the models. Some of these predictions were new and others represented a more rigorous basis for previous derivations.

Second, most models in MLT have theoretical 'learning-state' variables that completely represent the effects of past events on the current state of learning. The model is generally Markov in these learning-state variables, i.e., the probability that an organism is in a particular state of learning on the $n + 1^{th}$ trial depends only on the state of learning on the nth trial, the events that occur on the nth trial, and not on events or states of learning that occur prior to trial n. In fact, Equation 4 shows that the response probability distribution may be regarded as such a state variable for the linear model. The axiomatic development of both frameworks permitted the establishment of a series of theorems concerning the Markov character of several aspects of the underlying stochastic processes.

A third advantage of the work was that it gave rise to the clear statement of a number of open problems in the statistical analysis of the models. Suppes' success at axiomatizing the frameworks had a lot to do with attracting professional mathematicians such as Lamperti (Lamperti & Suppes, 1959; Suppes & Lamperti, 1960), Karlin (1953), and Norman (1972) to work on such problems in MLT.

Finally the foundational work permitted the mathematical comparison of the two frameworks. Of particular importance were a number of theorems showing that certain linear models were limiting cases of stimulus sampling models[4] as the number of stimulus elements increased to infinity (Estes & Suppes, 1974, p. 166). Thus linear models, with their deterministic equations, can be regarded as 'macro-models' for the underlying statistical models of stimulus sampling theory. This conceptually pleasant result was a direct byproduct of the work of Estes and Suppes.

B. *Models for a Continuum of Responses*

The area of MLT most uniquely associated with Suppes concerns models for a continuum of responses (Suppes, 1959, 1960, 1964; Suppes and Frankman, 1961; Suppes and Zinnes, 1961, 1966; Suppes and Rouanet, 1964; Suppes, Rouanet, Levine, and Frankmann, 1964).

In terms of our stimulus-response-outcome scheme, the idea is to make the response set $\mathcal{R}$ correspond to some natural continuum such as a circle, line segment, etc. Furthermore, outcomes are not discrete but, rather, correspond to the points on the response continuum, i.e., $\mathcal{O} = \mathcal{R}$. Learning to steer a car, track an object, or guess the length of a time interval are examples of situations involving a natural response continuum. Also, most discrete response settings can be viewed as defining equivalence classes of more microscopic acts on a response continuum, i.e., two acts are equivalent if they accomplish the same 'instrumental' act in the world of the experiment.

To simplify matters, suppose there is but one stimulus (or setting) involving the continuum $\mathcal{R}$. Then one may postulate that on any trial n, the organism's response is determined by a response density $r_n(x)$, $x \in \mathcal{R}$. The effect of reinforcement is to change $r_n(x)$ over trials. Suppose that on each trial n, following the response x_n some point y_n on the continuum is reinforced, i.e., y_n is where the organism should have responded. One would expect $r_{n+1}(x)$ to 'gravitate' toward y_n. A natural rule in the spirit of the linear model framework would be that

$$(5) \qquad r_{n+1}(x) = (1 - \theta)r_n(x) + \theta k(x, y_n),$$

where $0 < \theta < 1$ and $k(x, y_n)$ is a density function centered at y_n which reflects the spread of the effect of the reinforcer at y_n.

In Suppes (1959), the implications of an assumption like that in Equation 5 are developed. By selecting various rules for reinforcer delivery, the theory makes rich and complex predictions about empirical response distributions. Although complex properties of probability theory and integral equations were required, analogous predictions to those from the discrete models were obtained.

In the other articles devoted to the response continuum, Suppes and his colleagues formulated other varieties of models and provided empirical evidence for them. The empirical setting for much of this work involved the subjects in predicting where on the perimeter of a circle a point of light would appear. Actual points of appearance (y_n) were determined by various probabilistic rules and various properties of the response data were compared with the model predictions.

While the models scored many empirical successes, the response continuum models failed to attract much attention from other workers in MLT. This neglect seems unfortunate. For example, the work offers the closest point of contact between MLT and the literature on learning or adaptive systems in engineering and computer science (e.g., Tsypkin, 1973). There has been little interplay between these two formally related areas. One can imagine a range of interesting man-machine interaction questions that could be studied in light of both approaches. Perhaps such developments will occur, but even if they do not, Suppes was responsible for founding and developing a theoretically interesting area of MLT.

In a related project, Suppes (Karsh & Suppes, 1964; Suppes & Donio, 1967) extended simulus sampling models to the continuous time rather than discrete trial case. It can be argued that learning in 'continuous time' more closely approximates the conditions of actual learning in the world, and Skinner's extensive work on operant conditioning of animals (see Hilgard and Bower, 1966) provides ample evidence for the feasibility of studying such learning. While Suppes' work on this project was limited, later researchers such as Norman (1966), and Ambler (1973) have considered such problems.

C. Markov Learning Models

In the 1960s, MLT developed a new framework known as Markov learning models. It was a natural outgrowth of stimulus sampling theory; however, it was mathematically simpler and less theoretically committing than its predecessors. While the framework was developed mostly by the work of F. Restle, G. Bower, and J. Greeno and others, some of Suppes' early work contributed a great deal to popularizing it.

The Markov framework assumes that a given learning situation can be "decomposed" into a small number of discrete stages. Each stage has its own characteristic response rule, and learning consists of making discrete transitions through the stages. The 'terminal' or 'absorbing stage' of the learning situation is characterized by a response rule that implies that only correct responses are made.

The framework represents these informal ideas by postulating a learning state for each stage. Transitions among states are governed by a finite state (discrete trial, homogeneous) Markov chain (see Kemeny and Snell, 1960). Further, each state has its characteristic response probabilities that remain constant throughout learning, i.e., response probabilities for an organism can only change by making state transitions. The reader familiar with automata theory can think of such structures as finite probabilistic automata with a single input. The outputs are the responses and the state transition and output functions specify the probabilistic processes in the model.

The framework became more popular than its predecessors – stimulus sampling theory and linear learning models – for several reasons. First, many different learning situations could be represented in the same framework. Substantive differences between them would be reflected in different numbers of states and associated transition and response probabilities but not in the basic structure itself.

Second, the statistical theory of such models was relatively easy; and, in fact, general purpose algorithmic procedures were developed for parameter estimation and for fitting the models to response string data (Milward, 1969). Finally, for reasons that are still not well understood, the Markov learning models were much better than their predecessors in fitting learning data and in providing interpretable parameter estimates.

The 1960's saw the successful application of finite Markov models to such tasks as learning paired-associates, recalling or recognizing items from a list, discovering simple hypotheses from Boolean valued stimuli, solving reasoning problems, conditioning eyeblinks of a rabbit to tones followed by airpuffs, training a rat to jump a barrier to avoid a shock, transferring prior habits to related situations, etc. The models not only provided a formal scheme for data fitting, but they also provided a number of insights into traditional questions about the learning process in such settings (see Greeno, 1974 for a comprehensive survey).

Even though Suppes was not a major figure in later use and development of these models, he was one of the first to use them, and he interested others in their development. In Suppes and Atkinson (1960), two and three state Markov models were first developed and then applied to two-person gaming experiments (to be described). In that work, the connection between the Markov models and their forerunner in stimulus sampling theory was formally derived. Later Suppes applied the models to concept formation in children (Suppes, 1965a, 1965b; Suppes and Ginsberg, 1962, 1963) and to aspects of second language learning (Crothers and Suppes, 1967).

In another development, Suppes extended the predictive domain of the Markov models to include response latency (Schlag-Rey, Groen & Suppes, 1965; Suppes, Groen & Schlag-Rey, 1966). In principle, MLT ought to account for any observable behavior relevant to learning. In addition to

157

the response made to a stimulus, the time required to make the response (the latency) is another observable datum. By associating a latency distribution with each learning state, prediction of response times was made possible.

Suppes' most important role in the development of Markov models was less tangible. He was a teacher of MLT to many of those who went on to develop that framework.

D. Applications to Areas Outside Learning

It has always been fashionable in American psychology to attempt to explain a given behavioral domain in terms of traditional learning theory. Child psychology, thinking, personality, social psychology, and even clinical psychology all have major positions that are learning-theoretic in character. Once the foundations of MLT had been developed, it was natural to apply them to areas outside of learning. Suppes was the most active person in applying MLT to social psychology. His bias is revealed in a quote from Suppes and Krasne (1961, p. 46).

. . . we hold that ultimately group behavior can be explained entirely in terms of the behavior of the individuals who constitute the group. . . . Furthermore, to our minds recent quantitative formulations of stimulus-response-reinforcement theory provide excellent conceptual tools for effecting such a subsumption.

The most extensive application of MLT to phenomena in social psychology was the work on two-person, noncooperative games. (Atkinson and Suppes, 1958, 1959; Suppes and Atkinson, 1960). In such games there are two players who do not communicate directly. Each player must select one of a finite number of (mutually exclusive) responses $\mathscr{R} = \{R_1, \ldots, R_L\}$ on each of a series of plays of the game, $n = 1, 2, \ldots$. The outcome (or reward) for each player is determined jointly by their responses. The outcome delivery rule can be represented by a payoff matrix in the usual game-theoretic sense. Suppes and Atkinson concentrated their work on the special case where on each trial a player gets either $+1$ or -1 units of reward, i.e., either wins or loses on that trial (both can win, however). In that case, the 'payoff matrix' can be viewed as a table whose entries give the probabilities of winning for each player as a function of their joint response pair.

Since the players only communicate indirectly through their responses and resulting outcomes, it is natural to view each player as in a simple learning situation and test various models from MLT against the behavioral data from both subjects. This reduction of a fragment of game theory to MLT was quite successful in the experimental prediction sense.

Nowadays it is a growing area within economics to develop behaviorally adequate as opposed to 'rational' or 'prescriptive' theories for economic phenomena. Other less well known examples of Suppes' application of MLT to social psychology are (Suppes & Krasne, 1961; Suppes & Carlsmith, 1962; Suppes & Schlag-Rey, 1962). While economists continue their interests in the gaming work, there is not a great deal of current effort to apply S-R notions to problems in social psychology within psychology itself.

III. Cognitive Psychology

Just as Suppes and others were giving to learning theory its most precise formulation, the field itself was being called into question as never before in American psychology. Extensive developments in many fields, including biology, computer science, linguistics, mathematics and philosophy, were converging on the viewpoint that theories with greater structural complexity were necessary to account for human behavior. In fact, one might argue that it is a virtue of the formalist movement in learning theory that its very clarity helped to make clear its limitations. Along with the shift in viewpoint in psychology came a name change. Whereas for many years 'learning theory' had been at the center of theoretical attention, one now spoke in the same contexts of 'cognitive psychology' (after Neisser's 1967 book of that title). Suppes' later work in psychology also reflected this development. As we discuss this work in Section III (and also in Section IV) we will be able to evaluate MLT in more detail.

A. Automata

The work on learning theory which has been the focus of our discussion so far has been relatively easy to describe and evaluate, because the goals of the work were relatively straightforward. They involved the formalization of current ideas, the building of models within a generally accepted psychological framework, the extension of the framework (as in the case of continuous models) and the application of models to experiments. These activities, in the contemporary scientific climate in psychology, seem to fall within 'normal science' (Kuhn). Thus we can note that Suppes played a major role in helping to formalize theories, developed some new models himself and tested these models against experiment. Within the 'normal science viewpoint' of stimulus-response psychology, our critical and evaluative role is completed.

In the next area of our concern, however, the case is more complicated. This area of Suppes' work bears upon the theoretical adequacy of the viewpoint exemplified by the work that we have discussed. There is much at stake here and evaluation is complex.

In the 1960s the study of linguistics was playing an increasing role in psychological discussions. Linguistics has a long history, as does the relation between linguistics and psychology. In earlier periods of American structural linguistics, linguists (e.g., Bloomfield) accepted the theoretical foundations of learning theory (i.e., some form of Behaviorism or stimulus-response psychology), at least in principle. (It is often said that their practice in linguistic description did not always follow their methodological statements). But since the work of Chomsky, many linguists were not only arguing that they gave a better account in detail of linguistic phenomena than did psychologists (which psychologists could shrug off by a division of labor argument), but they also claimed that their work showed that the theoretical foundations of learning theory were seriously inadequate, at least with respect to its ability to explain characteristic human behavior.

Learning theory, as our earlier discussion suggests, deals with rather simple learning situations. One might doubt (and it has often been doubted) that the theories and methodologies involved in these areas might be of much use in the study of more complex learning. In particular, one might argue that humans have abilities which in no reasonable way may be analyzed or understood by stimulus-response theory. The argument might run: S-R theory assumes that observable stimuli are related to observable responses. There is no mention of internal states or internal processes. Therefore S-R theory is incapable of explaining any behavior which depends on internal states or processes. Human behavior depends on internal states and processes. Therefore S-R theory cannot analyze or understand or explain human behavior.

Arguments of this form (and counter-arguments) have an extensive history that need not be reiterated here. The arguments that Suppes (1969) refers to are those of Chomsky and other scholars and are based on human language. We should note, though, that Chomsky's argument is quite a bit more complex than the above argument, depending on more than the existence of internal states. Rather the arguments depend on the complexity of linguistic abilities, and the distant relation between these abilities and the kind of evidence upon which their learning could be built.

Suppes (1969) takes as his goal the demonstration that S-R theory can explain in principle the learning of complex behavior. In particular, Suppes claims that finite automata can be 'learned' by S-R models. This means that for any finite automaton there is an S-R model which becomes isomorphic to the finite automaton in the limit (as more and more 'trials' with reinforcement are run). Before we discuss the details of this work, we should note that on the surface, at least, the claim itself seems very strong. Despite the fact that finite automata are still significantly weaker than what linguists claim are necessary to represent linguistic competence, still they crucially have internal states. Since S-R models start out without internal states and can use only quite indirect means of obtaining information about these states (i.e., reinforcement) it seems as if such S-R models could not 'become' any finite automaton. Thus Suppes' result is surprising. Some scholars also consider finite automata to be *general* limited-memory, performance models. From this viewpoint the result is *very* strong, since it implies that there is a sense in which S-R models can learn any human performance.

Since the interpretation of the results are quite controversial it is worth spending some time on details. First let us remind the reader of the definition of a finite automaton.[5] This definition is taken from Suppes (1969) who in turn takes it from Rabin and Scott (1959).

A structure $\mathfrak{A} = \langle A, \Sigma, M, s_0, F \rangle$ *is a finite* (*deterministic*) *automaton if and only if*

(i)   *A is a finite nonempty set* (*the set of states of* $\mathfrak{A}$),

(ii) Σ *is a finite, nonempty set* (*the alphabet*)

(iii)   *M is a function from the Cartesian product* $A \times \Sigma$ *to* A
        (*M defines the transition table of* $\mathfrak{A}$),

(iv) s_0 *is in A* (s_0 *is the initial state of* $\mathfrak{A}$)

(v)   *F is a subset of A* (*F is the set of final states of* $\mathfrak{A}$).

The interpretation of this definition is that the automaton starts in s_0. A sequence of elements (a tape) of Σ is fed into the automaton. That is, starting in s_0, the automaton moves from state to state and letter (of Σ), to letter, according to M. A tape is *accepted* if and only if after processing it the automaton winds up in a final state, that is, a member of F. The language generated by $\mathfrak{A}$ is the set of accepted tapes. Formal definitions of the senotions may be found in Suppes' article.

The question of how one might relate stimulus sampling theory to finite automata at all may be looked at in the following general way. A class of automata has a certain 'computing power'. Stimulus sampling theory contains models which change over time (i.e., learn). At any given time one of these models 'computes' in a particular way. In particular, a model has a limiting (as trials increase) computation. The problem then becomes to relate the computational power of a class of automata to the computational power of the class of limiting stimulus sampling models.

The puzzle for Suppes is to figure out how S-R theory, or more particularly, a stimulus sampling model (see Section IIA) can become isomorphic in the limit to a finite automaton. Suppes pursues this problem by trying to find a useful sense of isomorphism between stimulus sampling theory models and finite automata. The inputs to a finite automaton (alphabet, extended to tapes) correspond in a natural way to the stimuli in stimulus sampling theory. For various reasons Suppes rejects the idea that the conditioning state of a stimulus sampling theory model is to be identified with the state of finite automaton. The idea that he does accept is that a state of a finite automaton corresponds to the *response* of a stimulus sampling model. On the face of it, this seems odd. States are *internal* (not observable) while responses are *external* (observable). But Suppes is proposing that internal states can nevertheless be reinforced, and in fact Suppes (1969, p. 354) gives an example (the vebalization of the 'carry' in an adding problem, the carry being associated with an internal state) as part of an argument that internal states can be externalized as responses. The crux of the proof then depends on defining a reinforcement schedule such that an originally unconditioned stimulus sampling model will become isomorphic to the finite automaton.

Suppose that for a state r, and an input a, the state-transition function for the automaton is $M(r, a) = q$. That is, the automaton moves from state r and input a to state q. Then Suppes assumes that the reinforcement schedule is such that for any trial n, if the stimulus-response model made response r on trial $n - 1$ and the stimulus a is presented on trial n, then the response q is reinforced and no other responses are reinforced on that trial. Given this schedule of reinforcement, Suppes then proves that for any connected finite automaton (i.e., any state can be reached) a stimulus response model exists, which starts off with no stimuli conditioned, but which in the limit *becomes* the finite automaton. This result is called the

Representation Theorem for Finite Automata. The definition of *becomes* is fairly natural, given this framework and appears in (Suppes, 1969, p. 344). The essence of the definition is that if $M(r, a) = q$ for the automaton, then in the limit the probability is 1 that response q is made on trial n given that response r was made on trial $n - 1$ and a was the stimulus on trial n.

Problems with Suppes' analysis have been the subject of at least three articles, each of which raises the same crucial point. Arbib (1969) was the first. The most important point that Arbib raises is the claim that Suppes' results only hold for automata in which for each state of the automaton there is only one output or response. Now Suppes' automata don't *have* responses or outputs, as he formally defines them. But in discussion he talks as if they do and, in fact, the one example that he gives, an adding automaton, *does* have outputs.

The essential point is that when the stimulus-response model makes a response on trial $n - 1$ (as it does on every trial), the trainer cannot use this response to determine which response to reinforce on trial n because the trial $n - 1$ response (see next paragraph) in general will *not* determine the *state* of the automaton on trial $n - 1$. This state will *only* be determined if for each response there is only 1 state that makes that response. Of course, as all three critics point out in one form or other, assuming that the state can be determined from the response defeats the whole purpose of assuming finite automata, which depends on the existence of internal (non-observable) states.

This controversy has a certain obscurity because in fact Suppes used a definition of *finite automaton* which does not contain the notion of *response*. But automata *with* responses are more natural for the kinds of behavior to which the automata are supposed to be relevant. In fact, the one worked out example which Suppes gives (an adding automaton) has responses. In light of later criticisms, this shift from definition to example is more than a casual problem. Also note that the power of responses in defining behavior is taken over in the given definition by the role of the final states (F). However (as Suppes, 1969 footnote 4, points out) the definition of isomorphism between a stimulus sampling model and a finite automaton does not require that any of the states (responses) of the limiting stimulus sampling model be distinguished in a way corresponding to the final states of the automaton.

Kieras (1976) gives the most complete mathematical development. He defines an *S* machine as one in which the current *response* (not state) and input determine the next response. He then shows that there are finite automata which are not S machines, and whose behavior cannot be represented by S machines. (Of course in general the most interesting will not be). Thus Suppes' result is that S machines can be learned by stimulus-response models. Kieras then goes on to show that stimulus-response models can learn *only* S machines, i.e., there is no stimulus-response model that can learn a finite automaton that is not an S machine. As Kieras (and the others) point out, S machines are *not* typical of human (or animal or computer) behavior. Rather, finite automata which are more complex than S machines are typical. Nelson (1975) makes the same point in somewhat different guise. It seems to us though that some of his discussion misses the point when he tries to indicate that Suppes' result holds only for finite state *acceptors*, but not for Moore or Mealy machines, which have outputs. Nelson obtains some interesting further results. He shows that taking further 'observable' information, (for example a sequence of responses) will still not allow the full range of finite automata to be represented.

To try to explicate the problem a bit further, in the hope of making the reader more aware of the difficulty in trying to conceptualize complex learning with internal states as a form of stimulus-response learning, we can take a slightly different tack than the three critics. They write sometimes as if Suppes' result has a mathematical problem, or has a hidden, non-stated assumption. But the same problem can be looked at from another point of view. We can say that there is nothing wrong mathematically with Suppes' result and that it applies to the full class of finite automata. Instead what is wrong is wrong both conceptually and empirically. It seems to us that the critics took Suppes' claim, which seemed empirically wrong to them and tried to make some sense of it. Mathematically, the Representation Theorem is easily defended. What it does, however, is to strain our empirical sense. Presented from another viewpoint (e.g., Kieras') the work can be taken to demonstrate the limitations of S-R models.

Consider a learner in a Suppes situation. He makes a response. Then he is presented with a stimulus. The response-stimulus pair provides sufficient information to tell the reinforcer which reinforcement to apply. Now we shouldn't think of the response as the usual kind of response. Rather the response *is* the state (or rather is in 1–1 relation with the state) of the organism. Possibly the learner outputs *two* responses after each input, one for the internal state. The problem is that the responses have to be interpretable as the internal states. It is difficult to think of very many interesting abilities that one would want to characterize in this way.

Of course, when looked at in this way, the Representation Theorem is not at all surprising. Suppose we have an automaton with n states. We conceive of the learner as some kind of 'non-connected automaton' S (i.e., without all the connections between states, but originally with n states). Say, S starts in state r on trial $n - 1$. Now stimulus input a comes in. The learner notices this. Now in the automaton, $M(r, a) = q$. Now the trainer (or God, or whoever) knows that the learner was in state r on the last trial. Then the trainer flashes: q. The learner could learn deterministically here, but Suppes' S-R model says that he learns probabilistically. So with probability c, the learner draws an arrow from state r to state q, labeled a.

To see how easy and non-surprising this is, and to get a feel for how the model learns, the reader might play the following game. Draw a finite automaton on a piece of paper (i.e., circles for states, numbered 1 on up, arrows between states, labeled with input letters). Tell a friend how many states the automaton has, say 4. The friend then draws four circles on a piece of paper, numbered 1 to 4. The friend now starts in any state. He announces which state he is in, say state 3. You then announce one of the stimuli (letters) and also the state which that letter takes your automaton to. For example, you might say, "b, 2." You will, of course, have chosen an intelligent friend, and explained to him what is going on. With paper and pencil in hand, he learns deterministically, that is, his conditioning parameter $c = 1$. He will, of course, draw an arrow from circle 3 to circle 2 and label it b. Before long, if you make sure to give him all possible (state, input) pairs, your friend will have "become" the automaton. The situation in the Representation Theorem is only slightly more complicated than this game by (1) the worry about beginning states, which we have omitted for simplicity, (2) the general probabilistic set-up, including a probabilistic presentation of stimuli and only a probability of stamping in the information on a trial.

So far as we can see, there is no reason why the Representation Theorem couldn't be proved for a Turing machine, or any other form of complex automaton which is finitely statable. All that has to be assumed is that all internal information which represents in a more general form the machine's 'state' at any given time can be externalized, so that the trainer can reinforce the appropriate next state (including left and right moves, instructions to write in memory, etc.). These seem to be natural extensions of the reinforcement of internal states.

Probably in response to the kinds of issues that we have just discussed

Suppes' student Rottmayer (1970 – c.f. also Suppes and Rottmayer 1974) developed a theory of learning in which the possibilities for reinforcement were considerably weaker. There are now only two reinforcers – Correct and Error – and they apply only at the end of entire tapes, not after each response or state transition. This definition is more in accordance with the view that a sentence, say, may be corrected if it is ungrammatical. (The actual developments take place in a perceptual rather than linguistic context, but Suppes' theoretical points are made generally). Given this 'weaker' form of reinforcement, an asymptotic convergence theorem can still be proved. Now, as one would suspect, there is only behavioral, as opposed to isomorphic, equivalence between the stimulus sampling model and the finite automaton.

In terms of the game that we introduced earlier, the learning procedure may be conceived to work as follows. A tape of inputs is presented to the learner. After each input, the learner guesses the next state and keeps record of these guesses. If, at the end of an entire tape, the learner is told "correct," then he stores these transitions. If, on the other hand, he is told "wrong," then he destroys these transitions. Once again, there is a general probabilistic framework, and the proof involves showing that there is convergence to a model which is behaviorally equivalent to the finite automaton. In Suppes (in press) there is an extension of the result to register machines, which are more powerful than finite automata.

Although this weakening of the possibilities of reinforcement is a step forward from the earlier assumptions, there appears to be a fundamental empirical and conceptual issue that must be raised. Suppes considers that the type of reinforcement that he has postulated is the *weakest* conceivable kind of reinforcement, and that advances will be made by analyzing theoretically and empirically richer kinds of reinforcement. He writes (in press, p. 20):

The other conceptual matter is the clear recognition of the great gains to be obtained from using methods of reinforcement that are stronger than the weakest nondeterminate ones. This fact is recognized in all ordinary teaching. It is the purpose of explanations, of didactic lectures, of verbal corrections of students, of attempts at explaining to them why they have made a mistake, and of a variety of other diagnostic approaches that lead to explicit verbal communication to students. I have discussed earlier the reasons for not going all the way in the other direction to completely determinate reinforcement. In this case, we end up with methods that are too strong and that cannot be practically realized. The conceptual subtlety of the reinforcement-information problem is the difficulty of giving an explicit account of how the student processes the complex verbal information that is given to him.

The problem is that what empirical evidence exists seems to show that for many abilities (e.g., syntax) children are *not* explicitly corrected when they make errors (Brown and Hanlon, 1970). Nor does anybody believe that in general children are explicitly taught the rules of grammar. There *is* information available to them, of course, but this seems to be mostly of the exemplar variety, the kind of minforation that would most naturally be mirrored in Suppes' framework by the *stimuli* (tapes), not by reinforcement. It is always possible, of course, that there is some exceedingly subtle kind of reinforcement of which psychologists have not yet been able to find evidence (e.g., eye movements of a parent correlated with grammaticality of a children's utterance). But all this seems unlikely, especially in a very strong form. Thus, rather than representing the *weakest* form of conceivable reinforcement, the yes-no correction scheme probably represents far too strong a form of reinforcement.

Even if there were such strong reinforcement available, an opposing point of view might point out the limitations in the Representation Theorem that can be proved. It is a fundamental conclusion of modern linguistics that not only is a native speaker of a language able to recognize the set of grammatical sentences, but that people's grammars are the same in essential respects. From the kind of learning procedure sketched above, one would suspect that the limiting stimulus sampling model could be very different from learner to learner, even given the same environment, and that these differences would magnify when differences in order of input of tapes, etc., were taken into consideration.

The opposing viewpoint, then would not look for the solutions to these fundamental problems of psychology in the discovery of subtle reinforcement schedules. Rather it would put the complexity into the learning model to begin with. That is, rather than start the learning model in a completely undifferentiated condition, one might assume that there were interesting structural complexities in the learner to begin with. Weak forms of 'reinforcement' would then suffice to allow learning to take place. (See Wexler, Culicover and Hamburger (1975) for a formal approach starting from this viewpoint). It seems to us that Suppes' work in this area is at the heart of the theoretical issue that has dominated psychology in recent years. Is learning of complex human abilities to be accounted for by subtle reinforcement schedules or by biologically given complex structures?

B. Probabilistic Grammars

In the last section we discussed how Suppes responded to the conceptual challenge laid down by linguists and others. But there is a second major area of Suppes' psychological work which is involved with linguistics. This concerns the development of 'probabilistic grammars' and studies of children's utterances (Suppes, 1970, 1973, 1974a, 1974b, 1974c; Suppes, Smith & Léveillé, 1973). We will enter into somewhat more detail on this topic than on previous subjects because probabilistic grammars provide a miniature setting in which to survey major features of Suppes' work, especially with respect to important questions concerning the empirical validation of theories.

The idea of a probabilistic grammar is quite simple given familiarity with the notions of grammar. Suppes for the most part restricts his attention to context-free grammars. A rule of a context-free grammar rewrites a non-terminal symbol (category) as a string of symbols. In general a category may be rewritten in a given grammar in several different ways. In the usual (deterministic) grammars a choice is arbitrarily made among the possibilities, and the set of derivations of the grammar includes all possibilities. In a probabilistic grammar, as Suppes defines it, on the other hand, a probability is assigned to each rewriting rule, and the probabilities of all rules which rewrite a given category add up to 1. Thus, to take an example, suppose that in some language a noun phrase (NP) could rewrite as either a pronoun, or a proper noun or an article plus a common noun and there are no other ways to rewrite a noun phrase. Then we would have

$$NP \xrightarrow{\ p\ } \text{pronoun,}$$
$$NP \xrightarrow{\ q\ } \text{proper noun,}$$
$$NP \xrightarrow{\ r\ } \text{article} + \text{common noun.}$$

Here the letter 'p' indicates that the probability of rewriting NP as pronoun is p. A requirement is that $p + q + r = 1$.

The point of introducing probabilities is to be able to calculate the probability of each sentence or 'terminal string' in a corpus. The assumption is made that each category rewrites according to the associated probabilities, and that rewriting one category in a particular way is independent of rewriting any other category in a particular way. For example:

Pr (NP rewrites as pronoun given VP rewrites as Verb)
= Pr (NP rewrites as pronoun given VP rewrites as Verb + NP)
= Pr (NP rewrites as pronoun) = p.

The problem that Suppes formulates is to test a grammar statistically against a corpus of sentences from the language. Each probability is taken as a parameter of the grammar, viewed as a model which is to be tested against data consisting of the corpus. As with MLT, various statistics of the corpus can be accounted for by such models.

Since Suppes wants to use the statistical properties of these grammars (models) in order to differentiate the fit of grammars to the corpus, a natural question to ask is whether, indeed, this is possible. That is, can the statistical properties, as opposed to the set of generated sentences of the grammar, differentiate grammars? Suppes and his co-workers test the fit of grammars to data, but since the situation is complicated, perhaps we can construct an artificial example to show that in fact the statistical properties of grammars do differentiate them, when they are viewed as models of a corpus. First, we will look upon a grammar as generating *types*, where a type is the sequence of nodes just above lexical items (words) in the derivation tree. For example, a type of English might be Article Noun Verb, as in 'The man walked'. In general, the set of *types* will be infinite, just as the set of sentences is infinite.

We want to show that the statistical properties of grammars with respect to a corpus can differentiate them. In particular we will construct an artificial example to show how 2 grammars can generate exactly the same set of types and yet have a different statistical fit. In the following constructed grammars, if there is no probability above the arrow in a rewrite rule, then the rule applies with probability 1. We will construct two grammars, G_1 and G_2. Each grammar will have 3 parameters (probabilities), p, q and r. The rules for the grammar (excluding the lexicon rules which put in terminal symbols) are

G_1:
$$S \longrightarrow ABC$$
$$A \longrightarrow BD$$
$$B \xrightarrow{p} E$$
$$B \xrightarrow{1-p} F$$
$$C \xrightarrow{q} G$$
$$C \xrightarrow{1-q} H$$
$$D \xrightarrow{r} G$$
$$D \xrightarrow{1-r} H$$

G_2:
$$S \longrightarrow ABC$$
$$A \longrightarrow DC$$
$$B \xrightarrow{p'} E$$
$$B \xrightarrow{1-p'} F$$
$$C \xrightarrow{q'} G$$
$$C \xrightarrow{1-q'} H$$
$$D \xrightarrow{r'} E$$
$$D \xrightarrow{1-r'} F$$

It is a simple calculation to see that the set of types of G_1 equals the set of types of G_2 equals $\{E, F\} \times \{G, H\} \times \{E, F\} \times \{G, H\}$. In (6 a) appears the tree associated with the derivation of the type $EGFG$ in G_1, and in

(6 b) appears the tree associated with the derivation of the same type in G_2.

(6 a)   (6 b)

We can obtain the probability of the type by multiplying the probabilities of each rule used in the derivation of the type. Thus, in G_1, $Pr(EGFG) = pr(1 - p)q$. In G_2, $Pr(EGFG) = r'q'(1 - p')q' = r'(q')^2(1 - p')$.

We have deliberately constructed the example so that the sets of types are equal, but the statistical properties of the grammars are different. Let W_i be a random variable denoting 'word i', that is the bottom category in position i (i runs from 1 to 4). Then notice that the penultimate category in first and third position is always B. Therefore, for G_1, $Pr(W_1 = E) = Pr(W_3 = E)$. This property doesn't hold in general for G_2, since there the penultimate categories in position 1 and 3 are D and B, respectively, and we don't have in general that $r' = p'$. On the other hand, for G_2 we have $Pr(W_2 = G) = Pr(W_4 = G)$. This equality doesn't hold in general for G_1. It is an elementary application of the statistical method to show how frequency data could distinguish these two probabilistic grammars taken as models of a corpus. Note that we have also arranged the situation so that the two different probabilistic grammars have the same number of parameters, so that the statistical superiority of one cannot be said to be due to a greater number of 'degrees of freedom' than the other.

It is difficult to see how these statistical considerations could ever be useful in helping to select a grammar for a language. They are simply not as powerful as the methods that linguists use for the same purpose. It is probably worth turning to a discussion of what Suppes considers the rationale for the use of these methods. Suppes (1974b, pp. 284–285) writes that "the central thesis of this paper is that objective probabilistic criteria of a standard scientific sort may be used to select a grammar."

The first question to ask is, why do relative frequencies of types of utterances have anything to do with theory of grammar? In Suppes (1974b), Suppes recognizes this question, and even gives an analogy; namely, the relative frequency of shapes is not pertinent to geometry. But Suppes has chosen one particular kind of example. He can take geometry as a branch of mathematics and not of science. (It is well known by now that some parts of geometry may be interpreted as physical theories.) Then he goes on to say that, in physics, however, many aspects of the frequencies of shapes are relevant, for example in the study of the shapes of clouds and their explanation or in the study of the shapes of complex organic molecules.

But this discussion misses the point. The question to ask is not whether relative frequencies are *ever* relevant data in science, but whether they are relevant to a particular theory or subject matter. Thus one should not move in this discussion from geometry to the study of the shapes of clouds. Rather one should consider mechanics. As far as we know, no one would claim that relative frequencies of shapes of objects were relevant data in the theory of mechanics. At any rate, such data is not used in the development of the theory of mechanics.

Suppes recognizes this objection also. For he goes on to say that "in any application of concepts to a complex empirical domain, there is always a degree of uncertainty as to the level of abstraction we should reach for". As an example he mentions that mechanics does not take account of the color of objects. But he then goes on to argue that:

Ignoring major features of empirical phenomena is in all cases surely a defect and not a virtue. We ignore major features because it is difficult to account for them, not because they are uninteresting or improper subjects for investigation. In the case of grammars, the features of utterance length and utterance complexity seem central; the distribution of these features is of primary importance in understanding the character of actual language use.

But labeling the ignoring of phenomena a defect rather than a virtue is really a misleading way of representing the actual practice of science. The history of successful science shows that in most important cases science cannot proceed *without* ignoring many (most) phenomena. A science chooses its subject matter and its phenomena, and it is well known that phenomena 'central' to a science are not always given before the science has developed. Rather, theories point toward the relevant phenomena.

In a mechanics which is trying to understand gross movements of particles (say), color is irrelevant. Thus one has to ask what linguists who study grammars are trying to understand. Suppes, in the quote above, argues that relative frequencies are of central importance in understanding "actual language use". We are not sure what Suppes is referring to here. Is "actual language use" supposed to be taken as something like the subject matter of the field of pragmatics, in the well known division of the subject matter of the study of language into syntax, semantics and pragmatics? If so, then it is difficult to see how relative frequencies are at the heart of this subject matter. Pragmatics, of course, can mean different things to different scholars. For example, some scholars would include the study of indexical expressions as part of semantics while some would consider that study to be part of pragmatics. It seems to us that many scholars these days would take as central to pragmatics the study of inferences which do not follow from sentences but which do follow if various kinds of hidden assumptions are included. An example would be Grice's maxims. One would not completely rule out frequency as having a role here. For example, unlikely sentences might have a special effect. But it is difficult to see how relative frequencies could be 'central' to this subject matter.

We suspect that Suppes must therefore have something else in mind when he mentions "actual language use." Presumably he has in mind a performance theory of, say, language production and comprehension. Then, for example, very long sentences would be unlikely because of memory limitations on the part of the hearer or speaker. But it is important to note that here we have moved from the realm of competence into performance. Also, once again the relevance of relative frequencies is still not clear. It can only be made clear when theories are constructed which deal with the important problems of language production and comprehension, and within the context of these theories it is shown that relative frequency is an important phenomenon for the elucidation of theories. In the linguistic, psycholinguistic and computer literature there are a number of suggestions towards beginnings of performance theories. Whether Suppes' statistical studies (which are methodologically more sophisticated than the usual studies in statistical linguistics) will be of value to those theories will be for the future to decide.

Suppes offers the probabilistic grammar methodology as a way of choosing competing grammars. In doing this he criticizes linguists who try to use a criterion of 'simplicity' in selecting grammars (e.g., Suppes, 1974b, pp. 284–285). His point is that other scientific fields (e.g., physics) do not have formalized criteria of simplicity to use in selecting theories, and therefore it is fairly hopeless to expect linguistics to come up with one. Rather linguists should look for new kinds of data, such as relative frequencies, to use in choosing grammars.

Suppes' discussion characterizes incorrectly the use of simplicity in linguistics. Since this notion is central to modern theoretical linguistics, and is also central to linguistics looked upon as a branch of psychology, it is worth devoting attention to clarifying matters here. It is true that some linguists have misused the notion, in the way that Suppes suggests, but Suppes is presumably referring to the use of simplicity by Chomsky, with whom the notion is most prominently identified, and thus we should characterize Chomsky's position.

First, simplicity must be set within a framework for linguistic theory. The central problem for linguistic theory is taken to be the restriction on the notion of 'possible language' to the point where it is possible to see how language can be learned by a human child, under the empirically correct limitations on time and access to data about the language. At the same time the restriction cannot be so severe as to not allow an existing natural language. Given the class of possible grammars, there is an 'evaluation metric', that is, a linear ordering of the grammars, so that the first is preferred to the second which is preferred to the third, and so on. We can conceive of the child as selecting the first grammar in this order which is compatible with the data that he receives about his language. Thus, although in general there are a large number of languages compatible with the data that the child receives, the evaluation metric chooses one of these.

The measure of 'simplicity' is to be associated with this evaluation metric. The choice of the term 'simplicity' is perhaps unfortunate, because simplicity is not supposed to be the same as some *a priori* or commonsensical notion of simplicity. Rather simplicity (the evaluation metric) is a theoretical construct which is justified on empirical grounds. If the metric makes the wrong choice of grammar (that is if a grammar is selected by the theory which is not the actual grammar that a human selects) then the metric is judged wrong.[6]

In the study of adult language, linguists use informant judgments of grammaticality of sentences, logical implications, synonymy, etc. These judgments are a classical form of data in psychology. For example, one of the 'hardest' areas of psychology is psychophysics, and the basic data of psychophysics are such judgments as whether the subject perceived a certain signal. It might be thought by non-psychologists that the number of subjects in linguistic 'experiments' (often one, seldom more than a few) might be a particular problem for linguistics. But once again psychophysics provides a nice analogy, because rarely are more than a few (often two or three) subjects used in an experiment. What is important is not average responses across subjects, but rather the fine-grained analysis of the single subject's response. And, in fact, the data are typically presented and analyzed for each individual subject. It might be thought that the fact that the linguist is often his own (and perhaps only) subject might be a problem, but, once again, the psychophysicist uses himself as a subject. There is one difference between psychophysics and linguistics, it seems to us. In psychophysics the task of the subject is to determine whether he perceives a signal, say, but the subject does not know on a particular trial whether a signal was actually presented. Thus it is easy in many cases for an experimenter to be his own subject and to be 'objective', On the other hand, the derivations of sentences in linguistic theory are relatively straightforward. Thus a linguist will often know whether his theory predicts that a sentence is grammatical or not. Linguists are aware of this problem, of course, which goes under the name of 'theory-dependent judgments'. But in many cases of interest there is no problem in making the judgments, and in other cases one can let the theory decide. Also, in some cases the obvious solution is to let a non-linguist make the judgment. Once again there is a psychological analogy, not to psychophysics, but rather to the broader field of perception which actually is quite close in spirit to linguistics. The crucial data might be whether a psychologist sees a visual illusion or not, and, of course, the psychologist knows whether his theory predicts whether he should see an illusion. There are various ways, theoretical and empirical, of getting around these problems. Our only purpose here is to set linguistic methodology within the broader context of psychological methodology.

The study of child language presents large problems for this methodology because it appears that children cannot make grammaticality judgments, or at least nobody has figured out a good way to entice them to make such judgments. Therefore much of child language research has been concerned with analysis of a corpus of utterances. As should be obvious this is a much less powerful method of data collection than is informant judgment. It is of course because of these methodological problems that the field of developmental psycholinguistics is not in a very advanced state. It might be that major empirical breakthroughs in this field can only be accomplished with the development of techniques to find out what competence the child has. Meanwhile if psychologists are going to continue to analyze corpuses, then probabilistic grammar techniques could conceivably have some value. For example, as Suppes points out, suppose a form doesn't occur in a corpus. We want to judge whether this means that the form is not generated by the child's grammar or, on the other hand, whether the form is generated by the child's grammar but simply didn't occur. The application of probabilistic methods, in particular probabilistic grammars, might allow us to make some kind of statistical inference about which is the case.

These are really very weak inferences, compared to relatively powerful linguistic methods, but they might have some use. For example, Suppes, Smith & Levéillé (1973), analyze the noun-phrase productions of a French child. They compare two probabilistic grammars. Both grammars generate about the same percentage of noun-phrase types in the corpus (about 65%). Also, both grammars generate about the same percentage of the tokens of noun-phrases in the corpus (about 95%). Yet Grammar II was distinctly superior to Grammar I in the statistical fit, that is in predicting relative frequencies.

Thus in the case of the French child, Grammar II might be said to be preferred to Grammar I. Grammar II, based on modern work in generative grammar, is probably closer to being a correct linguistic grammar than is Grammar I, based on work in traditional French grammar. One wonders if the same techniques would be useful in a child where the adult structure was not so recapitulated. What is interesting here is that the preferred grammar is one for which the noun phrase and determiner system have a kind of rich structure that has been considered only in about the last 10 years of linguistic work. Presumably these devices would be part of general linguistic theory, and, given the explanation of a child's learning of grammar as the goal of linguistic theory, a linguist would expect that the structures would be reflected in a child's grammar. Paradoxically, although Suppes has been associated with a stimulus-response, strong learning, non-nativist approach to language acquisition, what he seems to be claiming here is that the child has some rich and non-surface structures quite early.

One might imagine a number of barriers to a fuller development of the statistical theory. Consider a category B that can be produced in various parts of a phrase structure. Suppose that B can be rewritten as C or D. But suppose that the probabilities of rewriting B as C or D are different depending on whether B is in one of two different positions in the sentence. For example, a noun-phrase may rewrite differently depending on whether it is subject or object. Now, how is this to be represented in the probabilistic grammar? The obvious solution seems to be to make the probabilities context-sensitive, but the assumption in Suppes' work to date has been to make the probabilities context-free. There is an alternative, however. We can make the category *B* a different category *B'* when it occurs in position 2, say. For example the rule that introduces noun-phrase into object position might be *Verb Phrase → Verb + NP'*. Then we let *B'* rewrite in exactly the same ways as *B*, but with different probabilities. Essentially this way of hiding context-sensitive probabilities was utilized by Suppes, Smith and Levéillé (1973) when they distinguished between an adjective phrase and a post adjective phrase, depending on whether the adjective phrase came before or after the noun (which happens in French).

But so far as we can tell, the probabilistic restrictions set by the fact that two categories in different parts of a phrase-structure are the same are really the only statistical restrictions that probabilistic grammars make. Thus the move to *B'*, given that the deterministic grammar generates the correct types, can, if carried out wherever necessary, lead to a perfect fit. Of course, this is the standard situation in fitting statistical theories, where one can always increase the number of parameters until perfect fit is attained. But there is another problem here. How is one to know whether a new category or context-sensitive probabilities should be introduced? In general, one would expect that probabilities of rewrite rules applying *are* context-sensitive. Not only that, but as Suppes points out, semantic and pragmatic considerations will play a major role in altering these probabilities. In cases where the data or theory is available, the linguistic evidence will determine what the category is *B* or *B'*. Suppose the linguistic evidence says that category *B* is right in both positions. Would there then be a move to context-sensitive probabilities? Or would there be a challenge to the much more powerful linguistic evidence?

The analogy to perception might be taken up again. We don't know, say, exactly how a young child perceives the visual world. We could monitor the child's drawings and calculate the frequencies of circles, triangles, rectangles, etc., in those drawings. Would these frequencies tell us anything about his visual system?

Another aspect of Suppes' work on child language corpuses is the application of model-theoretic semantics to child language, as in Suppes (1970; 1973; 1974a; 1974b and 1974c). Here standard techniques are applied to try to formalize the semantics of children's utterances. These utterances are often ungrammatical in the adult language, but nevertheless, if one interprets them as one would a closely related adult expression, the appropriate semantic function can be written. To give just one example (Suppes, 1974c, p. 58), the child says, "Mommy eyes". An adult then judges that this has the same meaning as "Mommy's eyes" would for an adult, that is, it indicates "possession". Associated with a syntactic rule $NP \rightarrow NP + NP$ then would be a semantic function, in particular, a 'choice function for possession', as in the following 'semantic tree' (Suppes, 1974c, p. 58).

$$NP: f_A(B)$$

$$NP: A \quad NP: B$$

Of course there is a problem with this kind of analysis, as developmental psycholinguists are aware. Namely it is often difficult for an adult to judge what the meaning of a child's expression is. Consider other cases of what Suppes judges to involve possession: *rabbit splinter, horse feet, dolly dress.* Here, without context we can't be sure of the meanings of these expressions. The last, for example, might have the same meaning as 'The dolly is on the dress'. Context will sometimes help us to understand, sometimes not. Thus the use of a corpus in order to conclude via these methods that children have certain semantic functions is fraught with difficulties. Also the data are once again weak. In linguistic theory it is often thought necessary on both syntactic and semantic grounds in English to distinguish between 'alienable' and 'inalienable' possession. 'The rabbit's eyes' would involve inalienable possession, while 'the rabbit's splinter' would not. One would like to know whether such a distinction is present in a child's language, and what role it plays. Nevertheless, formalization as opposed to no formalization, everything else held equal, is always good (in our judgment). Thus the bringing in of model theory to the area of developmental psycholinguistics can be looked upon as 'good', as long as it does not mislead us into thinking that any crucial problems have been solved.

It seems to us that in the development of this area Suppes tried to play a role not unlike his earlier role in MLT. He tried to formalize certain theoretical notions with an aim to empirical testing of descriptive statistics. There was a major difference between the impact of the work in learning theory and in probabilistic grammar, however. In learning theory, Suppes worked in a field in which numerical experimental data already played a key role. Given an acceptance of the tenets and methodology of learning theory, the development of formal theories was a natural next step. In grammatical theory, on the other hand, numerical and statistical considerations played a quite minor role (except for the field of statistical linguistics, which had never been at the center of theoretical interest in linguistics). Most issues in linguistics are not touched by Suppes' models for corpuses. Nevertheless the application of precise statistical methods can be looked upon as an advance in the methodology of analyzing such corpuses.

C. Other Work in Cognitive Psychology

In addition to work relating MLT to automata theory and probabilistic grammar, Suppes developed several other projects within cognitive psychology. The most extensive of these involved the study of young children performing simple arithmetical tasks (Suppes, 1966b, 1967; Suppes & Groen, 1967; Suppes, Hyman & Jerman, 1967; Loftus & Suppes, 1972; Suppes, Jerman & Brian, 1968; Suppes & Morningstar, 1972). The data base for this work involved collecting performance and response time (latency) data from young children solving simple arithmetic tasks such as "$n + m = $?" where n and m are integers. The thrust of the work was to develop mathematical performance models for predicting the response time and error data in such tasks.

The work went through three phases. In the first, efforts were made to correlate various structural features of such problems with both error and latency data. That work did not involve formal processing models. In the second phase, various counting algorithms were proposed and made to yield predictions of response time. For example, in solving "$n + m = $?", one might suppose that the child first loads the value of $\max(n, m)$ in a 'register'. Then he increments the register by $\min(n, m)$ and reads off the answer. If hunting for 'max' and reading off the answer from the register take a constant amount of time, predictable variations in response times come about by the number of incrementing operations required. Various counting models of this variety fit experimental data fairly well, and a number of other psychologists such as W. Banks, G. Groen and F. Restle continued to develop this framework extensively.

The later work is the most interesting. It involves the postulation of processing models as *register machines* – a variety of automata. Register machine models of arithmetic yield accurate predictions of a variety of behavioral measures in such problem tasks. Cognitive psychology often postulates models for response latency based on response generation algorithms; however, few of these projects involve a serious effort to formalize the machinery of the algorithm. It is a reasonable conjecture that others will follow Suppes in using machine theory for such purposes.

From time to time Suppes has dabbled in the perception area. His preference has been for formalisms that eschew the grounding of perception in biology. He was influenced by Minsky and Pappert's (1969) extensive efforts to provide a formal approach to simpler kinds of pattern recognition. Suppes and Rottmayer (1974) propose automata-theoretic models for a variety of simple pattern recognition situations. While their work is only a beginning, additional applications of their formal approach are likely to occur.

Finally, Suppes (Roberts & Suppes, 1967; Suppes, 1972, 1977) has provided some analysis of the geometric models that underly visual perception. None of the projects discussed in this section are as extensive as those in MLT, and they remain currently in a state of incompleteness. However, they do illustrate Suppes' continuing efforts to show that formal work in cognitive psychology can proceed with axiomatic underpinnings. This theme, despite its relatively low profile, is important in contrast to the more popular, but less formal, applications of computer simulation methods in cognitive psychology. While the axiomatic method is more constraining than the computer simulation approach, it does have the advantage of making more precise the underlying assumptions in a theory.

IV. Overview

Any overview of Suppes' work in psychology must deal with an evaluation of MLT itself. While the area was active and productive for a decade and a half, there has been relatively little work in MLT since the late '60's. Most of the researchers who developed MLT have moved to more complicated areas in cognitive psychology such as memory, thinking and psycholinguistics. While there are some who would regard such a shift as reflecting only current fashion, it seems to us that MLT has failed to develop for more substantive reasons. Basically MLT was never able to shed its underpinnings in the traditional stimulus-response-outcome scheme. The vision of many learning theorists that complex cognitive phenomena could be explained in stimulus-response terms has never been shown to work. Few hold that vision today.

Suppes, himself, recognized the shift away from S-R psychology (Suppes, 1975):

We are now in an era of neobehaviorism, . . ., I want to make the essential behavioral feature of neobehaviorism the retention of stimuli and responses as central on the one hand, and the introduction of unobservable internal structure as the 'neo' component on the other . . . it is quite appropriate to postulate a full range of internal structures, ranging from memory hierarchies to language production and language comprehension devices that cannot be, from the standpoint of the theory, directly observed.

In this quote, Suppes is acknowledging the explanatory inadequacy of the internal mechanisms of MLT based on stimulus-response notions. His idea is that internal mechanisms must have more structure; yet the vision of accounting for the detailed properties of the observable behavior protocols of Equation 1 is still valid.

It remains an open problem whether or not formal models of cognitive processes are best assessed by detailed data filling. There have been few such successes of this kind in complex settings, and there are alternatives. For example, one might validate a theory by showing that it correctly predicts the occurrence or non-occurrence of various phenomena. The physical and biological sciences utilize both this means as well as data fitting for evidence for the adequacy of a theory.

In the tasks analyzed by MLT, it was not of interest to show that the theory could or could not predict that learning would occur. On the other hand, in more complex tasks such as problem solving or language learning it is by no means trivial to develop a realistic theory that will predict that the task can be accomplished at all. If further developments in formal theory in these areas do not entail detailed data fitting, both the substance and methodology of MLT will be gone. There is good reason to think that this will happen. However, even if MLT fails to continue as a model for formalism in psychology, it will have served as a useful object lesson for the development of psychology as a serious formal science.

Suppes' research in cognitive psychology is again motivated by application of the formal method. Whatever our conclusions about the ultimate scientific truth of the conclusions drawn in this research, it seems to us that the spirit of the formal approach is useful and important for the long-term development of psychology. There are others, of course, who have exploited well the formal method in related questions (e.g., Chomsky, or Minsky and Papert in their *Perceptrons*). But we feel that a survey of the growing field of 'cognitive psychology' itself would show a plethora of vaguely argued flow diagrams and 'systems accounts', influenced mainly by work in computer simulation. Suppes' spirit of precise theorizing would be useful in the advance of this science.

We come finally to Suppes' formal methods themselves. Will the axiomatic method as espoused by Suppes prove to have long term validity as a tool in psychology? If the goal of science is to attain insight or knowledge about the world, then surely it is a reasonable sub-goal to use objective methods in this pursuit. It is clear then that it is a reasonable sub-sub goal to use precise methods of fitting numerical data against precise predictions from a formal theory. Suppes has consistently and relentlessly developed and applied the axiomatic approach in empirical science. On the principle that there can be too much of a good thing, one might worry that Suppes has sometimes concentrated too heavily on the sub-sub goal without looking up to see whether the goal was being reached. We may look upon Suppes as a philosopher with a method, who is going to demonstrate the method's validity by applying it. Suppes (1976) surveys some uses of statistical predictions and tests in physics, econometrics and psychology. About physics he concludes (p. 440): "In the testing of highly structured theories of the kind characteristic of physics, there is little use of the vast apparatus of modern statistics". On the assumption that physics in some areas has attained knowledge of the world, some scholars in psychology might want to emulate it and spend their research efforts on developing highly structured theories. Nevertheless, the remarkable energies, abilities and clarity of Suppes cannot help but to impress themselves on all observers.

A final point about Suppes' contributions is that he has served well in the capacity of a teacher and facilitator of others. In the late 50s, Suppes founded the Institute of Mathematical Studies in the Social Sciences at Stanford. The Institute has had on a long term basis such eminent psychologists as W. K. Estes and R. C. Atkinson, and, on a more temporary basis, has housed many other important figures in mathematical psychology. A number of others – including both authors of this essay – have profited from graduate study with Suppes in the Institute.

Independent of the details of the many projects Suppes has conducted, his indirect contributions to formal work in psychology through his teaching and facilitating efforts have been deep and will be longlasting.

University of California, Irvine

Notes

[1] The stimulus-response-outcome account of the learning process of course has its roots in the philosophical tradition of the British empiricists. However, it differs from classical associationism in two important ways. First, the stimuli and responses that become associated are grounded in observable events. Second, the word 'reinforcer' conveys the

idea that some event occurs which provides positive or negative affect to the organism. The idea is that organisms change their response probabilities in such a way as to increase the chance of positive affect. The more neutral word 'outcome' is sometimes used to avoid theoretical precommitment to this notion of why response probabilities change.
[2] Descriptive statistics refer to means, variances, and distributions of various quantities defined on the ordered behavioral protocols of Equation 1. For example, if T organisms each produce an ordered protocol, then one could tabulate such statistics as the mean and variance of the number of R_l responses, for $1 \leq l \leq L$. Many other such statistics suggest themselves.
[3] Actually Estes & Suppes (1959, 1974) were drawn respectively from two longer, important unpublished technical reports:

Estes, W. K., and Suppes, P. 'Foundations of statistical learning theory I. The linear model for simple learning', *Technical Report No. 16*, Contract Nonr 225 (1959), Applied Mathematics and Statistics Laboratory, Stanford University, Stanford, Calif. 1957.

Estes, W. K., and Suppes, P. 'Foundations of statistical learning theory, II. The stimulus sampling model', *Technical Report No. 26*. Stanford, Calif.: Institute for Mathematical Studies in the Social Sciences, Stanford University, 1959.

These two reports and related lecture notes by Estes and Suppes exerted a great deal of influence on the formal direction that MLT was developed.
[4] The first proof that, for large N, stimulus sampling theory models converge uniformally over trials to linear models was given in the 1959 technical report mentioned in the previous footnote. Also see Norman (1972, p. 205).
[5] An introduction to automata theory may be found in Hopcroft and Ullman (1969).
[6] There is actually a second, though related, use of simplicity in linguistics. A *theory* T_1 is *simpler* than a theory T_2 if the class of grammars that T_1 allows is a sub-set of the class of grammars that T_2 allows. The use of simplicity arguments in linguistic theory often center around preferring theory T_1 to T_2 for just these reasons, thus advancing toward the goal of restricting the definition of possible human natural language. The argument doesn't always apply, but there still may be ways of preferring one theory to another. See Culicover and Wexler (1977).

References

Ambler, S. (1973), 'A mathematical model of learning under schedules of interresponse time reinforcement', *Journal of Mathematical Psychology*, **10**, 364–386.

Arbib, M. A. (1969), 'Memory limitations of stimulus-response models', *Psychological Review*, **76**, 507–510.

Atkinson, R. C. and Estes, W. K. (1963), 'Stimulus sampling theory'. In R. D. Luce, R. R. Bush, and E. Galanter (Eds.), *Handbook of Mathematical Psychology*, Vol. II. New York: Wiley, 121–268.

Atkinson, R. C. and Suppes, P. (1958), 'An analysis of two-person game situations in terms of statistical learning theory', *Journal of Experimental Psychology*, **55**, 369–378.

Atkinson, R. C. and Suppes, P. (1959), 'Applications of a Markov model to two-person noncooperative games'. In R. R. Bush and W. K. Estes (Eds.), *Studies in Mathematical Learning Theory*. Stanford: Stanford University Press, 65–76.

Bush, R. R. and Mosteller, F. (1951), 'A mathematical model for simple learning', *Psychological Review*, **58**, 313–323.

Bush, R. R. and Mosteller, F. (1955), *Stochastic Models for Learning*. New York: Wiley.

Brown, R. and Hanlon, C. (1970), 'Derivational complexity and order of acquisition in child speech'. In J. R. Hayes (Ed.), *Cognition and the Development of Language*. New York: Wiley.

Crothers, E. and Suppes, P. (1967), *Experiments in Second Language Learning*. New York: Academic Press.

Culicover, P. W. and Wexler, K. (1977), 'Some syntactic implications of a theory of language acquisition'. In P. Culicover, T. Wasow and A. Akmajian (Eds.), *Studies in Formal Syntax*. New York: Academic Press.

Estes, W. K. (1950), 'Toward a statistical theory of learning', *Psychological Review*, **57**, 94–107.

Estes, W. K. and Suppes, P. (1959), 'Foundations of linear models'. In R. R. Bush and W. K. Estes (Eds.), *Studies in Mathematical Learning Theory*. Stanford: Stanford University Press, 137–179.

Estes, W. K. and Suppes, P. (1974), 'Foundations of stimulus sampling theory'. In D. H. Krantz, R. C. Atkinson, R. D. Luce, and P. Suppes (Eds), *Contemporary Developments in Mathematical Psychology* (Vol. 1). *Learning, Memory, and Thinking*. San Francisco: Freeman, 163–183.

Greeno, J. G. (1974), 'Representation of learning as discrete transitions in a finite state space'. In D. H. Krantz, R. C. Atkinson, R. D. Luce, and P. Suppes (Eds.), *Contemporary Developments in Mathematical Psychology*, Vol. I. San Francisco: W. H. Freeman, 1–43.

Hilgard, E. R. and Bower, H. G. (1966), *Theories of Learning*, 3rd edition. New York: Appleton-Century-Crofts.

Hopcroft, J. E. and Ullman, J. D. (1969), *Formal Languages and their Relation to Automata*. Reading, Massachusetts: Addision-Wesly.

Karlin, S. (1953), 'Some random walks arising in learning models', *Pacific Journal of Mathematics*, **3**, 725–756.

Karsh, E. and Suppes, P. (1964), 'Probability learning of rats in continuous-time experiments', *Psychonomic Science*, **1**, 361–362.

Kemeny, J. G. and Snell, J. L. (1960), *Finite Markov Chains*. Princeton: Van Nostrand.

Kieras, D. E. (1976), 'Finite automata and S-R models', *Journal of Mathematical Psychology*, **13**, 127–147.

Lamperti, J. and Suppes, P. (1959), 'Chains of infinite order and their application to learning theory', *Pacific Journal of Mathematics*, **9**, 739–754. (Correction to 'Chains of infinite order and their application to learning theory,' *Pacific Journal of Mathematics*, 1964, **15**, 1471–1472.)

Loève, M, (1963), *Probability Theory*, 3rd edition. Princeton: Van Nostrand-Reinhold.

Loftus, E. F. and Suppes, P. (1972), 'Structural variables that determine problem-solving difficulty in computer-assisted instruction', *Journal of Educational Psychology*, **63**, 531–542.

Millward, R. B. (1969), 'Derivations of learning statistics from absorbing Markov chains', *Psychometrika*, **34**, 215–232.

Minsky, M. and Papert, S. (1969), *Perceptrons*. Cambridge, Massachusetts: MIT Press.

Neisser, U. (1967), *Cognitive Psychology*. New York: Appleton century-crofts.

Nelson, R. J. (1975), 'Behaviorism, finite automata and stimulus-response theory', *Theory and Decision*, **6**, 249–268.

Norman, M. F. (1966), 'An approach to free responding on schedules that prescribe reinforcement probability as a function of interresponse time', *Journal of Mathematical Psychology*, **3**, 235–268.

Norman, M. F. (1972), *Markov Processes and Learning Models*. New York: Academic Press.

Rabin, M. O. and Scott, D. (1959), 'Finite automata and their decision problems', *IBM Journal of Research and Development*, **3**, 114–125; reprinted in E. F. Moore (Ed.), *Sequential Machines*. Reading, Massachusetts: Addison-Wesley, 1964, 63–91.

Roberts, F. S. and Suppes, P. (1967), 'Some problems in the geometry of visual perception', *Synthese*, **17**, 173–201.

Rottmayer, W. A. (1970), 'A formal theory of perception', *Technical Report* No. 161, Stanford University, Institute for Mathematical Studies in the Social Sciences.

Schlag-Rey, M., Groen, G., and Suppes, P. (1965), 'Latencies on last error in paired-associate learning', *Psychonomic Science*, **2**, 15–16.

Suppes, P. (1954), 'Some remarks on problems and methods in the philosophy of science', *Philosophy of Science*, **21**, 242–248.

Suppes, P. (1959), 'A linear model for a continuum of responses'. In R. R. Bush and W. K. Estes (Eds.), *Studies in Mathematical Learning Theory*. Stanford: Stanford University Press, 400–414.

Suppes, P. (1960), 'Stimulus sampling theory for a continuum of responses'. In K. J. Arrow, S. Karlin and P. Suppes (Eds.), *Mathematical Methods in the Social Sciences, 1959*. Stanford: Stanford University Press, 348–365.

Suppes, P. (1964), 'Some current developments in models of learning for a continuum of responses'. (Discrete Adaptive Processes Symposium, American Institute of Electrical Engineers, June 1962). *The Institute of Electrical and Electronics Engineers Transactions on Applications and Industry*, **83**, 297–305.

Suppes, P. (1965a), 'On the behavioral foundations of mathematical concepts', *Monographs of the Society for Research in Child Development*, **30**, 60–69.

Suppes, P. (1965b), 'The kinematics and dynamics of concept formation'. In Y. Bar-Hillel (Ed.), *Proceedings for the 1964 International Congress for Logic, Methodology and Philosophy of Science*. Amsterdam: North-Holland, 405–414.

Suppes, P. (1966a), 'Mathematical concept formation in children', *American Psychologist*, **21**, 139–150.

Suppes, P. (1966b), 'The psychology of arithmetic'. In J. Bruner (Ed.), *Learning about Learning* (a conference report). Washington, D. C.: U.S. Government Printing Office, 235–242.

Suppes, P. (1967), 'The case for information-oriented (basic) research in mathematics education'. In J. M. Scandura (Ed.), *Research in Mathematics Education*. Washington, D.C.: National Council of Teachers of Mathematics, 1–5. Reprinted in J. A. McIntosh (Ed.), *Perspectives on Secondary Mathematics Education*. Englewood Cliffs, N.J.: Prentice-Hall, 1971, 233–236.

Suppes, P. (1969), 'Stimulus-response theory of finite automata', *Journal of Mathematical Psychology*, **6**, 327–355.

Suppes, P. (1970), 'Probabilistic grammars for natural languages', *Synthese*, 22, 95–116. Reprinted in D. Davidson and G. Harman (Eds.), *Semantics of Natural Language*. Dordrecht: Reidel, 1972, 741–762.

Suppes, P. (1973), 'Some open problems in the philosophy of space and time', *Synthese*, 1972, 24, 298–316. Reprinted in P. Suppes (Ed.), *Space, Time and Geometry*. Dordrecht: Reidel, 383–401.

Suppes, P. (1973). 'Semantics of context-free fragments of natural languages'. In K.J.J. Hintikka, J.M.E. Moravcsik, and P. Suppes (Eds.), *Approaches to Natural Language*. Dordrecht: Reidel, 370–394.

Suppes, P. (1974a), 'The semantics of children's language', *American Psychologist*, 29, 103–114.

Suppes, P. (1974b) 'Model-theoretic semantics for natural language'. In C. H. Heidrich (Ed.), *Semantics and Communication*. Amsterdam: North-Holland, 285–344.

Suppes, P. (1974c) 'On the grammar and model-theoretic semantics of children's noun phrases'. Colloques Internationaux du C.N.R.S. *Problèms Actuels en Psycholinguistique*, 206, 49–60.

Suppes, P. (1975), 'From behaviorism to neobehaviorism,' *Theory and Decision*, 6, 269–285.

Suppes, P. (1976), 'Testing theories and the foundations of statistics'. In W. L. Harper and C. A. Hooker (Eds.), *Foundations of Probability Theory, Statistical Inference, and Statistical Theories of Science* (Vol. 2). Dordrecht: Reidel, 437–455.

Suppes, P. (1977), 'Is Visual Space Euclidean', *Synthese*, 1977, 35, 397–422.

Suppes, P. 'Learning theory for probabilistic automata and register machines, with applications to educational research'. In Spada and Kempf (Eds.), *Structural Models of Thinking and Learning*, in press.

Suppes, P. and Atkinson, R. C. (1960), *Markov Learning Models for Multiperson Interaction*. Stanford: Stanford University Press, 1960.

Suppes, P. and Carlsmith, J. M. (1962), 'Experimental analysis of a duopoly situation from the standpoint of mathematical learning theory', *International Economic Review*, 3, 60–78.

Suppes, P. and Donio, J. (1967), 'Foundations of stimulus-sampling theory for continuous-time processes', *Journal of Mathematical Psychology*, 4, 202–225.

Suppes, P. and Frankmann, R. W. (1961), 'Test of stimulus sampling theory for a continuum of responses with unimodal noncontingent determinate reinforcement', *Journal of Experimental Psychology*, 61, 122–132.

Suppes, P. and and Ginsberg, R. (1962), 'Application of a stimulus sampling model to children's concept formation with and without overt correction responses', *Journal of Experimental Psychology*, 63, 330–336.

Suppes, P. and Ginsberg, R. (1963), 'A fundamental property of all-or-none models, binomial distribution of responses piror to conditioning, with application to concept formation in children', *Psychological Review*, 1963, 70, 139–161.

Suppes, P. and Groen, G. (1967), 'Some counting models for first-grade performance data on simple addition facts'. In J. M. Scandura (Ed.), *Research in Mathematics Education*. Washington, D.C.: National Council of Teachers of Mathematics, 35–43.

Suppes, P., Groen, G. and Schlag-Rey, M. (1966), 'A model for response latency in paired-associate learning', *Journal of Mathematical Psychology*, 3, 99–128.

Suppes, P., Hyman, L., and Jerman, M. (1967), 'Linear structural models for response and latency performance in arithmetic on computer-controlled terminals'. In J. P. Hill (Ed.), *Minnesota Symposia on Child Psychology*. Minneapolis: University of Minnesota Press, 160–200.

Suppes, P., Jerman, M. and Brian, D. (1968), *Computer-Assisted Instruction: Stanford's 1965–1966 Arithmetic Program*. New York: Academic Press.

Suppes, P. and Krasne, F. (1961), 'Applications of stimulus sampling theory to situations involving social pressure', *Psychological Review*, **68**, 46–59.

Suppes, P. and Lamperti, J. (1960), 'Some asymptotic properties of Luce's beta learning model', *Psychometrika, **25**, 233–241.

Suppes, P. and Morningstar, M. (1972), *Computer-Assisted Instruction at Stanford, 1966–68: Data, Models, and Evaluation of the Arithmetic Programs*. New York: Academic Press.

Suppes, P. and Rottmayer, W. (1974), 'Automata'. In E. C. Carterette and M. P. Friedman (Eds.), *Handbook of Perception* (Vol. 1). *Historical and Philosophical Roots of Perception*. New York: Academic Press, 335–362.

Suppes, P. and Rouanet, H. (1964), 'A simple discrimination experiment with a continuum of responses'. In R. C. Atkinson (Ed.), *Studies in Mathematical Psychology*. Stanford: Stanford University Press, 317–357.

Suppes, P., Rouanet, H., Levine, M. and Frankmann, R. W. (1964), 'Empirical comparison of models for a continuum of responses with noncontingent bimodal reinforcement'. In R. C. Atkinson (Ed.), *Studies in Mathematical Psychology*. Stanford: Stanford University Press, 358–359.

Suppes, P. and Schlag-Rey, M. (1962), 'Analysis of social conformity in terms of generalized conditioning models'. In J. H. Criswell, H. Solomon and P. Suppes (Eds.), *Mathematical Methods in Small Group Processes*. Stanford: Stanford University Press, 334–361.

Suppes, P., Smith, R. and Léveillé, M. (1973), 'The French syntax of a child's noun phrases', *Archives de Psychologie*, **42**, 207–269.

Suppes, P. and Zinnes, J. (1961), 'Stochastic learning theories for a response continuum with nondeterminate reinforcement', *Psychometrika*, **26**, 373–390.

Suppes, P. and Zinnes, J. (1966), 'A continuous-response task with nondeterminate, contingent reinforcement', *Journal of Mathematical Psychology*, **3**, 197–216.

Tyspkin, Ya. Z. (1973), *Foundations of the Theory of Learning Systems*. New York: Academic Press.

Wexler, K., Culicover, P. W. and Hamburger, H. (1975), 'Learning theoretic foundations of linguistic universals', *Theoretical Linguistics*, **2**, 215–253.

DEAN T. JAMISON

SUPPES' CONTRIBUTION TO EDUCATION*

The study of education differs from most academic disciplines in that its subject is a major economic sector; the United States alone currently spends over $120 thousand million per year on education. The criteria for considering Suppes' contributions to education must thus go beyond those employed in the chapters of this volume that deal with his contributions to philosophy and psychology. For Suppes has not only contributed through academic research to our thinking about education, but he has also pioneered the introduction of new techniques for instruction, particularly techniques involving computers. Indeed Suppes' practical work in education will, I expect, change the practice of education more profoundly than his research on education is likely to affect academic thinking. Thus the following pages will deal more with Suppes as a technocrat, manager, and entrepreneur than with Suppes as a scholar.[1]

This chapter has three sections. In the first I discuss Suppes' contribution to the development of instructional methods. Over the past 15 years his efforts – and those of institutions he has helped to create and manage – have been the major factors in adapting the computer into a workable medium for the delivery of instruction; the bulk of the first section discusses this development, and the remainder deals with efforts Suppes now has underway to use radio as an effective method of education in low-income countries. The second section of this chapter discusses Suppes' contribution to educational research – to detailed studies of learning and to research on optimal teaching. The final section ventures a few conclusions.

1. Suppes and the New Media of Education

In sharp contrast to many of the social and economic sectors that influence our lives the methods of education change slowly. This pace imposes the necessity for an historical perspective to highlight the fundamental changes that education has indeed undergone, and in two speculative papers Suppes (1971, 1975a) outlined his perception of the major technological advances in the history of education. The first major technological change – occuring in classical Greece and Alexandria – separated the learner from his tutor by using books and libraries to transmit knowledge. One and a half millennia later the invention of printing dramatically reduced the cost of books, allowing for much greater geographical dispersion of education for elites. A third technological advance was the introduction of tests which allow a clear separation to be drawn between an educational system's pedagogical function, and its role in the selection of economic and social elites. Tests played an important role in social selection in China as early as the twelfth century and are by now, of course, pervasive in that role around the world. A fourth and recent technological innovation is the school; schools organize students into blocks of sufficient size that face-to-face instruction (using lectures and recitation) can become an economically viable technique of basic education for a substantial fraction of a country's population.[2]

Reviewing this progression of educational media – from tutors to manuscripts then to printed books and classrooms – provides a context for considering Suppes' work in developing the potential of computers and electronic media for instruction. In the period since 1963 Suppes has overseen the expenditure of perhaps $25,000,000 to adapt and program a rapidly evolving computer technology into an instrument for high-quality individualized instruction. This computer revolution in the technology of instruction would, if it succeeds, combine the mass availability of present-day classroom instruction with the possibilities for individual tutoring hitherto available to only a tiny elite. Thus Suppes (1966, p. 207) has predicted:

. . . in a few more years millions of school-children will have access to what Philip of Macedon's son Alexander enjoyed as a royal prerogative: the personal services of a tutor as well-informed and responsive as Aristotle.

The full realization of this hope will likely remain unrealized for the remainder of this century or longer; nonetheless, in the 12 years following this prediction, Suppes and his co-workers have transformed a collection of possibilities and program fragments into a substantial body of operating computer-assisted instruction (CAI) curriculums.

My principal purpose in this section to summarize briefly Suppes' CAI development work; I also briefly discuss his educational development activities in other areas. To provide a context for the ensuing discussion, Table 1 overviews the areas in which Suppes and his colleagues have prepared curriculum materials; the table includes textbooks and radio as well as CAI.

Table 1
Curriculum Materials Prepared by Suppes[a]

Print	Radio	Computer-assisted Instruction
	Elementary school level	
Geometry for Primary Grades, Books 1 and 2, (Suppes & Hawley, 1960).	Beginning in 1973 Suppes has been Principal Investigator on the Nicaragua Radio Mathematics Project (Searle, Friend, & Suppes, 1976). The project uses radio to teach mathematics at grades 1 to 4, and may expand to other subjects and countries.	1963–65: Logic; drill-and-practice in arithmetic (Suppes, Jerman, & Brian, 1968).
Sets and Numbers, Books K-2, (Suppes, 1968).		1966–68: Tutorial instruction in mathematics and, with R. C. Atkinson, reading (Suppes & Morningstar, 1972; Suppes, 1972).
Sets and Numbers, Books 3–6, (Suppes, 1966, 1969).		1969– : Final development and expanded operational use of drill-and-practice curriculums in mathematics, reading, and language arts (Suppes et al., 1973); Fletcher & Suppes, 1972).
	University level	
Introduction to Logic, (Suppes, 1957).		1967–70: Tutorial course in first-year Russian developed and implemented with J. Van Campen (Suppes & Morningstar, 1969).
Axiomatic Set Theory, (Suppes, 1972).		1972– : Elementary logic (Goldberg & Suppes, 1976); set theory; computer programming; Bulgarian; Old Church Slavonic; courses in music (Suppes, Smith, & Beard, 1977).

[a]This listing is not exhaustive.

189

Computer-assisted Instruction

CAI relies on the computational and data storage capacities of modern computer systems to assist instruction in several ways. CAI systems transfer information to students, assist them with computations, and pose problems for them to solve. Depending on a student's response to a problem, or his instructions to the computer, the CAI system decides what next to display to the student. Because of the capacity of computers to present problems or instruction that is tightly tied to a student's needs, and to provide immediate corrective feedback to students on their responses, CAI has great *potential* for providing highly individualized and effective instruction.

Suppes was surely one of the first to recognize the potential of CAI but others did so as well, and by 1972 a selected bibliography on CAI filled 235 pages (Barnes and Schreiber, 1972). During the period from 1965 to 1971 the United States Office of Education spent $161,000,000 on approximately 500 projects involving CAI (Grayson, 1971), and in subsequent years the National Science Foundation spent several million dollars supporting Suppes' work as well as over $10,000,000 on two other major projects at the University of Illinois and the MITRE Corporation. Questions about where the money had gone soon followed. Computer equipment was in place, as were tantalizing demonstrations of CAI's rich potential. But few projects indeed had produced working CAI curriculums, usable in the schools or universities.[3] By 1972 the Office of Education had virtually ceased supporting CAI and by 1977 the National Science Foundation, too, had drastically reduced its commitments. Realizing the potential of CAI proved far more difficult than recognizing it; neither the funding agencies nor, by and large, had the developers pursued CAI's potential to its operational realization. In contrast, what perhaps most characterizes Suppes' work in CAI is the tenacity and long-term character of his commitment to producing operational CAI curriculums, and his success in doing so.

Technology and management

An operational CAI system has three major technical components. The first of these is the central processing unit and its associated data storage and input-output facilities. The second component is the student terminal. Each terminal usually consists of a keyboard and an alphanumeric display device. The display device may be either a cathode-ray tube, with an appearance like a television screen, or a teletype; changing costs and technical factors increasingly combine to dictate the choice of cathode-ray tube terminals. In addition, the terminals may include headsets for provision of aural messages to students, mechanisms for graphic or pictorial display, and mechanisms other than keyboards that allow students to communicate with the computer.

The third technical component of a CAI system is the communication system that links the computer to the student terminal. For a small CAI system serving only a few students in a single classroom the communication system can be simple indeed; on the other hand, there may occasionally be a need for a large computer system that serves a highly dispersed population. In this case the cost and technical complexity of communication becomes an important factor in the design of the system. Figure 1 shows the national communication network of Suppes' CAI system in 1972–73, when it reached its most widely dispersed population; as shown, the network covered locations across broad reaches of the United States. While communication services were generally provided by lines leased from the telephone company, problems of cost and service reliability in rural areas led to an exploration of the use of communication satellites for remote users. A link between Stanford and Isleta Pueblo, New Mexico, was operated for several months through the ATS-3 communication satellite of the National Aeronautics and Space Administration. The increasing availability and sophistication of mini- and micro-computers will likely obviate the future need for complex communication components of CAI systems.

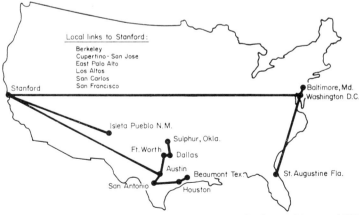

Fig. 1. IMSSS National Network, 1972–73. Source: Fletcher and Suppes (1976).

191

None of the technical components of a CAI system – the terminals, the computer system itself, and the communication system – are commercially available in a form well adapted to CAI usage. Thus there is a major technical design problem in modifying available equipment and in choosing components that perform in a technically satisfactory way at reasonable cost. There is, in addition, the problem of appropriately modifying computer software for CAI use (see Suppes, Smith, and Beard, 1977, pp. 180–182) and, most important, the problem of preparing the CAI curriculum materials for students' use. Solving the interrelated problems of hardware, software, and curriculum preparation requires the creation and management of a large and technically sophisticated organization. To solve these problems Suppes participated in the creation of two organizations that handle different aspects of his CAI development work.

The first organization is the Stanford University Institute for Mathematical Studies in the Social Sciences (IMSSS). Patrick Suppes and Kenneth Arrow, an economist, established the IMSSS in 1959 and Suppes then became and now remains its Director. The founding purpose of the IMSSS was to conduct quantitative research in economics, psychology, and other social sciences, and that has remained a fundamental aspect of the Institute's work. In 1963, however, in part to provide a realistic school-based setting in which to conduct psychological research, the IMSSS began development of a computer system to deliver CAI. The IMSSS's CAI system has grown, been modified, and become far more flexible and reliable in the ensuing 14 years. Its purpose has been primarily to develop CAI techniques and courses, to test and evaluate them in an operational environment, and (particularly recently) to provide operational CAI to Stanford University students.

The second organization that Suppes has created is Computer Curriculum Corporation (CCC) of which he is the President and principal owner. In contrast to the research and development orientation of the IMSSS's CAI activities, CCC's purpose is to develop CAI curriculums and to make them available at a reasonable cost on computer systems sufficiently simple and reliable that they can be operated in ordinary schools. CCC is a profit-making business that has expanded rapidly in recent years to a staff of over 90 employees; there are now close to 5,000 terminals in use throughout the United States that were either supplied by CCC or that use, under license, CCC curriculums. This number is growing rapidly. On the assumption that CCC curriculums are principally used for compensatory education, and that the population of students

eligible for compensatory education in the United States is about 10%
of the students in grades 1 through 6, CCC's terminals now probably
reach 2% or 3% of the compensatory population. This is a substantial
market share given the strong institutional pressures on school system
administrators to use compensatory education funds for additional staff.

In large part because of the decline in federal funding for CAI, the
Stanford-based staff of the IMSSS has declined from a peak of about 200
individuals (including graduate students) 7 or 8 years ago to a present
level of about 35. This decline, combined with the growth of CCC, reflects a definite move away from research and exploratory development
and toward implementation, though an active CAI research activity remains in place at the IMSSS.

Elementary-school curriculums
The first CAI activities of the IMSSS were in the areas of arithmetic and
logic for elementary school students, and these evolved into a series of
substantial curriculum development activities. Suppes (1972a) provides
a succinct and highly readable summary of the history of elementary
school curriculums at Stanford, and I refer the reader to that paper for a
more comprehensive overview. Basically, however, there were two major
lines of development of elementary school curriculums, and I touch on
these briefly in the paragraphs that follow.

Beginning in 1964 the United States Office of Education, as a part of the
general wave of hopefulness concerning CAI's future, provided the
IMSSS with a large grant to develop tutorial CAI in reading and mathematics in collaboration with Brentwood Elementary School in East Palo
Alto, California. The CAI curriculums were designed to provide complete
coverage for students' instruction in reading and mathematics, and a
complex and elaborate computer system was designed and built in collaboration with IBM to effect this task (Suppes and Morningstar, 1972,
Part II). Richard C. Atkinson was responsible for curriculum design in
reading and Suppes was responsible for mathematics as well as for the
overall implementation and operation of the system. The Brentwood
project lasted two years before funding ceased. The type of CAI provided
students under the Brentwood project seems, in retrospect, to have cost
too much to justify resulting improvements in students performance, and
that line of CAI development at the IMSSS has come to an end. Much was
learned, however, about CAI technology and curriculum development.

The second line of development of curriculum at the elementary school level involved creation of drill-and-practice curriculums to supplement students' ongoing instruction in mathematics, reading, and language arts. These curriculums provide students with a rapid sequence of problems in lessons that last from 5 to 10 minutes each; the students receive immediate feedback on the correctness of their responses and the CAI system individually tailors the presentation pattern of problems to the past history of the student's responses. Figure 2 shows a small child pondering his response to an arithmetic problem on a CCC system.

Available evaluation data strongly suggest that this type of CAI can be effective for compensatory education, a finding that is particularly important given evidence that few (if any) effective and replicable alternative compensatory interventions are available.[4] CCC makes available a mathematics curriculum for grades 1 through 6 and reading and language arts curriculum for grades 3 through 6. As soon as a low-cost, reliable mechanism for providing audio messages becomes available CCC plans to provide reading and language arts for grades 1 and 2.

University level curriculums
The thrust of recent CAI work at the IMSSS has been to extend the range and deepen the sophistication of its course offerings at the university level. The first university level course to be extensively used on the IMSSS CAI system was an introductory course in Russian developed by Professor Joseph van Campen; students in this course performed much better on examinations than did students in a comparison course that was traditionally taught. 73% of the CAI students finished the course, whereas only 32% finished in the regular class; requested enrollments in subsequent years exceeded the IMSSS's capacity to provide places (Suppes and Morningstar, 1969). The IMSSS also developed and implemented a 2nd-year Russian course, but, because of difficulties in financing these courses, the IMSSS no longer offers them.

Suppes, Smith, and Beard (1977) overview the IMSSS's current CAI activities at the university level and describe the IMSSS's present computer facilities. CAI courses are now available in logic, axiomatic set theory, several Slavic languages, computer programming, Chinese, and music. In addition IMSSS staff continue their efforts to improve the technology of CAI, particularly in the areas of computer generated speech and computer processing of natural language fragments.

A note on CAI economics
The IMSSS's CAI system principally serves as a vehicle for curriculum

Fig. 2. Terminal of CCC CAI System installed at Westminster Avenue Elementary School, Los Angeles.

development and research, and only secondarily as an operational delivery system for CAI curriculums. It would thus be both difficult and inappropriate to calculate its cost per student-hour of instruction, say, and to compare those costs with the range of costs of classroom instruction at Stanford. However the CAI systems that CCC produces serve only an operational role, and the cost of the service they provide can be calculated in a straightforward way (including the costs of maintenance and of the teachers and aides required to manage the systems in the schools). Use of this type of CAI for compensatory education costs less than the add-on amounts typically allocated per-student for compensatory education – substantially less, in fact, than the amount allocated by the largest source of compensatory funds, Title I of the Elementary and Secondary Education Act of 1965. For this purpose, at least, CAI is now thoroughly economically viable.

The economic viability of operational CAI at the university level remains, however, to be established. Suppes (1975b) offers the argument that for low-enrollment courses at universities CAI can be justified on the ground that the student-to-teacher ratio with these courses is so low that they can be extraordinarily costly when conventionally taught. (Suppes, Smith, and Beard, 1977, present evidence that enrollments at Stanford in such courses as Bulgarian and Old Church Slavonic can indeed be low.) Suppes' argument is somewhat strange, even though there is a sense in which he is correct. If one *must* offer these courses, if CAI curriculum development costs are low or sunk, and if the economic shadow price of, say, an Assistant Professor of Bulgarian is as high as his wage, then CAI *might* be justified in low-enrollment courses. But this is surely a slender economic justification for so major a development effort as that of the IMSSS in CAI.

The fundamental economic arguments for continued substantial investment in CAI development seem to me to rest on three propositions: (i) the value of many individuals' time is high and will be as high or higher in the future; (ii) cumulative investment in CAI will produce a growing set of high-quality, easily delivered courses; and (iii) the hardware cost of providing CAI will continue to decline. From propositions (i) and (iii) I conclude that the increasing cost of providing traditional instruction relative to that of providing CAI will cause CAI to be economically attractive for an ever-broadening range of purposes. From propositions (i) and (ii) I would conclude that an increasingly important benefit of CAI will be to reduce the time required of students (particularly adult students) to acquire education. Finally, proposition (ii) of course stands on its own; higher quality is, for example, the basic economic justification for CAI's present use in compensatory education.

Instructional Radio

CAI is the most recent application of electronic media to education; but as early as the 1920s radio was widely used for instruction and in the years following the 1950s there have been many and varied efforts to use television. One important purpose to which use of the media has been addressed is that of improving the generally poor quality of education available in low-income countries,[5] and in the early 1970s the IMSSS proposed that the United States Agency for International Development (AID) fund a project using radio to teach elementary mathematics. The project would draw heavily on the curriculum structure and psychological principles underlying Suppes' mathematics CAI work, attempting to apply them at low cost. By early 1975 the IMSSS's Radio Mathematics Project (RMP) was underway in Nicaragua (Searle, Friend, and Suppes, 1976).

At present the IMSSS operates an office in Nicaragua with two Stanford staff members and 30 Nicaraguans. The RMP has initiated its third operational year and is reaching several thousand first- and second-grade students. Searle, Suppes, and Friend (1977) describe the present status of the project in detail and, of particular importance to other project developers, they emphasize the psychological principles underlying the project's use of extremely frequent student response as a pedagogical technique. Two other salient features of the RMP that Searle, Suppes and

Friend describe are its heavy use of formative evaluation in curriculum preparation and its concern from the outset with problems of cost and operational implementation of the project results. Initial evaluations (Searle, Matthews, Suppes, and Friend) suggest the RMP to be highly successful.

The RMP remains to be implemented operationally, but, if operational implementation is even half as effective as the pilot project, the implications for quality improvement in elementary education in low-income countries could be profound. AID and the IMSSS are exploring techniques for operational implementation, development of radio lessons in curriculums other than mathematics, and extension of the results to other countries.

2. Suppes's Research in Education

Today's educational research literature contains virtually no systematic theory. The research methods used include description, simple experimentation, and more or less systematic searching for statistical associations in large data sets. These are all methods of research from which we can learn, but they certainly lack the satisfying mathematical structure that is to be found in parts of other of the behavioral sciences, for example psychology or economics.

Suppes' research in education stands generally outside the mainstream in that much of it is theoretical. In his presidential address to the American Educational Research Association, Suppes (1974) strongly argues the case for more theory in educational research, and two quotations from that address provide a good sense of his views:

The best general argument for theory in educational research I have left for last. This is the obvious triviality of bare empiricism as an approach to knowledge. Those parts of science that have been beset by bare empiricism have suffered accordingly. . . . At its most extreme level, bare empiricism is simply the recording of individual facts, and with no apparatus of generalization or theory, these bare facts duly recorded lead nowhere. They do not provide even a practical guide for future experience or policy. They do not provide methods of prediction or analysis. In short, bare empiricism does not generalize.

The same triviality may be claimed for the bare intuition of the romantics. Either bare empiricism or bare intuition leads not only to triviality, but also to chaos in practice . . . (p. 6)

It is often thought and said that what we most need in education is wisdom and broad understanding of the issues that confront us. Not at all, I say. What we need are deeply structured theories in education that drastically reduce, if not eliminate. the need for wisdom. I do not want wise men to design or build the airplane I fly in, but rather technical men who understand the theory of aerodynamics and the structural properties of metal. (p. 9)

The area of educational research most amenable to theoretical work is almost certainly learning theory, and most of Suppes' research in education deals with learning. Batchelder and Wexler (1979), in an accompanying paper in this volume, deal at length with Suppes' extensive contributions to mathematical learning theory and cognitive psychology, and I will make no attempt to cover that material here.[6] The work in learning theory that Batchelder and Wexler discuss is sufficiently mathematical to have penetrated into educational psychology only a little (if at all), and my discussion here will focus on those aspects of Suppes' work in learning theory that bear directly on education. The discussion divides naturally into two parts – Suppes' research on learning and his research on optimal teaching.

Studies of Learning

In discussing Suppes' contribution to the theory of learning as applied to education, it is useful to categorize learning by the level of aggregation of the material to be learned. A basic level from the point of view of educational psychologists is that of the individual *item*; examples of items include specific problems in arithmetic, phoneme-grapheme correspondences in initial reading, or foreign language vocabulary. I shall first discuss Suppes' work at the level of learning of the underlying *components* of the basic items in a curriculum. The next level to be discussed is the item level itself, and the third level is that of performance on item sequences (Suppes calls them "trajectories") within a curriculum. The final level I shall discuss is that of the gross learning of the material within a curriculum that would be measured by a standardized achievement test. This latter type of study forms the basis of most educational evaluation, the activity in which a large proportion of educational researchers spend the bulk of their time.

Item component analysis

Suppes has long been concerned with models for predicting students' performance on problems in the elementary mathematics curriculum, but in some of his more recent work he has turned to the question of how a student learns and performs on the *components* of individual items in arithmetic. This work focuses on individual steps students take toward a solution rather than simply on the correctness of the response. The mathematical models underlying this work are based on the theory of automata and register machines, and Suppes postulates a model of the student as a register machine that processes the components of arithmetic problems as the input tape to the machine. The output tape consists of the student's response to the problems. A highly readable description of this work may be found in Suppes (1973); a more extensive description and data analysis is contained in Suppes and Morningstar (1972, Chapter 4).

In order to test empirically models of this sort a great deal of highly detailed information on student response patterns is required, and the existence of the IMSSS's CAI laboratory provides an ideal mechanism for accurately gathering such data in a real-world environment. The formative evaluation that is an integral part of the Nicaragua Radio Mathematics Project also provides data for testing these models. It is through this interplay of the detailed modelling of student item learning and data collection from operational projects that Suppes utilizes research in improving instruction.

Research at the item level
Suppes has published a great deal more research on learning at the item level than he has at other levels. This is perhaps a natural consequence of his work in mathematical learning theory, since mathematical models for paired-associate learning can be altered very naturally to model educationally-relevant learning at the item level. Suppes' extensive collaboration with Edward Crothers on second-language learning (Crothers and Suppes, 1967) draws heavily on models of Suppes and others in mathematical psychology to develop and test a theory of second-language learning. Crothers and Suppes' work on second-language learning must rank as one of the most comprehensive attempts to combine theoretical and experimental methods in the understanding of an applied educational problem.

Another line of investigation at the item level concerns predictions of error probabilities and response latencies for items in the elementary mathematics curriculum. In contrast to the work at the item component level the thrust of this research is toward assessing performance on the problem as a whole. In a series of publications (Suppes, Jerman, and Brian, 1968, Chapters 6 and 7; Loftus and Suppes, 1972; Suppes and Morningstar, 1972, Chapter 3; Searle, Lorton, and Suppes, 1974) Suppes and a number of collaborators have developed this work. The methods are, however, distinctly less theoretical than the mathematical models of paired-associate learning. The method consists principally of regression analysis of item difficulty as a function of characteristics of the problems.

Trajectories of learning
The performance of students moving through a curriculum within a school year has been modeled relatively rarely. Educational psychologists have focused the bulk of their attention on learning at the item level, whereas educational evaluators (and the economists and sociologists who have an interest in education) have focused on end-of-year performance on a standardized test, while the detailed study of student growth within a school year has been neglected. In several recent papers (Suppes, Fletcher, and Zanotti, 1975, 1976; Suppes, Macken, and Zanotti, in press) Suppes and his coworkers have initiated an attempt to fill this gap.

In this line of research, as in others, Suppes' interplay of theoretical and empirical studies is closely tied to the availability of extensive data generated from his CAI operations. The structure of the elementary-school CAI curriculums is such that they provide for each student at each point in time a grade-placement measure of the student's current position in the curriculum. Suppes' work in this area consists of modelling the "trajectory" that a student's grade placement traces out as a function of time. By estimating parameters of learning models that are specific to individual students, Suppes is able to provide accurate predictions indeed of students' trajectories through the elementary mathematics curriculum.

This attempt to model student performance within a curriculum constitutes an important departure from traditional educational research. Nonetheless both the empirical and the theoretical conclusions of this effort have limitations. The basic theoretical specification is a nonlinear regression model that results from solving a stochastic differential equation; but a range of alternative specifications would seem to be equally plausible. The closeness of the fits of data to prediction that the trajectory models provide is rare in educational research; however, it is generally true that closely-spaced time series data can be accurately fit, and these results would seem to fall in that pattern.

Educational evaluation
Given Suppes' involvement both in research and in the development of instructional interventions, it would seem natural that he undertake thorough evaluations of the effectiveness of his interventions in operational environments. Evaluational research seems, however, to hold little interest for him, and I would think it fair to say that much of his evaluational

research has been undertaken under pressure from funding agencies. However, the evaluation research that Suppes has participated in provides valuable information on the effectiveness of a number of the IMSSS's curriculums, and I will thus report briefly on it here.

Suppes and Morningstar (1969) and Suppes, Fletcher, Zanotti, Lorton, and Searle (1973) provide evaluations of the effectiveness of CAI in raising student achievement test scores. The first of these papers, which is a widely cited document on CAI, examined the elementary school mathematics and university-level Russian curriculums; I have already discussed the results of the Russian evaluation, and the results at the elementary level were likewise favorable to CAI. The second paper utilizes a variety of regression models to evaluate the effectiveness of mathematics CAI for hearing-impaired students; the results again affirm CAI's effectiveness. (Fletcher and Beard, 1973, concluded, however, that CAI in language arts may actually have had a negative impact on hearing-impaired students.)

In part because of a general impression that the elementary school CAI curriculum was relatively more effective for disadvantaged groups, Jamison, Fletcher, Suppes, and Atkinson (1976) evaluated a number of CAI implementations explicitly in terms of their effect on inequality in the distribution of educational achievements. They applied measures used by economists to assess income inequality and concluded, as predicted, that CAI, if uniformly applied to a population, would likely reduce educational inequality.

Evaluators seldom assign students randomly to treatment and comparison conditions, but in the series of evaluations being undertaken of the Nicaragua Radio Mathematics Project this is systematically being done. The first of these evaluations (Searle, Matthews, Suppes, and Friend, 1978) has just been completed, and its results were noted earlier in this paper. This evaluation of the RMP will, I expect, soon come to be regarded as one of the most definitive evaluations in the education literature – both because of the strong impact of the intervention and the clear-cut experimental design of the evaluation.

Optimal Teaching

The principal practical purpose of research into how students learn is, of course, to improve teaching. Yet, just as the science of clestial mechanics is unable to tell us which of many potentially feasible orbits is optimal (in terms, say, of a tradeoff between payload weight and time-of-flight), so would even a highly perfected theory of learning remain short of a theory of instruction. Suppes (1968) provides a valuable general discussion of these issues, as does Bruner (1966) from quite a different perspective.

There is by now a substantial theoretical literature on optimal teaching that takes as its starting point various mathematical theories of learning. Much of this theoretical work has been undertaken by or under the direction of Richard C. Atkinson at the IMSSS, and there have been a number of efforts to implement through CAI the results of these optimizations (Atkinson, 1972).

Suppes' later contributions to this literature are small, but in a seminal paper (Suppes, 1964) he initiated this entire line of work by being the first to state explicitly and to solve the problem of optimal teaching for a specified mathematical theory of learning. The problem of optimal teaching is one to which Suppes' research is now returning.

3. Conclusions

I have in this chapter traced two major channels of Patrick Suppes' influence on education – his contributions to the development of computers and other media of instruction, and his contributions to theory in educational research. To these two channels I would add the possibility of a third: the international reputation[7] he has earned for his research and development accomplishments has provided him a political forum for advancing his views on directions in education and educational research.

Rather than directly influencing the process of choice in education, however, I predict Suppes' lasting contribution will have been to enlarge the set from which choice is possible. The simple economics of the situation makes the eventual widespread adoption of CAI inevitable. Suppes' work is recognized as the first substantial pioneering of that technology, and Suppes' name will remain inextricably linked to the computer revolution in education. Suppes and his co-workers have also greatly expanded the potential of radio to enrich the quality of education in low-income countries. If that venture succeeds, educational change in at least some of these countries could differ markedly from what it would otherwise be. That radio could become a potent educational tool has none of the inevitability that CAI has, and the role of Suppes and the IMSSS is for that reason the more important.

And what of Suppes' emphasis on theory in educational research? I predict that Suppes' views on the importance of theory will prove wrong, that our knowledge of the process and of the influence of education will advance through simple, routine empirical research. The best of this work will be competently conceived and competently executed – but not brilliant. While there will be room for relevant and powerful theory – as Suppes' own work amply demonstrates – most theoretical work in education will, I predict, be tangential to the advance of knowledge.

The World Bank

Notes

*The views and opinions expressed herein are those of the author and do not necessarily reflect those of the World Bank Group.

[1] It was precisely because his practical work in education constitutes so substantial a proportion of Suppes' career that the editor of this volume wished to include a chapter dealing with education. However, these matters do deviate from the thrust of the volume, and, for that reason, the editor requested that this chapter be brief.

[2] It is the use of schools for mass education that Suppes refers to as 'recent'; philosophers will of course be familiar with the medieval schools of Paris, which are also of interest to economists because of their use of competitive market (nowadays 'voucher') financing mechanisms.

[3] Experiences outside the United States, though generally less costly, paralleled the U.S. experience.

[4] The Finance and Productivity Group of the U.S. National Institute of Education, under the direction of Arthur S. Melmed, has funded a longitudinal experiment to provide definitive information on the long-term effectiveness of CCC's Drill-and-Practice curriculum for compensatory education.

[5] Only recently has systematic empirical evidence become available to document the widely held impressionistic view that educational quality is poor in low-income countries. In a review of the findings of the 19-country 'International Evaluation of Educational Achievement', Inkeles (1977, p. 157) concluded: "What was distinctive about the less developed countries was the extremely poor showing they made on the tests, at all ages and largely without regard to the subject tested or the mode of testing."

[6] It is with some reluctance that I eschew discussion of mathematical learning theory, for my own first protracted contact with Suppes was a collaboration on a lengthy and rather technical paper in this area (Jamison, Lhamon, and Suppes, 1970). This joint work was the most stimulating activity of my student years.

[7] Suppes' list of honors for work in education is long. Perhaps the most significant is his Presidency of the U.S. National Academy of Education; he has just completed a four-year term as the Academy's third President.

References

Atkinson, R. C.: 1972, 'Ingredients for a Theory of Instruction', *American Psychologist* **27**, 921–931.

Barnes, O. D., and Schreiber, D. B.: 1972, *Computer-assisted Instruction: A Selected Bibliography*, Association for Educational Communications and Technology, Washington, D.C.

Batchelder, W. H., and Wexler, K.: 1979, 'Suppes's Work in the Foundations of Psychology', *this volume*.

Bruner, J.: 1966, *Toward a Theory of Instruction*, The Harvard University Press, Cambridge, Massachusetts.

Crothers, E., & Suppes, P.: 1967, *Experiments in Second-language Learning*, Academic Press, New York.

Flecther, J. D., and Beard, M. H.: 1973, *Computer-assisted Instruction in Language Arts for Hearing-impaired Students*, (Tech. Rep. 215), Institute for Mathematical Studies in the Social Sciences, Stanford University, Stanford, Calif.

Fletcher, J. D., & Suppes, P.: 1972, 'Computer-assisted Instruction in Reading: Grades 4–6', *Educational Technology* **12**, 45–49.

Fletcher, J. D., and Suppes, P.: 1976, 'The Stanford Project on Computer-assisted Instruction for Hearing-impaired Students', *Journal of Computer-based Instruction* **3**, 1–12.

Goldberg, A., and Suppes, P.: 1976, 'Computer-assisted Instruction in Elementary Logic at the University Level', *Educational Studies In Mathematics* **6**, 447–474.

Grayson, L. P.: 1971, 'The U.S. Office of Education and Computer Activities: A Summary of Support', *Educational Technology*, 51–54.

Hawley, N., & Suppes, P.: 1960, *Geometry for Primary Grades; Book 1*, Holden-Day, San Francisco, (Spanish translation: 1964, *Geometria para los Grados Primarios; Libra 1*, Editorial Depatamento de Instruccion Publica, San Juan, Puerto Rico.) (French translation: 1965, *Geometrie pour Classes Elementaires, Livre 1*, Gontran Trottier, Montreal, Canada.)

Hawley, N., & Suppes, P.: 1960, *Geometry for Primary Grades; Book 2*, Holden-Day, San Francisco. (Spanish translation: *Geometria para los Grados Primarios; Libra 2*, Editorial Depatamento de Instruccion Publica, San Juan, Puerto Rico).

Inkeles, A.: 1977, 'The International Evaluation of Educational Achievement: A Review', *Proceedings of the National Academy of Education* **4**, 139–200.

Jamison, D., Fletcher, R. D., Suppes, P., and Atkinson, R. C.: 1976, 'The Cost and Peformance of Computer-assisted Instruction for Education of Disadvantaged Students', in J. Froomkin, D. Jamison, and R. Radner (Eds.), *Education as an Industry*, National Bureau of Economic Research and Ballinger Publishing Co., Cambridge, Mass., pp. 201–240.

Jamison, D., Lhamon, D., & Suppes, P.: 1970, 'Learning and the Structure of Information', in J. Hintikka & P. Suppes (Eds.), *Information and Inference*, D. Reidel Publishing Company, Dordrecht, Holland, pp. 197–259.

Loftus, E. F., & Suppes, P.: 1972, 'Structural Variables that Determine Problem-solving Difficulty In Computer-assisted Instruction', *Journal of Educational Psychology* **63**, 531–542.

Searle, B., Friend, J., and Suppes, P.: 1976, *The Radio Mathematics Project: Nicaragua, 1974–1975*, Institute for Mathematical Studies in the Social Sciences, Stanford University, Stanford, Calif.

Searle, B., Lorton, P. Jr., & Suppes, P.: 1974, 'Structural Variables Affecting CAI Performance on Arithmetic Word Problems of Disadvantaged and Deaf Students', *Educational Studies in Mathematics* **5**, 371–384.

Searle, B., Matthews, P., Suppes, P., and Friend, J.: 1978, *Formal Evaluation of the Radio Mathematics Instructional Program: Nicaragua – Grade 1, 1976*, in Cook, T., and associates (Eds.), *Evaluation Studies Review Annual*, Vol. 3, Sage Publications, Beverly Hills, pp. 651–672.

Searle, B., Suppes, P., and Friend, J.: 1977, 'The Nicaraguan Radio Mathematics Project', in Spain, P., Jamison, D., and McAnany, E. (Eds.), *Radio for Education and Development: Case Studies*, Vol. 1, Staff Working Paper 266, The World Bank, Washington, D.C., pp. 2–32.

Suppes, P.: 1957, *Introduction to Logic*, Van Nostrand, New York. Translated into Spanish by G. A. Carrasco.: 1966, *Introduccion a la Logica Simbolica*, Compania Editorial Continential, Mexico.

Suppes, P.: 1964, 'Problems of Optimization in Learning a List of Simple Items', in M. W. Shelly, II, & G. L. Bryan (Eds.), *Human Judgements and Optimality*, John Wiley & Sons, New York, pp. 116–126.

Suppes, P.: 1966, 'The Uses of Computers in Education', *Scientific American*, **215**, 206–220.

Suppes, P.: 1966, 1969, *Sets and Numbers*, (Books 3–6) Random House, New York, revised editions.

Suppes, P.: 1968, 'Can There Be a Normative Philosophy of Education?', in G. L. Newsome, Jr. (Ed.), *Philosophy of Education 1968*, Studies in Philosophy and Education, Southern Illinois University, Edwardsville, Ill., pp. 1–12.

Suppes, P.: 1968, *Sets and Numbers*, (Books K–2), Random House, New York, revised editions.

Suppes, P.: 1971, 'Technology in Education', in S. M. Brownell (Ed.), *Issues in Urban Education*, Yale University Press, New Haven, Conn., pp. 119–146.

Suppes, P.: 1972a, 'Computer-assisted Instruction at Stanford', in *Man and Computer*, (Proceedings of international conference, Bordeaux, 1970), Karger, Basel, pp. 298–330.

Suppes, P.: 1972b, *Axiomatic Set Theory*, Dover Publications, New York. Original edition translated into Spanish by H. A. Castillo: 1968, *Teoria Axiomatica de Conjuntos*, Editorial Norma, Cali, Colombia.

Suppes, P.: 1973, 'Facts and Fantasies of Education', *Phi Delta Kappa Monograph*.

Suppes, P.: 1974, 'The Place of Theory in Educational Research', *Educational researcher* **3**(6), 3–10.

Suppes, P.: 1975a, 'The School of the Future: Technological Possibilities', in L. Rubin (Ed.), *The Future of Education: Perspectives on Tomorrow's Schooling*, Allyn & Becon, Boston, pp. 145–157.

Suppes, P.: 1975b, 'Impact of Computers on Curriculum in the Schools and Universities', in O. Lecarme & R. Lewis (Eds.), *Computers in Education, IFIP* (Part 1), North-Holland, Amsterdam, pp. 173–179.

Suppes, P., Fletcher, J. D., & Zanotti, M.: 1975, 'Performance Models of American Indian Students on Computer-assisted Instruction in Elementary Mathematics', *Instructional Science* **4**, pp. 303–313.

Suppes, P., Fletcher, J. D., & Zanotti, M.: 1976, 'Models of Individual Trajectories in Computer-assisted Instruction for Deaf Students', *Journal of Educational Psychology* **68**, 117–127.

Suppes, P., Fletcher, J. D., Zanotti, M., Lorton, P. V., & Searle, B. W.: 1973, *Evaluation of Computer-assisted Instruction in Elementary Mathematics for Hearing-impaired Students*, (Tech. Rep. 200), Institute for Mathematical Studies in the Social Sciences, Stanford University, Stanford, Calif.

Suppes., P., Jerman, M., & Brian, D.: 1968, *Computer-assisted Instruction: Stanford's 1965–66 Arithmetic Program*, Academic Press, New York.

Suppes, P., Macken, E., and Zanotti, M.: in press, 'The Role of Global Psychological Models in Instructional Technology', in R. Glaser (Ed.), *Advances in Instructional Psychology*, Lawrence Erlbaum Associates, Hillsdale, N. J.

Suppes, P., & Morningstar, M.: 1969, 'Computer-assisted Instruction', *Science,* **166**, pp. 343–350.

Suppes, P., & Morningstar, M.: 1972, *Computer-assisted Instruction at Stanford, 1966–68: Data, Models, and Evaluation of the Arithmetic Programs*, Academic Press, New York.

Suppes, P., Smith, R., and Beard, M.: 1977, 'University-level Computer-assisted Instruction at Stanford: 1975', *Instructional Science* **6**, 151–185.

PATRICK SUPPES

REPLIES

As should be evident, there is much that I agree with in the comments and criticisms of my work included in this volume. In this sense, it is perhaps incorrect to entitle my own further remarks as *replies*. What I have tried to do in several cases is to amplify my own views even where there is no real disagreement between the comments made and my own philosophical position. On the other hand, I do not want to overemphasize a tone of sweetness and light. I enjoy a good argument too much not to take this occasion to state points of disagreement.

To Moulines and Sneed

Semantics of Physical Theories

Moulines and Sneed's discussion of the semantics of physical theories raises problems for my own way of looking at these matters that I have not adequately dealt with. I have not used the term *semantics* in the discussion of the relation between physical theories and fundamental measurement but I am not unhappy to adopt their use for present purposes.

I certainly agree with Moulines and Sneed that it is not appropriate to look for fundamental measurement of all physical quantities. In *Foundations of Measurement* (1971a, pp. 539–544) we give a table of more than five pages, listing the dimensions and units of standard physical quantities. The list ranges from electrical charge through tensile strength, flux linkage to capacitance, and I do not think for a moment that a fundamental theory of measurement of this enormously long list would be appropriate.

Bogdan, R.J. (Ed.) 'Patrick Suppes' 207–232.
Copyright © 1979 by D. Reidel Publishing Company, Dordrecht, Holland.

Many of the physical quantities would certainly be treated in terms of derived measurement, and I also agree that many others are to be regarded as theoretical physical quantities not subject to direct measurement. The question of interest, it seems to me, is their query as to whether my sort of program can "be carried through for the remaining nontheoretical concepts."

In my younger and more formalistic days, I probably advocated a kind of minor Carnapian *Aufbau* in which we would proceed first with fundamental measurement, then move to definition of appropriate derived quantities and on to theoretical formulations in one massive structure. I now have a more open and schematic view of how even the most advanced parts of physics are done. I do not think it is important to construct in complete detail all of the steps required or to have as an explicit program such reconstruction. What seems important is to identify the key issues and to focus on their analysis. A good example would be to provide a thorough analysis of fundamental measurement for key concepts like mass and length. We should be able to give some account of these matters that corresponds rather closely to what is done at certain beginning stages in actual laboratory work, but I am less convinced than I used to be that it is fruitful to include all the details that would take us from elementary procedures of measurement to actual laboratory procedures in contemporary work. The unbelievably complex experimental lore that accumulates in any advanced branch of science does not lend itself to a totally explicit analysis. I suppose I believe that in some sense such an analysis can be given, but I am now skeptical of its fruitfulness as a central endeavor for the philosophy of science.

There are a great variety of subsidiary questions that can be asked and that tell us a lot about the 'semantics' of physical theories. For example, what kind of statistical methods are used in the analysis of data and how are these statistical methods related to testing theories? It does not take much delving into *Physical Review* to find that a vast assortment of statistical methods is used, some naive and some not so naive, and it seems to me of some interest to investigate this kind of synoptic question. Again, it is of interest to determine in different parts of science to what extent formal methods of experimental design are used and where they are, according to the best current lore, not considered necessary.

Perhaps what is most important to emphasize is the very large gap between the theoretical literature in any developed branch of science and the untraversable thicket of technical language used in the corresponding experimental work. I have recently tried reading some of the experimental work in quantum mechanics and I find a complete difference in the character of the vocabulary, the use of language, and especially in the difficulty of tracing the variety of technical assumptions about the performance of experimental apparatus. It would be useful philosophical work for some of the key experiments to be related in a closer and better way to important physical theories like quantum mechanics, but I am skeptical of anyone's providing a semantics in the sense discussed by Moulines and Sneed for any theories that are not dead and buried, or not of such an artificial character that they were never born.

Classical Particle Mechanics

Moulines and Sneed focus much of their detailed discussion on the axiomatization of classical particle mechanics, and so I turn to some specific comments on these matters. They list three difficulties in successfully exhibiting the internal structure of classical particle mechanics. One is claimed to be in not separating sharply enough the role of the kinematical and dynamical primitive concepts. To some extent I think this claim is correct in the original work. In later versions kinematical and dynamical concepts have been separated, but there is an additional invariance theorem that has not been brought to the surface explicitly and that helps clarify more sharply the difference between kinematical and dynamical notions. This is to prove that the clearly kinematical concepts and axioms characterize the invariance of models in a much looser way. Essentially any continuous one-one transformation will preserve the kinematical concepts, whereas the dynamical concepts and axioms are only invariant under the much more restricted Galilean group of transformations.

The second criticism concerns the fact that the axioms only characterize the structure of single models and not the relation between models. Consequently the historically important relations between different special laws of force, for example, have no natural place. It seems to me that the proper response is that much of the detail that one would like to have included has not been worked out. But this is not a criticism of the basic axiomatization. For this purpose I would like to draw an analogy to group theory. There is quite wide agreement on the appropriate axioms for groups in the ordinary mathematical sense, but it is not a responsibility of these axioms to characterize the great variety of special groups that are of interest and that have been studied so intensively by mathematicians

PATRICK SUPPES

over the past hundred years. Secondly, an enormous mathematical effort has been put into studying the relations between different groups, that is, between different models of the same general theory, but again the statement of this relation is not a matter for the fundamental axiomatization of groups but a matter for additional and further mathematical study. This seems to me to be the situation in the case of mechanics. By adding further axioms or hypotheses we can narrow the class of models and focus on particular force laws. We can also study the relation between various models satisfying various laws by standard mathematical methods but such studies do not change the basic framework of the original axiomatization – they just constitute elaborate and, in many cases, much more ingenious extensions of the original work. There is a variety of such questions that can be asked about mechanics and there is a certain body of work that has been done over a long period of time. It is not clear, however, how much the details of this work are of general philosophical interest.

As a third criticism, Moulines and Sneed emphasize the complex way in which the meaning of mechanical concepts is built up by additional applications of the theory and by the development of related theories. I do not really disagree with what they say but I think it is appropriate to separate a general concept of meaning of physical concepts from the more restricted concept relevant to a particular theoretical formulation. Thus, it seems appropriate to talk about the theoretical meaning of mass as the concept is characterized in the axioms of particle mechanics and to distinguish this restricted theoretical meaning from the bewildering variety of ways in which masses are measured and dealt with in empirical applications. If we want to enhance the meaning every time a new application is developed, then it is appropriate that we think of this wider sense of mass as open and continually changing. I see no harm in this, but I also see a virtue in continuing to insist on a narrower, more fixed meaning that does not change with changing applications.

Quantum Mechanics

In several different ways, Moulines and Sneed point out how I have shifted from a concentration on the nonstandard probability theory characteristic of orthodox quantum mechanics to a focus on the possibility of analyzing quantum mechanical phenomena from the viewpoint of standard stochastic processes. Relative to the history of quantum mechanics over the past fifty years, it is a radical thesis to maintain that orthodox probability theory will win out over orthodox quantum mechanics in providing a satisfactory theoretical framework. To a large extent, a philosophical viewpoint that derives from classical realism motivates my own increasing acceptance of the orthodox probabilistic viewpoint. I find it very much easier to think about particles as having continuous trajectories. The Copenhagen interpretation is lacking intuitive persuasiveness and is too closely allied to narrow positivistic views that no longer seem plausible.

If what I am saying is at all correct, then the current interest among philosophers in quantum logic will wane and will not have the fundamental importance that has been attached to it in many discussions. I realize that a great many philosophers will disagree with this view, and it is this very fact of controversy on almost all major questions that makes the foundations of quantum mechanics currently one of the most active areas in the philosophy of science.

I agree with the final remarks of Moulines and Sneed that whether the stochastic viewpoint I have been urging will turn out to be adequate for the foundations of quantum mechanics must certainly be treated as an open problem. My intuitions on the matter are increasingly strong, but I am trying hard to resist adopting a dogmatic position.

I shall finish by making two observations about wave functions that illustrate what I consider to be the enlightening results of adopting a throughly probabilistic viewpoint toward quantum mechanics. It is a standard remark that the interpretation of wave functions as waves does not make any sense at all once we talk about several particles and the dimension of the space is at least six for the spatial coordinates. The vivid original picture of waves disappears entirely as the dimension of the space increases, but if we think about the wave function as being a simple and convenient way to express the joint distribution of random variables, which are in general dependent, then we have a natural and familiar conceptual framework for development.

The second and more interesting point concerns the interpretation of the meaning of the linear law of superposition for wave functions. How are we to interpret the deeper meaning of this linear superposition? Again, a probabilistic viewpoint provides a useful conceptual answer. The linear superposition of wave functions is an elegant way of determining a new probability distribution of a random variable from two other random variables in such a way that the arduous task of finding the joint distribution of the two initial random variables is bypassed. The superposition of wave functions permits a relatively easy and direct computation of the new distribution. What these last remarks suggest is a thorough probabilistic analysis of the essential quantum mechanical phenomenon of inter-ference. In many ways a proper theory of the classical two-slit experiment and the interference patterns that result is one of the best testing grounds for the viability of the stochastic approach to quantum mechanics. In the past two years I have done a lot of work on this problem and I am opti-mistic about the solution, but I am not ready to offer an analysis satis-factory in all details.

To Luce

My basic agreement with Luce's view of what is important in theories of measurement and what the central problems are is so nearly complete that it is hard to find issues to comment upon that divide us. This degree of accord is not surprising in view of the extensive character of our collaboration over a period of almost two decades. There are some things I would like to say, however, about the major topics he mentions.

Invariance and Meaningfulness

As Luce mentions, we have not yet been able to agree about how concepts of invariance are to be brought into the interpretation of proper uses of statistics. The controversy is not only between us but has involved almost everybody who works in the theory of measurement, and no definitive resolution seems in sight. Let me illustrate some of the difficulties. On the one hand, nobody would argue for an absolute center of the universe and thus a natural origin for spatial measurements. A spatial probability dis-tribution, for example, that depended in an essential way on such a natural zero would scarcely be taken seriously. On the other hand, it is common practice to apply a wide variety of quantitative statistical analyses to data that are ordinal in character, for example, rank orderings of objects or phenomena according to some particular property – qualification as a candidate for election, rank-order judgments of configurations as in dog shows, or any other of a great number of rank-order judgments of merit or relative conformity to a standard.

One of the cases of considerable philosophical interest is: What are the restrictions in the analytical theory and analysis of ordinal data on pref-erences among different individuals? In the past I have pretty much adopted a hard line: If the underlying measurements are invariant only up to a certain group of transformations, then only those statistics that have the same invariance properties make sense. Thus, for example, talking about the mean of a sample of data that are measured only on an ordinal scale is, on this criterion, a meaningless statement. From the standpoint of the axiomatic theory of measurement, I still see good grounds for holding to this position, but in the actual practice of measurement there are many situations in which procedures are engaged in that do not have a good axiomatic foundation.

There are background intuitive reasons for thinking that the measurement is a tighter one from the standpoint of its uniqueness of numerical representation than a strict analysis might suggest. Suppose, for example, that we ask two expert judges of apples to place each of 400 apples in one of four graded categories. The first judge ends up with 100 apples in each category; the second judge puts 150 in the lowest category, 50 in the second, 50 in the third, and 150 in the highest category. If we express the distribution of classification first by the mean, then the two judges have the same mean, but if we apply an arbitrary transformation to make the fourth category be assigned not the number four for the highest category but some arbitrarily large number, then we can make the mean of the second judge be significantly higher than the mean of the classifications of the first judge. But surely there is something quite unnatural about this transformation. It does not make intuitive sense to assign the numbers 1 to the first category, 2 to the second, 3 to the third, and then 517 to the fourth category, even though such a transformation is permitted in the general theory of ordinal scales.

Back of the judgment procedure and back of our intuitive evaluation of it there is a strong natural tendency to treat the ordered categories as being equally spaced, even though an explicit theory of this equal spacing is not part of the account ordinarily given of the ordering of the categories. This kind of example seems to me not to invalidate the axiomatic viewpoint toward meaningfulness but rather to bring out the fact that it is often the case in measurement that we do not have an explicit axiomatic theory and yet we proceed on the assumption that the measurements we are making are richer than the surface analysis would suggest. I am not at all certain how Luce feels about this example. I know it does not catch all of the aspects of the argument that concern me, but it perhaps will illustrate some of the muddle we find ourselves in about the question of meaningful statistics.

Finiteness

Luce properly emphasizes the concern that I have had with finite measurement structures and, as he also states, he has himself been more concerned with characterizing axiomatically a variety of infinite structures. There is a subtle point about my recent work on approximating finite structures that I want to bring out to show how the issue of which view is more restricted is not a simple matter. The kind of axiomatizations that Luce has been concerned with require that the structures have an Archimedean property and that a representation preserving the operations and relations be homomorphically mapped into an appropriate numerical structure. In the kind of approximate finite structures I have been concerned with, such a homomorphic mapping into the reals is not required for the objects that are being measured but only for the basic scales or standard sequence, as it is sometimes called, that is finite. Thus, for example, in the simple case of the equal-arm balance, the basic scale is a finite set of standard weights, but the axioms are set up for structures that can be either finite or infinite. Any new object is measured in accordance with how it compares to the standard weights. The full structure with a potential infinity of new objects does not have an Archimedean property and, in fact, can violate infinite cardinality restrictions required for isomorphic representation into the real numbers. A philosophically interesting fact about this setup is that it is highly constructive in spirit and yet leaves room for a potential infinity of objects to be measured with quite simple restrictions on their relations to each other. In ordinary measurement procedures, approximations are the order of the day. In the context of theories, we represent measurements as being exact, but this is only for purposes of theoretical and especially computational convenience.

On the other hand, I do not want to give the view that I think all of the arguments are in favor of this new use of finiteness by means of approximating structures. When we go to more complex structures, as for example those of Euclidean geometry, the approximating finite structures are much harder to characterize and it is not clear that the viewpoint I have advocated for measurement structures extends in a natural way to the foundations of geometry. This difficulty of extension suggests that I may be oversold on the simplicity of the finite approximating structures and that the viewpoint will not be so successful as more complicated cases are studied.

Testing Decision Theories

Luce remarks on the approach I and my collaborators have used in the past toward testing decision theories. There is a point about this kind of test that I want to remark on. It is not a point that is especially favorable but is, I think, of some conceptual interest. In many cases, what has been done is to find a convex polyhedron of solutions that fit a finite set of data, or in more refractory cases to minimize a threshold parameter and then to find a convex polyhedron of solutions, each of which satisfies the minimum threshold value of the parameter. Such solutions arise naturally when a set of inequalities is solved. In many tests of decision theories the experimental data are naturally cast in the form of a set of inequalities. For example, judgments of preference and preference differences give rise in a very natural way to such sets of inequalities. One of the interesting and unsatisfactory features about such sets of solutions is their contextual character. The classical theory of measurement has insisted upon conceiving of the measurement of a given property of an object or of a relation between objects, etc., to be a number that is independent of the numbers assigned to other objects once the appropriate standards are fixed. Thus, for example, once the standard of mass is fixed, the weight of the desk in my study is not affected by consideration of the weights of desks in other people's studies. On the other hand, when we obtain data on preferences from individuals that consist of ordering of possible outcomes and ordering of differences of preferences among pairs of outcomes, the numerical solutions we obtain are affected by introducing a new outcome and asking for its ordering and difference orderings. In other words, the numbers we obtain are not independent of the numbers assigned to other objects; a direct contextual effect is immediately noticed. In the particular case mentioned it is evident at once because the convex polyhedron of solutions will, in general, always become a smaller set of solutions, once an additional outcome is included.

All of this is straightforward and not surprising to anyone familiar with these matters. My point is that the axiomatic analysis of such contextual effects has scarcely developed at all. The presence of such effects is striking, not only in phenomena of reference but also in a variety of psychological phenomena of perception. Judgments of symmetry, judgments of relative length, etc., are affected by the introduction of new perceptual objects into a given scene, but the theory of such contextual effects has, from an axiomatic or a geometrical standpoint, scarcely been touched.

There is a great deal of informal evidence that a person's beliefs are often subject to such contextual effects. Ask a question and the answer may depend not so much on the person's beliefs as on the way the question was asked. From this standpoint, subjective probabilities as the expression of partial beliefs must be looked upon as highly contextual in character. Recent systematic research of Amos Tversky and Daniel Kahneman (1971, 1973, 1974) shows that this is very much the case. Their work strongly suggests that a deep rethinking of psychological theories of measurement to include contextual effects could have interesting theoretical consequences.

To Rosenkrantz

Measurement of Subjective Probability and Utility

Rosenkrantz gives a rather detailed presentation of the methods for measuring subjective probability and utility developed many years ago by Davidson and me, and he also suggests some improvements in the methods that would be practical to adopt in future experiments of the same sort. His detailed analysis stimulated me to think again, after more than twenty years, about the conceptual framework of the methods Davidson and I used. Because of some of my current interests I especially thought about the not necessarily additive probability measure that is implied by the axioms. What is interesting is that this unique measure is not in general either an upper or lower measure. That it is neither an upper nor a lower measure can be seen from the following considerations. It is an accepted property for upper and lower probability measures that for every event E

$$(1) \qquad P_*(E) + P^*(\neg E) = 1.$$

But then if the measure that follows from the axioms were a lower measure we would have

$$(2) \qquad P_*(E) + P_*(\neg E) = 1,$$

because (2) follows from our axioms. Thus the upper measure and the lower measure would be identical, whence we would have a genuine probability measure. A similar argument applies if the measure is an upper measure.

It is evident in the work that Rosenkrantz describes that we did not do nearly as much with subjective probability as with utility. I regret not seeing the opportunity in the foreseeable future to return to these matters and investigate more extensively the measurement of subjective probability.

Comparative Probability and Expectation

Rosenkrantz comments on the recent work by Mario Zanotti and me (1976n) on necessary and sufficient conditions for the existence of a measure strictly agreeing with a qualitative comparative probability ordering of events. As he notes, and as I discussed earlier in my own reflections on the foundations of probability, we found a simple solution by considering extended indicator functions.

There are two remarks of Rosenkrantz about these matters that I want to follow up on. He mentions the well-known historical precedent in the early work of Huyghens. It is also to be found in the later but still quite early work of Bayes, who defines probability in terms of expectation. Rosenkrantz also comments on the naturalness of expectations when dealing with certain problems and I want to expand upon that point.

In many ordinary situations it is natural to talk about expectations rather than probabilities. I think I understand the reason for this usage. Let us first consider some examples. It is natural for someone to say, "I expect to lose about five pounds in the next two weeks," or "I expect to get about eighteen miles per gallon in my new car," or again "I expect to spend more than I can really afford on the house that I am buying." The reason that expectation rather than probability is the right concept is that these kinds of examples are naturally quantitative in character.

The logic of events works quite satisfactorily for cases that are purely yes-no decisions. For example, there is no difference between saying "I expect to go to France next year" and saying "I shall probably go to France next year," because the expectation of the indicator function and the probability of the event are identical. This is not at all the case for quantitative variables. In the case of weight, for example, the full probability statement about what is going to happen would be made, if at all, only by a medical specialist, that is, by attempting to give the full probability distribution of the random variable representing the number of pounds that will be lost in the period indicated. This is a continuous random variable in theory, and even in practice it has a large number of discrete values. The most that we ordinarily think about is in terms of expectations of such random variables. Only the statistically sophisticated would even ask for the variance. The full distribution is out of the question.

In the recent flurry of interest in probability matters in philosophy this importance of expectations as opposed to probabilities or, put another way, this importance of random variables as opposed to events has not been sufficiently noticed. To emphasize the point I am making, let me underscore the fact that it is not the move from events to random variables that is at issue. The issue is giving only the expectations of the random variables and not their full distributions. If the full distribution of the random variables is given, then of course we can move back to formulating everything in terms of the probability of events, although this is not even then the most natural way to think about such matters. The significant thing is that we never do think about the full distribution in these quantitative cases. We are usually only interested in the expectations, and ordinary talk reflects this matter extremely well.

Learning and Conceptual Change

What Rosenkrantz has to say under this heading is of considerable interest, not least because he has himself contributed considerably to the analysis of this fundamental problem (I refer to his recent book).

Rather than attempt to defend the viewpoint of stimulus sampling theory and to criticize his own proposals, I would like to concentrate on the broad features that I think have not yet received sufficient attention in a detailed and technical way by any of us concerned with learning and conceptual change.

The essential idea of what I want to say is to be found in work on memory that goes back all the way to Bartlett. It is a mistake to think of memory in analogy with a passive data bank waiting for computer-like retrieval. The evidence from many investigations is strongly in support of the idea that memories of past events are constructed in complicated ways by operations that we yet understand very poorly. What is stored in memory is something much more abstract and remote from the concrete experience than the memory we bring into consciousness after some considerable effort at reconstruction. The same aspect of construction applies when we look forward to the finding of new concepts. Bayesian analysis, or any generalization formulated by Rosenkrantz or me in different directions, would give a very poor account of the most elementary learning of geometry by students just being introduced to the subject. What students need to learn is how to actively make constructions – the process of using concepts they have to construct new concepts, a sequence that in rational development is well exemplified in Book I of Euclid's *Elements*. It is this sort of thing we have not yet been successful in capturing. If we want to put it in different terms to follow out the computer analogies popular in current cognitive psychology, the problem is not to look for a set of natural kinds but to construct a program appropriately using subroutines that are already familiar.

I took some first steps in this direction with my 1969 article on stimulus-responce theory of finite automata and in a number of recent publications have tried to go further, but I am under no illusion that I have yet presented anything like a satisfactory theory. I do think that the more constructive approach implicit in the procedural or programming way of looking at matters will prove fruitful. On the other hand, I want to emphasize that it seems to me we are still lacking some major concepts that are needed for a really successful theory in this area. I am not hopeful that either an extension of Bayesian ideas or any simple extension of the stimulus-response theory of learning will be adequate. The failure of current theory is well marked by our almost total inability to construct computer programs that themselves have the capacity to learn. Once we understand the theory in some deeper way we should be able to write very much more powerful programs than we now can.

Causality

Rosenkrantz queries at the end of his article how I would handle the case of two theories, one of which fits more possibilities than the other. His query, with particular reference to Copernicus and Ptolemy, brings out a general lacuna in my monograph on causality. I really do not discuss adequately the causal comparison of theories as such. The systematic developments I give are much more related to the study of causal questions within a theory or in straight empirical applications, as, for example, the statistical study of whether smoking is a cause of lung cancer. I think there are ways of bringing in the kinds of examples Rosenkrantz mentions, but it is also a fair criticism that I have not dealt with such matters in any explicit detail.

Concluding Remarks

I have not commented on many issues raised by Rosenkrantz. For example, I have not responded to his remarks about justice because I said about all I have to say at the moment in my own earlier statement in this volume. It should be clear that Rosenkrantz's many comments and analyses of my work touch issues that are central to my interests and that I hope to continue to contribute to in the future.

To Grandy

Logic of Measurement

Grandy's proposed Boolean-valued semantics to replace the three-valued logic I proposed in (1965d) has the merit, as he points out, of giving a standard truth-functional semantics for conjunction, disjunction and negation. The point at issue that he discusses is my assignment of the truth value of *meaningless* to instances of the law of excluded middle.

I suppose I am unreconstructed on this point but I continue to see virtue in assigning to classical instances of the law of excluded middle some value other than true when the two components are themselves meaningless. He gives examples taken from my discussion of theories of measurement, but the same remarks apply in a general way to such examples as *This mountain is in love* or *this mountain is not in love*. My objective was to thoroughly fence off all meaningless expressions, and not to let a complex sentence have the value of true when it is built up from meaningless sentential components.

The issue between us is not a formal one but a philosophical one about intuitions concerning meaningfulness. In my view, ordinary usage and scientific practice are on my side in this particular debate, but I will not try to push the argument further in the present context.

Syntax

I have no quarrel with Grandy's basic description of my use of probabilistic grammars. There are one or two points I want to comment on. The first concerns the comparison of two different grammars, neither of which fits the data exactly. Grandy seems to think that in such a situation a conclusion about the relative merits of the two grammars is not really possible, but this is in fact a very common situation in applied statistics. It is not at all uncommon to have no model that fits the data very well but to be able to discriminate in a very strong sense between two proposed models. From the standpoint of classical statistics, for example, if each model's fit can be expressed by a chi-square and we can use independent samples of data, then the ratio of the two chi-squares is distributed as an F-statistic and we can draw standard conclusions about the level of significance at which we can reject the null hypothesis that the two models fit equally well.

A quite detailed comparison of the probabilistic fit of two different grammars for the same corpus, in this case for the French syntax of a child's noun phrases, is to be found in my article with Smith and Léveillé (1973g). In comparison with the detailed work referred to in this article, it seems to me that Grandy's remarks are on too general a level when he says, "The second possibility is simply that the grammar is not an adequate one for the language." It may well be that the completely detailed account of a young child's (or an adult's) language will not be provided by any grammar, but this does not mean that we cannot get better and better approximations to the actual language spoken.

In the present instance we are fishing in deep waters and we do not really have a very clear idea of what kinds of theories to expect. It may be that our initial idealized ambitions will not be realized but at the same time very considerable progress in a variety of directions can be made. There are many other areas of science that have this character. A classical one of great importance is aerodynamics. The models are in general rather poor approximations to the detailed phenomena but much that is useful can be gained from study and further development of them. I feel the same way about grammars of children's language.

Semantics

Grandy's focus on my development of a theory of congruence of meaning to replace a single notion of synonymity represents an emphasis that I agree with, and his summary of my ideas is sufficiently accurate and detailed that I can make my own remarks supplementary in character.

There are three main points in his analysis that I want to take up. First, Grandy emphasizes the desirability of finding a basic set of congruence relations "such that all others of interest can be generated by various operations on the basic set." Within the framework of permutations, for example, this seems natural and fairly easily achievable. It does not seem out of reach to obtain results corresponding to classical results in the theory of permutation groups. For example, in the theory of such groups it can be shown that every permutation can be written as a product of cycles of length two, that is, transpositions of adjacent elements. On the other hand, I am skeptical that any reasonable basic set of congruence relations that deal with matters of this kind can be found to also deal with such a general notion as that of paraphrase. It is rather like looking for operations that are common to both affine and topological spaces in geometry. Within a general concept, as for example that of affine spaces, a basic set of operations can be found, but to expect to find a set that runs across quite different notions of congruence seems unrealistic and unlikely of successful realization.

It is perhaps worth noting that the idea of using a basic set of simple transformations to generate more complex ones is exactly the device used by Warren and me (1975h) in giving a theory for generating and classifying defense mechanisms. The transformations introduced are transformations that apply to the main parts of sentences, for example, subject, verb, and object. An extension of this view to get actor-congruence, action-congruence, etc., seems to have some promise.

Grandy comments next on the desirability of looking at more details of the grammar and introduces his notion of nonterminal phrasal congruence. I am in firm agreement with this concept and in fact introduced a very similar notion in my 1973 lectures on mathematical linguistics at Stanford. In those lectures I moved up from the bottom of the tree rather than worked down from the top of the tree as Grandy suggests, but in whichever direction we go, it seems to me there are difficulties in getting an elegant mathematical theory. For example, unless we restrict Grandy's notion of "portions of phrasal terminal subtrees below the top node," any two paraphrases of each other would be congruent in his nonterminal phrasal sense because we could simply include under "portions" everything below the top node of the tree. In my 1973 lectures I used a counting device and thus talked about, for example, n-strong congruence if we looked for a congruence having moved up everywhere n nodes from the terminal nodes. However, this notion is unsatisfactory because we really do not want to move up the same distance from each terminal node. The same thing applies to Grandy's approach. We do not want to move down from the top node the same distance along each branch, but on the other hand we do not want to introduce some ordered sequence of integers corresponding to the branches read from left to right with the ith integer indicating how far down we go from the top node along the ith branch in asking for identity in order to have nonterminal phrasal congruence. A simple device would be to count the number of nodes, starting from the top node, that are identical when one tree is superimposed on the other. But such a simple counting device seems to do violence to our intuitions about similarity of shape. We want somehow to have the isomorphism about equally distributed from the top and not lie along certain special branches to the exclusion of all others.

This takes me to Grandy's third point that I want to discuss: his query as to whether it is not a mistake to look for sameness of meaning because, in fact, sameness does not seem to be a transitive relation. Again, this is a point I made in my 1973 lectures by introducing the notion of ε-congruence. Such notions of similarity that are not transitive are familiar in psychology, especially in the theory of perception. It does not mean that there is not a reasonable theory of congruence for such matters – it is just that it is a good deal more complicated. It is a mistake to think that because we do not have a transitive relation we cannot have a concept of sameness or similarity of meaning.

This is a subject on which I have written a great deal in the past, not necessarily directed toward sameness of meaning but directed in general toward problems of similarity, because these matters have been extensively treated in the theory of measurement. The modern literature on the subject goes back to Luce (1956) on semiorders, the theory of which was simplified by Scott and me (1958b). A characteristic feature of semiorders is that a strong ordering relation is introduced that carries with it a symmetric similarity relation that is not transitive. I am in complete agreement with Grandy's examples and believe that such a modification of the theory is conceptually natural. It is just that we already know from the corresponding problem in geometry how complicated it is to develop a thoroughly satisfactory approximate theory of congruence. Some of the remarks I made earlier in my reply to Luce about contextual geometries are also applicable here.

Contrary to Grandy's final paragraph, I do not think it is necessary to introduce a metric of meaning differences but rather to use the ideas that have already been extensively developed in the theory of measurement for dealing with approximations. The ideas introduced in my article on the measurement of belief (1974g) provide another way of thinking about such approximations.

Grandy's final remarks suggest specific empirical investigations that would relate intuitive judgments of similarity of meaning to specific transformations. It is my own guess that we could obtain quite reasonable results by such an attack and probably would learn a good deal more than we now know about the way in which such judgments are made.

To Batchelder and Wexler

Batchelder and Wexler touch on many issues dear to my heart. In responding to their many insightful criticisms and evaluations of my work, it would be easy to get carried away and to go deeper into details than is appropriate. Some of the issues they deal with are closely related to my current research interests; I will indicate at appropriate points where I plan a more detailed treatment in the future. My comments follow the main divisions of their article.

Mathematical learning theory

I agree with their assessment that mathematical learning theory is in a relatively dormant stage within psychology and has been so through most of the 1970s. In a recent survey article on contemporary learning theories (1977f), I identified seven different approaches to learning currently receiving attention. Six of the seven can properly be said to have their main centers of activity outside of psychology. These six are: perceptrons and pattern recognition, currently primarily studied by engineers; learnable functions, currently of interest primarily to computer scientists; biologically adaptive systems, currently being studied most intensely by computer scientists; artificial intelligence approaches; language acquisition devices, a subject to which Wexler has contributed extensively (but I think of his work in many ways as being more linguistic than psychological in spirit); and, finally, rational changes of belief, a problem mostly contributed to by statisticians and philosophers. The earlier work on linear learning models, especially, has received widespread application in the literature of engineering mentioned above. This wide range of interest in learning, much of it of a mathematical sort and many parts of it having connection to the earlier work in mathematical learning theory, is evidence that the subject in itself has simply become of interest in other disciplines.

Moreover, some of the recent work in cognitive psychology, especially work centering around Allen Newell's use of production systems, is increasingly concerned with problems of learning. I do not mean to suggest that production systems or the main concepts of all of the various areas mentioned above are in any sense primarily derivative from the earlier work in mathematical learning theory, but I do emphasize the point that mathematically oriented work in learning theory is continuing at a vigorous pace, even if under different intellectual sponsorship.

Automata

Batchelder and Wexler give a detailed presentation of my results on a representation theorem for finite automata in terms of stimulus-response models (1969g). In connection with the representation theorem itself, I want to remark here only that the objections of Kieras and Nelson that they mention will be responded to in more detail in the future. The basis of the more detailed response is that too severe a restriction is placed on the form of the representation, especially by Kieras, who gives the most detailed discussion. As they point out, Kieras defines an S machine as one in which the current response and input determine the next response, but what is mistaken in Kieras's analysis is the assumption that the responses of the S machine are the same as the responses of the S–R model. This is typically never the case in mathematical representation theorems, and once this very strong assumption, which was not part of my original assumptions, is dropped, then it is easy to show that any finite automaton can be represented by a stimulus-response model. It is true that this point was not adequately dealt with in my 1969 paper because the formal models I considered did not have outputs as a formal part of the definition. I shall not go into technical details here but just mention two well-known examples that illustrate my point about representation theorems. When the real numbers are built up from set-theoretical entities defined in terms of the natural numbers, no one-one correspondence is intended between the natural numbers and the real numbers. When the mechanics of rigid bodies is represented by a finite set of particles whose mutual distances are fixed, there is no natural correspondence whatsoever between the number of particles and the number of rigid bodies.

Where I do want to differ with Batchelder and Wexler's own account of these matters is in their claim that it is difficult to think of many interesting abilities in which responses can be interpreted as the internal states. It seems to me that they have not thought very deeply about many aspects of school learning, in which it is a familiar first step to require the students to verbalize the appropriate responses vocally, and only later to let those responses remain silent or internal. Indeed, the widespread contemporary practice of silent reading is a modern habit and not something that was at all widespread even a few hundred years ago. It is worth noting that one of the earliest treatises on memory, that of Simonides from about 400 B.C., exhorted those who wanted an excellent memory to "repeat again what you hear; for by often hearing and saying the same things, what you have learned becomes complete into your memory" (cited in Yates, 1966, p. 29). This emphasis on the oral tradition in learning with its explicit use of oral responses was not confined to Simonides but is powerfully reaffirmed in a variety of ways in many of Plato's writings. The early Greeks were suspicious of written records because of skepticism about their efficacy for conveying the proper tone and feeling. I cite the strongly held views of Plato and others as evidence of the importance of the oral tradition and, therefore, oral responses in ancient literature and philosophy.

On the issue of weak and strong forms of reinforcement, I agree with Batchelder and Wexler that there are certainly weaker forms of reinforcement than nondeterminate yes-no correction schemes. But their dismissal of the kinds of reinforcement that pass between mother and child is far too hasty and general for my taste. I am not prepared to say exactly how reinforcement works in these situations but the kind of symbiotic relationship that is established in most cases – the enormous ability of the child to detect subtle changes in mood, intonation, etc., on the part of the parent – is evidence for me of ability to detect unobvious kinds of reinforcement. Furthermore, the parent's language that is important to the child is directed to the child and not to some general audience. I certainly agree that we have not been successful in characterizing the exact nature of this relationship, but I am unconvinced by their arguments and those of others with a linguistic persuasion that there is no reinforcement that can be identified.

On their following point, that "people's grammars are the same in essential respects," it seems to me that at the level of complete detail this is certainly wrong. To me this is the same as saying that because students will write programs to correctly compute a certain mathematical function, for example, a polynomial in two variables and of the fourth degree, that the programs they write are the same. In fact, the programs will be different and the differences in this case can be easily identified. It would be my own view that the kind of software of subroutines and procedures each of us has for processing language, either as speakers or as listeners, has individual idiosyncratic features. Moreover, these idiosyncratic features, from the production standpoint, are easily detected in terms of differences in pronunciation, stress, prosodic features, stylistic variations, etc. What imposes constraints and forces an appropriate degree of congruence between different people's grammars is the strong desire to communicate. I accept without question also the presence of certain physical structures, for example, the structure of the ear and of the vocal tract, but these common features do not persuade me at all that individuals do not have grammars that have essential differences as well as essential common features.

In this connection, Batchelder and Wexler cite the long article of Wexler,

Culicover, and Hamburger (1975), which starts by assuming that something like a context-free grammar is known as a linguistic universal, and proceeds to a theory of language learning. What is remarkable, however, about this work, in spite of its formal interest, is its sketchy character from any serious empirical standpoint. I like the work and think it represents progress, but I find it far too removed from any empirical details of a systematic nature to yet be taken seriously as a substantive theory of learning.

Probabilistic grammars

What Batchelder and Wexler have to say about probabilistic grammars is in rather definite disagreement with my own views on several counts. Their objective description of such grammars, however, is accurate and requires no supplementary comments from me. What is apparent about Batchelder and Wexler's discussion of these matters is their strong adherence to what I would call an orthodox linguistic viewpoint. This is noticeable first in their discussion of whether relative frequencies are relevant to grammars, and more particularly their concession that perhaps after all they are relevant to performance if not to competence. I want to mention here that I do not consider the notion of competence well defined and consequently do not use the distinction in any systematic way myself.

When Batchelder and Wexler discuss the problem of statistical fit of probabilistic grammars to a child's corpus, for example, they admit that the problem of deciding how many parameters to introduce or, in the terms they use, how many context-sensitive probabilities to permit, is the standard one in fitting statistical theories. They seem to want to draw a contrast to what would ideally be an open-and-shut case when they say "in cases where the data or theory is available, the linguistic evidence will determine what the category is, B or B'," but this seems to me a wholly unrealistic view of linguistic evidence. I am fairly familiar with linguists' discussion of child or adult language. It does not appear that we yet have the kind of methodology that makes these matters at all certain or definite, and I am not impressed by their claims here or elsewhere about the strength of "powerful linguistic methods." I am also unimpressed with linguists' use of introspection among adults to make judgments of grammaticality. The methodology here is undeveloped and certainly scarcely agreed upon. There is not at all the kind of close agreement to psychophysics that they mention but rather, as they also indicate, agreement with the broader field of perception. I could cite a large number of papers in perception that have a precision of methodology in their analysis of data quite unmatched by anything within the linguistic framework they are upholding. On this point, let us linger a moment on the so-called "linguistic evidence" for determining whether to introduce one or two categories. The standard linguistic argument is in terms of distribution, but of course such distribution arguments are at heart probabilistic. It is just that linguists ordinarily do not develop such arguments with much systematic or quantitative care.

Perhaps the best argument for probabilistic grammars in psycholinguistics is to be found in our work on developmental models (1974t). In this long technical report, only parts of which are now being published, we use probabilistic methods to show that we get a better fit to a child's use of new grammatical rules if we consider how the probabilities of use change over time. Such incremental developmental models are compared explicitly with stage models that are often talked about in rather unsystematic fashion by some psycholinguists and Piagetians. Interestingly enough, this use of probabilistic models corresponds closely to the use of extensive data from single subjects in psychophysics. It is closer to psychophysics than the example mentioned from linguistics by Batchelder and Wexler because there is an attempt to analyze the entire body of data from a quantitative standpoint. There have not been many other systematic proposals for looking at the changes in a child's grammar as he matures from, say, 24 months to 40 months. The tradition has been to look at individual changes and only to speculate about systematic aspects. I do not believe that what we do with probabilistic models is the end of the story or even the best that can be done, but it does represent a systematic approach to constructive developmental models. I find the changes in relative frequency of use a good index to changes in the child's underlying grammar and I find it hard to believe that such data are not directly pertinent to a systematic linguistic view of changes in his performance with maturation.

Concerning the remarks about the application of model-theoretic semantics to children's utterances, I certainly agree that the methods are not entirely satisfactory, but this seems to be a remark I would be prepared to make about all other semantical approaches as well. This does not mean that semantics should somehow be neglected and sacrificed to a total interest in syntax, phonology, and prosody. In some recent work (1978f) we have been able to get what I believe is a more systematic grip on the semantics of children's talk. It seems to me important to continue such efforts; I find it hard to believe that anyone would propose that it is out of the question in principle to develop a systematic semantics for children's language. Batchelder and Wexler do not go so far as to say this, but lurking back of their discussion is such an idea and I want to disavow it explicitly myself.

Finally, let me comment on Batchelder and Wexler's remarks about simplicity. As they note, I have stated in prior publications that simplicity is not a serious notion in physics and I have queried why it should be taken as such in linguistics. They then respond with Chomsky's notion of an "evaluation metric." I find it surprising that two psychologists take this notion seriously as a procedure for how a child can go about selecting his first grammar. The simplest and most powerful objection is that the child certainly will not have in front of him, or in the interior of his mind or wherever, entire grammars to select from. It certainly seems completely implausible that he goes about the choice of a grammar in this way at all. Surely the procedure is one of constructing the grammar rule by rule or by small clusters of rules. It seems to me inconceivable that "we can conceive of the child as selecting the first grammar in this order which is compatible with the data that he receives about his language." My surprise at their making this claim is a reflection of the wide difference that separates us on the deeper issue of what is a feasible psychological approach to a child learning a language. Even if it is claimed that the metric is not meant to be a psychological notion but can indirectly make predictions about the grammar the child ends up with, I find the absence of details about such metrics, at least in all publications known to me, a ground for skepticism about the appropriateness of the notion. In a superficial way this notion of an evaluation metric is related to the notion of complexity that has recently become important in computer science, but the way in which the complexity of algorithms is discussed, and especially the way in which the notion is used, is very different from that envisaged for an evaluation metric.

My disagreements with Batchelder and Wexler about matters of importance are evident, but I want to conclude by emphasizing the deeper level at which we agree. Their own interest in systematic methods of attack on the problems of language learning, and especially the powerful recent results of Wexler on the learnability of transformational grammars, strikes a responsive note in my own thinking. I look forward to continuing our disagreements but in a framework that permits a constructive development of the argument because of the similarity of our general approaches to psychological theory and methodology.

To Jamison

Jamison's descriptive account of my work in education does not seem to require much comment. I have had my own say about computer-assisted instruction in my autobiographical part of this volume. I could quibble with Jamison about the importance and significance of using computer-assisted instruction for low-enrollment courses but the detailed issues would take me too far away from the general spirit of this set of replies.

Jamison does raise one important substantive issue about educational research that calls for detailed comment. This is his claim that the role of theory in educational research will be at best tangential to the advance of knowledge about education.

I want to put my remarks on this matter within a more general framework. In many ways, a good case can be made for the fact that in every branch of science the pursuit of empirical knowledge has overwhelmed theory. The ability of experimenters, or empiricists more generally if the field is not naturally experimental in character, to accumulate new and significant data beyond the ability of theory to account for them is in my view typical of every branch of science. It is perhaps one of the most outstanding features of science since World War II. The theorists have lost their grip and may never regain it in the spirit of earlier times. The disarray of theory in psychology, for example, a field close to education, has been commented upon by a wide variety of psychologists and with increasing frequency in the past decade. The hegemony of learning theory came to an end, as has been commented already in this volume, about 1965. Linguistics did not have the intellectual power to replace it as the dominant theoretical force, although I personally approve of the theoretical turmoil and rethinking that linguists have forced upon psychology. The recent flurry of cognitive psychology has many exciting ideas, but it certainly is a collection of ideas and cannot be properly baptized as a new theory. A similar absence of predominant theoretical ideas in economics has been widely commented upon and it seems generally agreed upon that the recalcitrant facts have badly outrun all theoretical attempts to explain them. Modern competitive equilibrium theory is a mathematically beautiful part of economics, but certainly no one claims it will provide a detailed analysis of any significant portion of the data. The less mathematical and more empirically oriented Keynesian theory has been moving toward the exit door for at least half a decade. It might seem that the situation is different in molecular biology but this is just because for the first time some serious theoretical ideas have been proposed. One can scarcely believe that very much biological behavior can be accounted for by the recent leading fundamental ideas. And so it goes.

Personally, I think this is a satisfying state of affairs. The Don Quixote romanticism of many physicists, who seem to continue to think that the ultimate simples of the physical universe will be found by yet one more significant increase in the energy available for the study of elementary particle collisions, seems wholly misplaced. I cannot but be completely skeptical of an adequate simple account ever being found. The oddity and chaos of the universe will, it seems to me, keep any theories at bay and require a fundamental change in philosophical attitude from the search for the ultimate constituents and the ultimate causes of any phenomena rich enough to be the subject of an entire scientific discipline.

It is against this background of skepticism about ultimate theories and ultimate accounts of phenomena that I want to reaffirm my belief in the importance of theory for education. Although I think that theories cannot be ultimate and that we shall be continually searching for improvements, I do not have any feeling of despair about the efficacy of scientific theories. As I sometimes like to put it, I just want to drive the last remnants of theology out of science. It does not seem to me that education is any different from its neighboring social sciences. It is as feasible and important to bring theory to bear on the process of teaching children to read as it is to study the psychophysics of vision or of hearing. It is as important to understand how children learn mathematics as it is to understand how we can program computers to do algorithms efficiently or to prove that the programs we have constructed are correct. A minor example of theory is easily illustrated here. In the earlier work on mathematics learning in young children, perhaps the feature most conspicuously missing was a clear theoretical concept of algorithm. The highly empirical early work of Thorndike and his associates suffered from this absence more than from any other feature. It is easy enough to see that Thorndike was struggling for a systematic formulation of such ideas but simply did not have the mathematical tools at hand.

It is a familiar view in philosophy that the common sense of today is the science of yesterday. Some rather different sorts of examples from the ones I have given can illustrate this very well in the case of education. The attitude of teachers and other adults in the school system toward childhood sexuality has been radically altered in this century by what originally were theoretical ideas of Freud that ran very counter to the commonsense concept of the child in the 19th century. The way in which Freud's ideas of childhood sexuality have altered attitudes toward students in school is one of the more profound changes of this century. Another example of a similar sort is the psychoanalytic recognition of the limits of education and especially of the limits of the role of the teacher. This theoretical view runs contrary to the populist and commonsense views of Dewey, and only lately has their theoretical import begun to have some impact in recognizing that it is not up to the schools or the colleges to act *in loco parentis*. It can be argued that other trends of the times have contributed to this view but I emphasize that the view was already expressed with theoretical vigor in psychoanalytic writings of the early 1920s.

It is easy enough to continue with other examples but I am not trying to make the point in detail and am not providing the right sort of documentation to persuade a skeptic. I want only in closing to emphasize my own view that we can expect as much of theory in education as we can in other parts of the social sciences, especially those concerned with issues of economic, political or social significance. No doubt the facts will outrun the theories in every area of serious interest, but who would expect or want matters to be otherwise?

References

Luce, R. D. (1956), 'Semiorders and a Theory of Utility Discrimination', *Econometrica* **24**, 178–191.

Tversky, A., and Kahneman, D. (1971), 'Belief in the Law of Small Numbers', *Psychological Bulletin* **76**, 105–110.

Tversky, A., and Kahneman, D. (1973), 'Availability: A Heuristic for Judging Frequency and Probability', *Cognitive Psychology* **5**, 207–232.

Tversky, A., and Kahneman, D. (1974), 'Judgment Under Uncertainty: Heuristics and Biases', *Science* **185**, 1124–1131.

Wexler, K., Culicover, P., and Hamburger, H. (1975), 'Learning-theoretic Foundations of Linguistic Universals', *Theoretical Linguistics* **2**, 215–253.

Yates, F. A. (1966), *The Art of Memory*, University of Chicago Press.

PART THREE

BIBLIOGRAPHY OF PATRICK SUPPES

1951

(a) A Set of Independent Axioms for Extensive Quantities', *Portugaliae Mathematica* **10**, 163–172.

1953

(a) With J.C.C. McKinsey. 'Philosophy and the Axiomatic Foundations of Physics', *Proceedings of the Eleventh International Congress of Philosophy* **6**, 49–54.

(b) With J.C.C. McKinsey. 'Transformations of Systems of Classical Particle Mechanics', *Journal of Rational Mechanics and Analysis* **2**, 273–289.

(c) With J.C.C. McKinsey and A.C. Sugar. 'Axiomatic Foundations of Classical Particle Mechanics', *Journal of Rational Mechanics and Analysis* **2**, 253–272.
   This article gives a well-defined set-theoretical characterization of classical particle mechanics. The problems of axiomatizing various parts of physics are discussed in some detail, and the relation of the axiomatization given to earlier work by Hamel, Simon, and others is examined.

1954

(a) 'Descartes and the Problem of Action at a Distance', *Journal of the History of Ideas* **15**, 146–152.

(b) 'Some Remarks on Problems and Methods in the Philosophy of Science', *Philosophy of Science* **21**, 242–248.

(c) With H. Rubin. 'Transformations of Systems of Relativistic Particle Mechanics', *Pacific Journal of Mathematics* **4**, 563–601.

1955

(a) With D. Davidson and J.C.C. McKinsey. 'Outlines of a Formal Theory of Value, I', *Philosophy of Science* **22**, 140–160.

(b) With J.C.C McKinsey. 'On the Notion of Invariance in Classical Mechanics', *British Journal for Philosophy of Science* **5**, 290–302.

(c) With H. Rubin. 'A Note on Two-place Predicates and Fitting Sequences of Measure

Functions' *Journal of Symbolic Logic* **20**, 121–122.
(d) With M. Winet. 'An Axiomatization of Utility Based on the Notion of Utility Difference', *Journal of Management Science* **1**, 259–270.

1956

(a) 'Nelson Goodman on the Concept of Logical Simplicity', *Philosophy of Science* **23**, 153–159.
(b) 'The Role of Subjective Probability and Utility in Decision-making', *Proceedings of the Third Berkeley Symposium on Mathematical Statistics and Probability, 1954–1955*, **5**, 61–73.

This article gives an axiomatization of decision theory which is similar to that of L. J. Savage's. The summary result concerning the role of subjective probability and utility is the same: one decision is preferred to a second if and only if the expected value of the first is greater than that of the second. The theory differs from Savage's in several important respects: (i) the number of states of nature is arbitrary rather than infinite; a 50–50 randomization of two pure decisions is permitted and used in an essential way; (ii) the definition of concepts required for stating axioms is considerably less complicated.
(c) With D. Davidson. 'A Finitistic Axiomatization of Subjective Probability and Utility', *Econometrica* **24**, 264–275.

1957

(a) *Introduction to Logic*, Van Nostrand, Princeton. (Spanish translation by G. A. Carrasco, Compañia Editorial Continental, S.A., Mexico, 1966.)
(b) With D. Davidson and S. Siegel. *Decision Making: An Experimental Approach*, Stanford University Press, Stanford, Calif. (Midway Reprint, 1977, Chicago.) University of Chicago Press.

This book presents several models and experimental tests of the models derived from the general concept that an individual chooses between alternatives involving uncertainty as if he were attempting to maximize expected utility. However, the detailed meaning given to this concept differs from model to model, and the models presented differ from the standard ones of von Neumann and Morgernstern and Savage. The differences have mainly arisen as part of the detailed effort to make the models thoroughly testable from an experimental standpoint. In important respects, the ideas developed in the paper are closely related to the early work of F. D. Ramsey.

The detailed experimental results are among the first published that deal with the problem of simultaneously and independently measuring utility and subjective probability.

1958

(a) With R. C. Atkinson. 'An Analysis of Two-person Game Situations in Terms of Statistical Learning Theory', *Journal of Experimental Psychology* **55**, 369–378.
(b) With D. Scott. 'Foundational Aspects of Theories of Measurement', *Journal of Symbolic Logic* **23**, 113–128.

The main point of this article is to show how foundational analyses of measurement may be grounded in the general theory of models as developed in recent years in logic. Even more, the effort is to indicate the kind of problems relevant to measurement, which may then be stated and, in some cases, answered in a precise manner but which is not possible without some explicit use of logical notions. A formal definition of a theory of measurement as a particular kind of class of relational system is given and the general problem of axiomatizing a particular theory of measurement is studied.

1959

(a) 'Axioms for Relativistic Kinematics with or without Parity' in *The Axiomatic Method With Special Reference to Geometry and Physics* (Proceedings of an international symposium held at the University of California, Berkeley, December 26, 1957 — January 4, 1958) (ed. by L. Henkin, P. Suppes, and A. Tarski), North-Holland, Amsterdam, pp. 291–307.

The primary aim of this article is to give an elementary derivation of the Lorentz transformations, without any assumptions of continuity or linearity, from a single axiom concerning invariance of the relativistic distance between any two space-time points connected by an inertial path.

(b) 'A Linear Model for a Continuum of Responses' in *Studies in Mathematical Learning Theory* (ed. by R.R. Bush and W.K. Estes), Stanford University Press, Stanford, Calif., pp. 400–414.

(c) 'Measurement, Empirical Meaningfulness and Three-valued Logic' in *Measurement: Definitions and Theories* (ed. by C. W. Churchman and P. Ratoosh), Wiley, New York, pp. 129–143.

(d) With R. C. Atkinson. 'Applications of a Markov Model to Two-person Noncooperative Games' in *Studies in Mathematical Learning Theory* (ed. by R. R. Bush and W. K. Estes), Stanford University Press, Stanford, Calif., pp. 65–75.

(e) With W. K. Estes. 'Foundations of Linear Models' in *Studies in Mathematical Learning Theory* (ed. by R. R. Bush and W. K. Estes), Stanford University Press, Stanford, Calif., pp. 137–179.

(f) With W. K. Estes. *Foundations of Statistical Learning Theory, II. The Stimulus Sampling Model*, (Technical Report 26, Psychology and Education Series), Stanford University, Institute for Mathematical Studies in the Social Sciences, Stanford, Calif.

This report is concerned to give an explicit and exact set-theoretical axiomatization of stimulus-sampling theory. In addition, basic general theorems of the theory are proved. The most important are the general Markov theorem and the representation theorem for linear models in terms of stimulus-sampling models. (This report was published in abbreviated form as 1974q.)

(g) With N. Hawley. 'Geometry in the First Grade', *American Mathematical Monthly* **66**, 505–506.

(h) With J. Lamperti. 'Chains of Infinite Order and Their Application to Learning Theory', *Pacific Journal of Mathematics* **9**, 739–754.

(i) With H. L. Royden and K. Walsh. 'A Model for the Experimental Measurement of the Utility of Gambling', *Behavioral Science* **4**, 11–18.

(j) With K. Walsh. 'A Non-linear Model for the Experimental Measurement of Utility', *Behavioral Science* **4**, 204–211.

1960

(a) *Axiomatic Set Theory*, Van Nostrand, Princeton. (Spanish translation by H. A. Castillo, Editorial Norma, Cali, Colombia, 1968.)
(b) With R. C. Atkinson. *Markov Learning Models for Multiperson Interactions*, Stanford University Press, Stanford, Calif.

This book represents an attempt to bridge the gap between statistical learning theory and social psychology by applying stimulus sampling models to social interaction situations, and particularly to multi-person situations that have a game structure. The first chapter presents the theory in considerable detail. Chapter 2 presents methods for the analysis of data, with particular emphasis on maximum likelihood methods. The next nine chapters describe and analyze the experiments which were performed to test the theory. The actual method used in several of these chapters constitutes substantial extensions of the basic theory as presented in Chapter 1.

In the final chapter the main conclusions are summarized, and various extensions of the theory are considered. These extensions range from the Asch-type situation of social conformity to an analysis of economic markets. A prominent feature of the book is the presentation and quantitative analysis of extensive bodies of experimental data.

(c) With N. Hawley. *Geometry for Primary Grades*, Book 1, Holden-Day, San Francisco. (Spanish translation, Editorial Departamento de Instrucción Pública, San Juan, Puerto Rico, 1964; French translation, Gontran Trottier, Montreal, 1965.)
(d) With N. Hawley. *Geometry for Primary Grades*, Book 2. Holden-Day, San Francisco. (Spanish translation, Editorial Departamento de Instrucción Pública, San Juan, Puerto Rico, 1966.)
(e) 'A Comparison of the Meaning and Uses of Models in Mathematics and the Empirical Sciences', *Synthese* **12**, 287–301. (Czechoslovakian translation in *Teorie modelu a modelování* (ed. by K. Berka and L. Tondl), 1967, pp. 208–222.)
(f) Problem Analysis and Ordinary Language', *Proceedings of the Twelfth International Congress of Philosophy* **4**, 331–337.
(g) 'Some Open Problems in the Foundations of Subjective Probability' in *Information and Decision Processes* (ed. by R. E. Machol), McGraw-Hill, New York, pp. 162–169.
(h) 'Stimulus Sampling Theory for a Continuum of Responses' in *Mathematical Methods in the Social Sciences, 1959* (ed. by K. J. Arrow, S. Karlin, and P. Suppes), Stanford University Press, Stanford, Calif., pp. 348–365.
(i) With J. Lamperti. 'Some Asymptotic Properties of Luce's Beta Learning Model', *Psychometrika* **25**, 233–241.

1961

(a) 'Behavioristic Foundations of Utility', *Econometrica* **29**, 186–202.
(b) 'The Philosophical Relevance of Decision Theory', *Journal of Philosophy* **58**, 605–614.
(c) 'Probability Concepts in Quantum Mechanics', *Philosophy of Science* **28**, 378–389.

This article examines in detail the nonstandard probability theory that is a consequence of the standard formalism of quantum mechanics. The nonexistence of
joint distributions of conjugate variables is stressed.

(d) With R. W. Frankmann. 'Test of Stimulus Sampling Theory for a Continuum of
Responses with Unimodal Noncontingent Determinate Reinforcement', *Journal of
Experimental Psychology* **61**, 122–132.

(e) With F. Krasne. 'Applications of Stimulus Sampling Theory to Situations Involving
Social Pressure', *Psychological Review* **68**, 46–59.

(f) With B. McKnight. 'Sets and Numbers in Grade One, 1959–1960', *The Arithmetic
Teacher* **8**, 287–290.

(g) With J. Zinnes. 'Stochastic Learning Theories for a Response Continuum With Nondeterminate Reinforcement', *Psychometrika* **26**, 373–390.

1962

(a) 'Models of Data' in *Logic, Methodology and Philosophy of Science: Proceedings of
the 1960 International Congress* (ed. by E. Nagel, P. Suppes, and A. Tarski), Stanford
University Press, Stanford, Calif., pp. 252–261. (Czechoslovakian translation in *Teorie
Modelu a Modelování* (ed. by K. Berka and L. Tondl), 1967, pp. 223–235.)

(b) 'Recent Developments in Utility Theory', *Recent Advances in Game Theory*, Princeton University Conference, 61–72.

(c) With J. M. Carlsmith. 'Experimental Analysis of a Duopoly Situation from the
Standpoint of Mathematical Learning Theory', *International Economic Review* **3**,
60–78.

(d) With R. Ginsberg. 'Application of a Stimulus Sampling Model to Children's Concept
Formation with and without Overt Correction Responses', *Journal of Experimental
Psychology* **63**, 330–336.

(e) With R. Ginsberg. 'Experimental Studies of Mathematical Concept Formation in
Young Children', *Science Education* **46**, 230–240.

(f) With S. Hill, 'The Concept of Set', *The Grade Teacher* **79**, 51, 86–90.

(g) With S. Hill, 'Mathematical Logic for the Schools', *The Arithmetic Teacher* **9**, 369–
399.

(h) With M. Schlag-Rey. 'Analysis of Social Conformity in Terms of Generalized Conditioning Models' in *Mathematical Methods in Small Group Processes* (ed. by J. H.
Criswell, H. Solomon, and P. Suppes), Stanford University Press, Stanford, Calif.,
pp. 334–361.

(i) With M. Schlag-Rey. 'Test of Some Learning Models for Double Contingent Reinforcement', *Psychological Reports* **10**, 259–268.

1963

(a) 'The Role of Probability in Quantum Mechanics' in *Philosophy of Science, the Delaware Seminar* (ed. by B. Baumrin), Wiley, New York, pp. 319–337.

(b) 'Set Theory in the Primary Grades', *New York State Mathematics Teacher's Journal*
13, 46–53.

(c) With R. Ginsberg. 'A Fundamental Property of All-or-None Models, Binominal
Distribution of Responses Prior to Conditioning, with Application to Concept Formation in Children', *Psychological Review* **70**, 139–161.

A basic assumption of the simple all-or-none conditioning model is that the probability of a correct response remains constant over trials before conditioning. Four implications of this assumption were tested: (a) prior to the last error there will be no evidence of learning, (b) the sequence of responses prior to the last error forms a sequence of Bernoulli trials, (c) responses prior to the last error exhibit a binomial distribution, and (d) specific sequences of errors and successes are distributed in accordance with the binomial hypothesis. These four tests were performed on the data from seven experiments concerned with concept formation in children, paired-associate learning and probability learning in adults, and T maze learning in rats. The statistical evidence from these various experimental groups provided substantial support of the all-or-none model. However, when Vincent curves were constructed for responses prior to the last error, some of the learning curves showed significant departures from stationarity.

(d) With J. Zinnes. 'Basic Measurement Theory' in *Handbook of Mathematical Psychology*, vol. I (ed. by R. D. Luce, R. R. Bush, and E. H. Galanter), Wiley, New York, pp. 3–76. (Russian translation in *Mathematica* (ed. by L. D. Meshalkin), Mir, Moscow, 1967, pp. 9–107).

This systematic approach to the subject of measurement begins with the formulation of two fundamental problems. The first problem is justification of the assignment of numbers to objects or phenomena. The second problem concerns the specification of the degree to which this assignment is unique. The first problem is usually referred to as the representation problem for a theory of measurement and the second as the uniqueness problem.

The general theory of both fundamental and derived measurement is developed with an emphasis always on the solution of these two fundamental problems for any particular measurement scale.

1964

(a) With S. Hill. *First Course in Mathematical Logic*, Blaisdell, New York. (Spanish translation by E. L. Escardo, Editorial, S. A., Barcelona, 1968.)

(b) 'The Ability of Elementary-school Children to Learn the New Mathematics', *Theory into Practice* **3**, 57–61.

(c) 'The Formation of Mathematical Concepts in Primary-grade Children' in *Papers from the ASCD Eighth Curriculum Research Institute* (ed. by A.H. Passow and R.R. Leeper), pp. 99–119.

(d) 'Modern Learning Theory and the Elementary-school Curriculum', *American Educational Research Journal* **1**, 79–93.

(e) 'On an Example of Unpredictability in Human Behavior', *Philosophy of Science* **31**, 143–148.

(f) 'Problems of Optimization in Learning a List of Simple Items' in *Human Judgments and* (ed.*Optimality'* by M.W. Shelly II and G.L. Bryan), Wiley, New York, pp. 116–126.

(g) 'Some Current Developments in Models of Learning for a Continuum of Responses' Discrete Adaptive Processes Symposium, American Institute of Electrical Engineers, June 1962), *The Institute of Electrical and Electronics Engineers Transactions on Applications and Industry* **83**, 297–305.

(h) With E. Crothers and R. Weir. 'Latency Phenomena in Prolonged Learning of

Visual Representations of Russian Sounds', *International Review of Applied Linguistics* **2**, 205–217.

(i) With E. Karsh. 'Probability Learning of Rats in Continuous-time Experiments', *Psychonomic Science* **1**, 316–362.

(j) With H. Rouanet. 'A Simple Discrimination Experiment with a Continuum of Responses' in *Studies in Mathematical Psychology* (ed. by R.C. Atkinson), Stanford University Press, Stanford, Calif., pp. 317–357.

(k) With H. Rouanet, M. Levine, and R.W. Frankmann. 'Empirical Comparison of Models for a Continuum of Responses with Noncontingent Bimodal Reinforcement' in *Studies in Mathematical Psychology* (ed. by R.C. Atkinson), Stanford University Press, Stanford, Calif., pp. 358–359.

1965

(a) 'Computer-based Mathematics Instruction', *Bulletin of the International Study Group for Mathematics Learning* **3**, 7–22.

(b) 'The Kinematics and Dynamics of Concept Formation' in *Proceedings for the 1964 International Congress for Logic, Methodology and Philosophy of Science* (ed. by Y. Bar-Hillel), North-Holland, Amsterdam, pp. 405–414.

(c) 'Learning the New Mathematics' in *New Directions in Mathematics*, Membership Service Bulletin 16–A, Association for Childhood Education International, pp. 57–64.

(d) 'Logics Appropiate to Empirical Theories' in *Theory of Models* (ed. by J.W. Addison, L. Henkin, and A. Tarski) (Proceedings of the 1963 International Symposium at Berkeley), North-Holland, Amsterdam, pp. 364–375.

(e) 'On the Behavioral Foundations of Mathematical Concepts', *Monographs of the Society for Research in Child Development* **30**, 60–96.

This article is concerned with the psychological foundations of mathematical concepts, especially as reflected in the learning of such concepts by young children. The first section of the article states explicitly a version of stimulus-sampling learning theory that is used in all of the detailed analyses. The second section reports six experiments dealing with mathematical concept formation in young children, to which the theory is applied. A particular emphasis is placed on whether the learning process in this context is represented better by all-or-none or incremental conditioning. The final section is concerned with behavioral aspects of logical inference and, in particular, of elementary mathematical proofs.

(f) 'Towards a Behavioral Foundation of Mathematical Proofs' in *The Foundations of Statements and Decisions* (Proceedings of the International Colloquium on Methodology of Science, September 18–23, 1961) (ed. by K. Ajdukiewicz), PWN-Polish Scientific Publishers, Warsaw, pp. 327–341.

(g) With F. Binford. 'Experimental Teaching of Mathematical Logic in the Elementary School', *The Arithmetic Teacher* **12**, 187–195.

(h) With D. Hansen. 'Accelerated Program in Elementary-school Mathematics – The First Year', *Psychology in the Schools* **2**, 195–203.

(i) With R.D. Luce. 'Preference, Utility and Subjective Probability' in *Handbook of Mathematical Psychology*, vol. III (ed. by R.D. Luce, R.R. Bush, and E.H. Galanter), Wiley, New York, pp. 249–410.

This long survey chapter has as its aim to give a detailed and technical analysis of the main results in the literature on models of preference, utility, and subjective probability, especially of those designed for experimental testing or as part of a general psychological theory of choice. The first division is between algebraic and probabilistic theories. The second main distinction in the theories examined is between those concerned with certain and those with uncertain outcomes. The third and final main distinction is between simple choice experiments and ranking experiments. Here the question is whether the individual is expected to select among several outcomes or whether he is asked to rank order them, that is, to select from the set of rankings.

(j) With M. Schlag-Rey. 'Observable Changes of Hypotheses under Positive Reinforcement', *Science* **148**, 661–662.

(k) With M. Schlag-Rey and G. Groen. 'Latencies on Last Error in Paired-associate Learning', *Psychonomic Science* **2**, 15–16.

1966

(a) *Sets and Numbers* (elementary-school mathematics series, Grades K–6), Random House, New York.

(b) 'Accelerated Program in Elementary-school Mathematics – The Second Year', *Psychology in the Schools* **3**, 294–307.

(c) 'Applications of Mathematical Models of Learning in Education' in *Model Building in the Human Sciences* (Entretiens de Monaco en Sciences Humaines, Session 1964) (H.O.A. Wold, Scientific Organizer), Union Europienne D'Editions, Monaco, pp. 39–49.

(d) 'The Axiomatic Method in High School Mathematics' in *The Role of Axiomatics and Problem Solving in Mathematics* (The Conference Board of the Mathematical Sciences), Ginn, Washington, D.C., pp. 69–76.

(e) 'A Bayesian Approach to the Paradoxes of Confirmation' in *Aspects of Inductive Logic* (ed. by J. Hintikka and P. Suppes), North-Holland, Amsterdam, pp. 198–207.

(f) 'Concept Formation and Bayesian Decisions' in *Aspects of Inductive Logic* (ed. by J. Hintikka and P. Suppes), North-Holland, Amsterdam, pp. 21–48.

(g) 'Mathematical Concept Formation in Children', *American Psychologist* **21** 139–150.

(h) 'Plug-in Instruction', *Saturday Review* **49**(30), 25, 29–30.

(i) 'The Probabilistic Argument for a Non-classical Logic of Quantum Mechanics', *Philosophy of Science* **33**, 14–21. (French translation in *Synthese* **16**, 74–85).

(j) 'Probabilistic Inference and the Concept of Total Evidence' in *Aspects of Inductive Logic* (ed. by J. Hintikka and P. Suppes), North-Holland, Amsterdam, pp. 49–65.

The purpose of this article is to examine a cluster of issues centering around the statistical syllogism and the concept of total evidence. A constructive theory of probabilistic inference that avoids the so-called paradoxes of the statistical syllogism is developed, and a Bayesian viewpoint that accepts as natural and as part of coherence the concept of total evidence is set forth.

(k) 'The Psychology of Arithmetic' in *Learning about Learning* (a conference report) (ed. by J. Bruner), United States Government Printing Office, pp. 235–242.

(l) 'Some Formal Models of Grading Principles', *Synthese* **16**, 284–306.

This article offers an analysis of grading principles from the viewpoint of statistical decision theory and game theory. The most original part of the article is in the final section concerned with a theory of two-person justice. The important concepts here are points of justice and justice-saturated strategies, but the underlying conceptual

device is the principle of requring an individual to rank not only his own consequences but the consequences of the other person as well.

(m) 'Tomorrow's Education', *Education Age* **2**, 4–11.

(n) 'Towards a Behavioral Psychology of Mathematical Thinking' in *Learning about
Learning* (a conference report) (ed. by J. Bruner), United States Government Printing
Office, Washington, D.C., pp. 226–234.

(o) 'The Uses of Computers in Education', *Scientific American* **215**, 206–220. (German
translation in *Information Computer und kunstliche Intelligenz*, Umschau, Frankfurt-
am-Main, 1967, pp. 157–172. Russian translation in *Informatsiya*, Mir, Moscow,
1968, pp. 165–182. Polish translation by T. Wiewiórowski in *Dziś i Jutro Maszyn
Cyfrowych*, Warsaw, 1969, pp. 231–256).

This article surveys the work of computer-assisted instruction at Stanford through
1967 and attempts to forecast some of the future developments that may be anticipated. There is an emphasis on fundamental problems that must be solved in
order for substantial progress to be made in the future.

(p) With G. Groen and M. Schlag-Rey. 'A Model for Response Latency in Paired-
associate Learning', *Journal of Mathematical Psychology* **3**, 99–128.

(q) With M. Jerman and G. Groen. 'Arithmetic Drills and Review on a Computer-based
Teletype', *The Arithmetic Teacher* **13**, 303–309.

(r) With J. L. Zinnes. 'A Continuous-response Task with Non-determinate, Contingent
Reinforcement', *Journal of Mathematical Psychology* **3**, 197–216.

1967

(a) With E. Crothers. *Experiments in Second-language Learning*, Academic Press, New
York.

(b) 'The Case for Information-oriented (Basic) Research in Mathematics Education' in *Research in Mathematics Education* (ed. by J.M. Scandura), National Council
of Teachers of Mathematics, Washington, D.C. pp. 1–5.

(c) 'The Computer and Excellence', *Saturday Review* **50**(2), 46–50.

(d) 'Computer-based Instruction', *Electronic Age* **26**, 2–6.

(e) 'Decision Theory' in *Encyclopedia of Philosophy*, vol. II, Macmillan and Free Press,
New York, pp. 310–314.

(f) 'On Using Computers to Individualize Instruction' in *The Computer in American
Education* (ed. by D.D. Bushnell and D.W. Allen), Wiley, New York, pp. 11–24.

(g) 'The Psychological Foundations of Mathematics' in *Les Modèles et la Formalisation
du Comportement* (Colloques Internationaux du Centre National de la Recherche
Scientifique), Editions du Centre National de la Recherche Scientifique, Paris, pp.
213–242.

(h) 'Some Extensions of Randall's Interpretation of Kant's Philosophy of Science' in
*Naturalism and Historical Understanding: Essays on the Philosophy of John Herman
Randall, Jr.* (ed. by J.P. Anton), State University of New York Press, New York, pp.
108–120.

(i) 'Some Theoretical Models for Mathematics Learning', *Journal of Research and Development in Education* **1**, 5–22.

(j) 'The Teacher and Computer-assisted Instruction', *National Education Association
Journal* **56** (2), 15–32.

(k) 'The Teaching Machine', *Christian Science Monitor*, August 10, p. 11.

(l) 'What Is a Scientific Theory?' in *Philosophy of Science Today* (ed. by S. Morgenbesser), Basic Books, New York, pp. 55–67.

(m) With J. Donio. 'Foundations of Stimulus-sampling Theory for Continuous-time Processes', *Journal of Mathematical Psychology* **4**, 202–225.

(n) With G. Groen. 'Some Counting Models for First-grade Performance Data on Simple Addition Facts' in *Research in Mathematics Education* (ed. by J.M. Scandura), National Council of Teachers of Mathematics, Washington, D.C., pp. 35–43.

(o) With L. Hyman and M. Jerman. 'Linear Structural Models for Response and Latency Performance in Arithmetic on Computer-controlled Terminals' in *Minnesota Symposia on Child Psychology* (ed. by J.P. Hill), University of Minnesota Press, Minneapolis, pp. 160–200.

(p) With C. Ihrke. 'Accelerated Program in Elementary-school Mathematics – The Third Year', *Psychology in the Schools* **4**, 293–309.

(q) With F. S. Roberts. 'Some Problems in the Geometry of Visual Perception', *Synthese* **17**, 173–201.

1968

(a) With M. Jerman and D. Brian. *Computer-assisted Instruction: Stanford's 1965–66 Arithmetic Program*, Academic Press, New York.

The main purpose of this book is to chronicle our first year's activities in computer-assisted instruction on a reasonably large scale and in a reasonably operational mode. The book describes in detail the 1965–66 arithmetic drill-and-practice program conducted at the Institute for Mathematical Studies in the Social Sciences, Stanford University, and at an elementary school located some miles south of Stanford. One chapter is devoted to an edited version of the daily log of the project operation. Another chapter concerns various aspects of the curriculum, and still another summarizes the results of questionnaires concerning reaction to the drill program that were submitted to students, parents, and teachers at the school involved. Chapters 5–8 present a detailed summary of research conducted on student performance in the program. The models developed and that are tested against the data are mainly directed toward obtaining a deeper understanding of the cognitive structure that differentiates the relative difficulty of problems for students at various age and grade levels. The models tested emphasize not only the analysis of the correctness of the response but also the latency or speed of response. As some of the performance models show, in many tasks involving basic skills, latency provides much more sensitive evidence of the degree of mastery than does the percentage of errors.

Chapter 9, the final chapter of the book, presents a fairly detailed description of the hardware aspects of the computer system and also of the programming logic and programming language developed for expeditious handling of the large number of drill exercises.

(b) 'Can There Be a Normative Philosophy of Education?' in *Philosophy of Education 1968* (ed. by G.L. Newsome, Jr.) (Proceedings of the Twenty-fourth Annual Meeting of the Philosophy of Education Society–Santa Monica, April 7–10, 1968), Studies in Philosophy and Education, Southern Illinois University, 1968, Edwardsville, pp. 1–12.

(c) 'Computer Technology and the Future of Education', *Phi Delta Kappan* **44**, 420–423.

(d) 'The Desirability of Formalization in Science', *Journal of Philosophy* **65**, 651–664.

(e) 'Information Processing and Choice Behavior' in *Problems in the Philosophy of Science* (ed. by I. Lakatos and A. Musgrave), North-Holland, Amsterdam, pp. 278–299.

(f) With R.R. Bush and R.D. Luce. 'Models, Mathematical' in *International Encyclopedia of the Social Sciences*, vol. X, Macmillan and Free Press, New York, pp. 378–386.

(g) With R.D. Luce. 'Mathematics' in *International Encyclopedia of the Social Sciences*, vol. X, Macmillan and Free Press, New York, pp. 65–76.

(h) With N. Moler. 'Quantifier-free Axioms for Constructive Plane Geometry', *Compositio Mathematica* **20**, 143–152.

(i) With I. Rosenthal-Hill. 'Concept Formation by Kindergarten Children in a Card-sorting Task', *Journal of Experimental Child Psychology* **6**, 212–230.

(j) With M. Schlag-Rey. 'Higher-order Dimensions in Concept Identification', *Psychonomic Science* **11**, 141–142.

1969

(a) *Studies in the Methodology and Foundations of Science: Selected Papers from 1951 to 1969*, Reidel, Dordrecht.

The twenty-three articles collected in this volume represent an important part of the author's published work up to this year. The articles have not been arranged chronologically, but under four main headings.

Part I contains articles on methodology concerned with models and measurement in the sciences. Part II also is concerned with methodology and includes articles on probability and utility.

The last two parts are concerned with the foundations of physics and the foundations of psychology. (The term 'foundations' is used rather than 'philosophy', because the articles are mainly concerned with specific axiomatic formulations for particular parts of physics or of psychology, and because the term 'foundations' describes such constructive axiomatic ventures more properly.) Several articles in Part IV are concerned with the psychological foundations of mathematics, and at least two with the philosophical foundations of behaviorism.

(b) With B. Meserve and P. Sears. *Sets, Numbers, and Systems*, Books 1 and 2, Random House, New York.

(c) With others. *Research for Tomorrow's Schools: Disciplined Inquiry for Education*, Macmillan, New York.

(d) 'Computer-assisted Instruction: An Overview of Operations and Problems' in *Information Processing 68*, vol. II (Proceedings of IFIP Congress 1968, Edinburgh) (ed. by A.J.H. Morrell), North-Holland, Amsterdam, pp. 1103–1113.

(e) 'Nagel's Lectures on Dewey's Logic' in *Philosophy, Science and Method: Essays in Honor of Ernest Nagel* (ed. by S. Morgenbesser, P. Suppes, and M. White), St. Martin's Press, New York, pp. 2–25.

(f) 'Stimulus-response Theory of Automata and TOTE Hierarchies: A Reply to Arbib', *Psychological Review* **76**, 511–514.

(g) 'Stimulus-response Theory of Finite Automata', *Journal of Mathematical Psychology* **6**, 327–355.

The central aim of this article is to state and prove a representation theorem for finite automata in terms of models of stimulus-response theory. The main theorem is that, given any connected finite automaton, there is a stimulus-response model that asymptotically becomes isomorphic to it. Implications of this result for language learning are discussed in some detail. In addition, an immediate corollary is that any tote hierarchy in the sense of Miller and Chomsky is isomorphic to some stimulus-response model at asymptote. Representations of probabilistic automata are also discussed, and an application to the learning of arithmetic algorithms is given.

(h) With M. Jerman. 'Computer-assisted Instruction at Stanford', *Educational Technology* 9(1), 22–24.

(i) With M. Jerman. 'Computer-assisted Instruction at Stanford', *Educational Television International* 3(3), 176–179.

(j) With M. Jerman. 'Some Perspectives on Computer-assisted Instruction', *Educational Media* 1(4), 4–7.

(k) With M. Jerman. 'A Workshop on Computer-assisted Instruction in Elementary Mathematics', *The Arithmetic Teacher* 16, 193–197.

(l) With E. Loftus and M. Jerman. 'Problem-solving on a Computer-based Teletype', *Educational Studies in Mathematics* 2, 1–15. (Romanian translation in *Invatamintul Matematic in Lumea Contemporana* (ed. by E. Fischbein and E. Rusu), Editura Didactica si Pedagogica, Bucharest, 1971, pp. 276–296.)

(m) With M. Morningstar. 'Computer-assisted Instruction', *Science* 166, 343–350.

1970

(a) *A Probabilistic Theory of Causality* (*Acta Philosophica Fennica* 24), North-Holland, Amsterdam.

In Hume's famous analysis of causality, causes and their effects are related in three essential ways: they are contiguous in space and time, causes precede their effects in time, and causes are followed by their effects in a constant fashion. The fundamental modification of Hume's analysis I propose is to say that one event is the cause of another if the appearance of the first event is followed with a high probability by the appearance of the second, and there is no third event that we can use to factor out the probability relationship between the first and second events.

It is the objective of this monograph to work out the technical details of this fundamental idea and to apply the results to some of the typical philosophical problems that arise in discussions of causality. Section 2 develops an analysis of causal relations among events within a standard probabilistic framework. Section 3 examines how much of this analysis can be retained when only qualitative probability relations are used, and Section 4 develops a qualitative causal algebra. Section 5 analyzes causal relations among quantitative variables or properties by using the central probabilistic concept of random variable. In Section 6, the final section, a large number of philosophical issues surrounding causality are discussed, some more extensively than others, but the problems considered range from those about the direction of time to those about the freedom of the will.

(b) 'Probabilistic Grammars for Natural Languages', *Synthese* 22, 95–116.

The purpose of this article is to define the framework in which empirical investigations of probabilistic grammars can take place. The full presentation of empirical results is left to other articles but some detailed examples are given to illustrate the ideas in concrete detail. Arguments for the importance of probabilistic considerations in the theory of grammars are advanced from the standpoint of accounting for some of the most salient features of actual spoken speech or written text, namely, the distribution of length of utterance, and the relatively sharp bounds on the complexity of utterances. The theory is developed from the standpoint of context-free grammars with probabilistic parameters applied to application of individual production rules. The resulting model is a Markov chain – not a Markov chain in the surface structure but in the terminal words together with the nonterminal vocabulary.

(c) 'Systems Analysis of Computer-assisted Instruction' in *The Challenge to Systems Analysis* (ed. by J. G. Kelleher), Wiley, New York, pp. 98–110.

(d) With C. Ihrke. 'Accelerated Program in Elementary-school Mathematics – The Fourth Year', *Psychology in the Schools* **7**, 111–126.

(e) With D. Jamison and C. Butler. 'Estimated Costs of Computer Assisted Instruction for Compensatory Education in Urban Areas', *Educational Technology* **10**, 49–57.

(f) With D. Jamison and D. Lhamon. 'Learning and the Structure of Information' in *Information and Inference* (ed. by J. Hintikka and P. Suppes), Reidel, Dordrecht, pp. 197–259.

(g) With M. Jerman. 'Computer-assisted Instruction', *The Bulletin of the National Association of Secondary School Principals* **54**(343), 27–40.

(h) With M. Morningstar. 'Four Programs in Computer-assisted Instruction' in *Computer-assisted Instruction, Testing, and Guidance* (ed. by W. H. Holtzman), Harper and Row, New York, pp. 233–265.

(i) With M. Morningstar. 'Technological Innovations: Computer-assisted Instruction and Compensatory Education' in *Psychology and the Problems of Society* (ed. by F. Korten, S. Cook, and J. Lacey), American Psychological Association, Washington, D.C., pp. 221–236.

1971

(a) With D. H. Krantz, R. D. Luce, and A. Tversky. *Foundations of Measurement*, vol. I, Academic Press, New York.

This is the first of a two-volume work on fundamental measurement – that is, the systematic introduction of numbers to represent qualitative data. This volume assimilates most of the previously known results, while adding a number of new results concerning qualitative orderings for which an additive or a polynomial representation exists. It includes the classic theories of physical measurement, as well as the more recent ones proposed for both the physical and the behavioral sciences. The theories covered include extensive, difference, additive, and polynomial conjoint measurement. These theories are applied to basic physical variables, dimensional analysis, probability, and behavioral science problems such as cross modality ordering, risk, and expected utility.

Mathematical formulations are accompanied by explanatory discussions and examples, and detailed proofs are provided in separate sections. A comprehensive organization of the results is provided in which all major representations are reduced to one of three basic mathematical constructions.

(b) 'Alternatives through Computers' in *Alternatives in Education* (ed. by B. Rusk), General, Toronto, pp. 57–70.

(c) 'Archimedes's Anticipation of Conjoint Measurement' in *Role and Importance of Logic and Methodology of Science in the Study of the History of Science* (Paper presented at the XIII International Congress of the History of Science, Moscow, 1971), Nauka, Moscow.

(d) 'Computer Assisted Instruction for Deaf Students', *American Annals of the Deaf* **116**, 500–508.

(e) 'Technology in Education' in *Issues in Urban Education* (ed. by S. M. Brownell), Yale University Press, New Haven, Conn., pp. 119–146.

(f) With S. Feldman. 'Young Children's Comprehension of Logical Connectives', *Journal of Experimental Child Psychology* **12**, 304–317.

(g) With B. Searle. 'The Computer Teaches Arithmetic', *School Review* **79**(2), 213–225.

1972

(a) With M. Morningstar. *Computer-assisted Instruction at Stanford, 1966–68: Data, Models, and Evaluation of the Arithmetic Programs*, Academic Press, New York.

This book presents an analysis and evaluation of the arithmetic programs in computer-assisted instruction at Stanford for the years 1966–68. Part I describes the drill-and-practice program that was run in a large number of elementary schools in California, Kentucky, and Mississippi. Chapter 3 is concerned with research aspects of the project, in particular, identification of the structural aspects of problems that contributed to their ease or difficulty of solution. Chapter 4 applies still more detailed theoretical automaton models to the digit-by-digit responses in performing the algorithms of addition, subtraction, and multiplication. We believe that the detailed models analyzed in this chapter are the most explicit information-processing models yet to be used in the actual analysis of data in the history of research on arithmetic and related parts of elementary mathematics.

The four chapters of Part II are concerned with the tutorial program in elementary mathematics that was developed and tested at Brentwood Elementary School in East Palo Alto. After describing the operation and the curriculum, Chapter 8 provides a detailed evaluation of the curriculum, using student-performance data, and Chapter 9 is concerned with the analysis of individual student performance. Taking advantage of the data-collection potentialities of a computer-assisted-instruction program, we are able to present one of the most extensive analyses of individual student performance in primary-grade mathematics as yet available anywhere in the literature.

(b) 'Compter-assisted Instruction' in *Display Use for Man-Machine Dialog* (ed. by W. Handler and J. Weizenbaum), Hanser, Munich, pp. 155–185.

(c) 'Computer-assisted Instruction at Stanford' in *Man and Computer* (Proceedings of international conference, Bordeaux 1970), Karger, Basel, pp. 298–330.

(d) 'Finite Equal-interval Measurement Structures', *Theoria* **38**, 45–63.

(e) 'Measurement: Problems of Theory and Application' in *Mathematics in the Social Sciences in Australia*, Australian Government Publishing Service, Canberra, pp. 613–622.

(f) 'On the Problems of Using Mathematics in the Development of the Social Sciences' in

Mathematics in the Social Sciences in Australia, Australian Government Publishing Service, Canberra, pp. 3–15.

(g) 'A Probabilistic Theory of Causality' (in Russian), *Voprosi Filosofi* **4**, 90–112.

(h) 'Some Open Problems in the Philosophy of Space and Time', *Synthese* **24**, 298–316.

(i) 'Stochastic Models in Mathematical Learning Theory' in *Mathematics in the Social Sciences in Australia*, Australian Government Publishing Service, Canberra, pp. 265–273.

(j) With J. D. Fletcher. 'Computer Assisted Instruction in Reading: Grades 4–6', *Educational Technology* **12**(8), 45–49.

(k) With A. Goldberg. 'A Computer-assisted Instruction Program for Exercises on Finding Axioms', *Educational Studies in Mathematics* **4**, 429–449.

(l) With E. F. Loftus. 'Structural Variables that Determine Problem-solving Difficulty in Computer-assisted Instruction', *Journal of Educational Psychology* **63**, 531–542.

(m) With E. F. Loftus. 'Structural Variables that Determine the Speed of Retrieving Words from Long-term Memory', *Journal of Verbal Learning and Verbal Behavior* **11**, 770–777.

1973

(a) 'The Concept of Obligation in the Context of Decision Theory' in *Science, Decision and Value* (Proceedings of the Fifth University of Western Ontario Philosophy Colloquium, 1969) (ed. by J. Leach, R. Butts, and G. Pearce), Reidel, Dordrecht, pp. 1–14.

(b) 'Congruence of Meaning', *Proceedings and Addresses of the American Philosophical Association* **46**, 21–38.

This article develops the theme that by looking at the history of geometry, and the role played by the concept of congruence in that history, we can get a new perspective on how to think about the closeness in meaning of two sentences. Various weak and strong senses of congruence of meaning are defined. Talk about the sameness of meaning of two sentences or expressions is then generalized to talk about the congruence of meaning of two sentences or expressions. The basic notion of congruence is defined in terms of the concept of semantic tree for a context-free language. Extension to languages that include transformations is straightforward.

(c) 'Facts and Fantasies of Education', *Phi Delta Kappa Monograph*. (Reprinted in *Changing Education: Alternatives from Educational Research* (ed. by M.C. Wittrock), Prentice-Hall, Englewood Cliffs, N.J., pp. 6–45).

Without proper evidence, alleged facts on which educational policy or practice is based can only be classed as fantasies. It is the task of research to convert the 'right' fantasies into facts and to show that the others have a merely ethereal quality. The first part of the paper is concerned with first-order fantasies about general ways of organizing education in matters of theory, policy, or practice. Examples considered in detail are: Bloomfield's linguistic fantasies about readings, Piaget's fantasies about stages, and Skinner's fantasies about teaching arithmetic. Part II deals with second-order fantasies about methodology. Examples considered here are Campbell and Stanley on the role of randomness in experimentation, and Chomsky on the theory of competence. The article closes with an extended research example from elementary mathematics.

(d) 'New Foundations of Objective Probability: Axioms for Propensities' in *Logic,*

Methodology, and Philosophy of Science IV: Proceedings of the Fourth International Congress for Logic, Methodology and Philosophy of Science, Bucharest, 1971 (ed. by P. Suppes, L. Henkin, Gr. C. Moisil, and A. Joja), North-Holland, Amsterdam, pp. 515–529.

(e) 'Semantics of Context-free Fragments of Natural Languages' in *Approaches to Natural Language* (ed. by K.J.J. Hintikka, J.M.E. Moravcsik, and P. Suppes), Reidel, Dordrecht, pp. 370–394.

This article is concerned to develop a standard model-theoretic semantics for context-free languages. The standard notion of a derivation tree of a context-free grammar is extended to that of a semantic tree by (i) introducing denotations for terminal nodes and (ii) providing a semantic function for each production rule of the grammar. The semantic functions determine the denotations of nonterminal nodes. The article concludes by applying these ideas to the development of a noun-phrase semantics for the speech of a young child.

(f) 'Theory of Automata and Its Application to Psychology' in *Process Models for Psychology* (Lecture notes of the NUFFIC International Summer Course, 1972) (ed. by G.J. Dalenoort), Rotterdam University Press, Rotterdam, pp. 78–123.

(g) With R. Smith and M. Léveillé. 'The French Syntax of a Child's Noun Phrases', *Archives de Psychologie* 42, 207–269.

1974

(a) *Probabilistic Metaphysics*, vols. I–II, Philosophical Society and the Department of Philosophy, University of Uppsala, Uppsala, Sweden.

These volumes constitute the Hägerström lectures given in the spring of 1974 at the University of Uppsala. The set of ideas developed can be described as a philosophy of probabilistic empiricism. It is the basic thesis of the lectures that orthodox theology has been replaced by a new theology of philosophy and science that is, because of its adherence to determinism, certainty, and completeness, equally fallacious and mistaken in character. Six basic tenets of this new theology that are criticized in detail are these: (i) the future is determined by the past; (ii) every event has a sufficient determinant cause; (iii) knowledge must be grounded in certainty; (iv) scientific knowledge can in principle be made complete; (v) the meaning of propositional attitudes can be adequately characterized by a semantics of possible worlds; (vi) the grounds of rational belief and action can be made complete. The central topics of the six lectures correspond to these six issues.

(b) 'Aristotle's Concept of Matter and Its Relation to Modern Concepts of Matter', *Synthese* 28, 27–50.

This article analyzes in some detail Aristotle's concept of matter, and ten principles that characterize his concept of matter are identified. These principles are then compared with the theory of matter of Descartes, Boscovich, and Kant. The thinking of these three philosophers about matter is examined in order to get a perspective on the philosophical thinking that parallels the development of modern science. In the final section, Aristotle's concept of matter is related to specific scientific theories of matter. The claim is made that Aristotle's basic ideas are appropriate and proper for modern science.

(c) 'The Axiomatic Method in the Empirical Sciences' in *Proceedings of the Tarski Symposium, Proceedings of Symposia in Pure Mathematics* **25** (ed. by L. Henkin et al.), American Mathematical Society, Providence, R.I., pp. 465–479.

(d) 'Cognition: A Survey' in *Psychology and the Handicapped Child* (ed. by J.A. Swets and L.L. Elliott), United States Government Printing Office, Washington, D.C., pp. 109–126.

(e) 'The Essential but Implicit Role of Modal Concepts in Science' in *Boston Studies in the Philosophy of Science*, vol. XX (ed. by R.S. Cohen and M.W. Wartofsky), *PSA 1972, Proceedings of the 1972 Biennial Meeting of the Philosophy of Science Association* (ed. by K.F. Schaffner and R.S. Cohen), Synthese Library, vol. LXIV, Reidel, Dordrecht, pp. 305–314.

(f) 'Mathematical Models of Learning and Performance in a CAI Setting' in *Computers in the Instructional Process: Report of an International School* (ed. by K.L. Zinn, M. Refice, and A. Romano), Extend Publications, Ann Arbor, Mich., pp. 339–353.

(g) 'The Measurement of Belief', *Journal of the Royal Statistical Society* (Series B) **36**, 160–175.

> This article criticizes some of the claims of the standard theories of subjective probability. The criticisms are especially oriented toward the structural axioms that cannot be regarded as axioms of pure rationality and the general results that yield exact measurement of subjective probabilities. Qualitative axioms for upper and lower probability are introduced to provide a theory of inexact measurement of subjective probability. Only minor modifications of de Finetti's qualitative axioms yield the desired theory. The article concludes with a comparison of the measurement of belief to the measurement results characteristic of Euclidean geometry, and also examines briefly some possibilities for using learning models as simplified abstract processes for constructing beliefs.

(h) 'Model-theoretic Semantics for Natural Language' in *Semantics and Communication* (ed. by C.H. Heidrich), North-Holland, Amsterdam, pp. 285–344.

(i) 'On the Grammar and Model-theoretic Semantics of Children's Noun Phrases', Colloques Internationaux du C.N.R.S., in *Problèmes Actuels en Psycholinguistique* **206**, 49–60.

(j) 'The Place of Theory in Educational Research', *Educational Researcher* 3(6), 3–10.

(k) 'Popper's Analysis of Probability in Quantum Mechanics' in *The Philosophy of Karl Popper*, vol. II (ed. by P.A. Schilpp), Open Court, La Salle, Ill, pp., 760–774.

(l) 'The Promise of Universal Higher Education' in *The Idea of a Modern University* (ed. by S. Hook, P. Kurtz, and M. Todorovich), Prometheus Books, Buffalo, N.Y., pp. 21–32.

(m) 'The Semantics of Children's Language', *American Psychologist* **29**, 103–114.

> This article is concerned with developing the relevance of the logical tradition in semantics that begins with Frege and has been much stimulated by the important work of Tarski and his students to the analysis of children's language. Application of model-theoretic semantics or logical semantics to context-free grammars, to the semantics of the definite article in English, and to the semantics of adjectives and quantifiers is given. In addition, there is discussion of the early expression of propositional attitudes in children's speech and a sketch of how recent work in the semantics of modal logic can be applied to the analysis of such speech.

251

(n) 'The Structure of Theories and the Analysis of Data' in *The Structure of Scientific Theories* (ed. by F. Suppe), University of Illinois Press, Urbana, Ill,. pp. 267–283.
(o) 'A Survey of Cognition in Handicapped Children', *Review of Educational Research* **44**, 145–176.
(p) With J.B. Carroll. 'The Committee on Basic Research in Education: A Four Year Tryout of Basic Science Funding Procedures', *Educational Researcher* 3(2), 7–10.
(q) With W.K. Estes. 'Foundations of Stimulus Sampling Theory' in *Contemporary Developments in Mathematical Psychology*, vol. I, *Learning, Memory, and Thinking* (ed. by D.H. Krantz, R.C. Atkinson, R.D. Luce, and P. Suppes), Freeman, San Francisco, pp. 163–183.
(r) With J.D. Fletcher. 'Computer-assisted Instruction in Mathematics and Language Arts for Deaf Students' in *AFIPS Conference Proceedings*, vol. XLIII, *1974 National Conference*, AFIPS Press, Montvale, N.J., pp. 127–131.
(s) With D. Jamison and S. Wells. 'The Effectiveness of Alternative Instructional Media: A Survey', *Review of Educational Research* **44**, 1–67.
(t) With M. Léveillé and R.L. Smith. Developmental Models of a Child's French Syntax (Tech. Rep. 243, Psych. and Educ. Ser.), Stanford University, Institute for Mathematical Studies in the Social Sciences.
(u) With R.D. Luce. 'Measurement, Theory of', in *Encyclopedia Britannica*, vol. XI (15th ed.), pp. 739–745.
(v) With W. Rottmayer. 'Automata' in *Handbook of Perception*, vol. I, *Historical and Philosophical Roots of Perception* (ed. by E.C. Carterette and M.P. Friedman), Academic Press, New York, pp. 335–362.
(w) With B. Searle and P. Lorton, Jr. 'Structural Variables Affecting CAI Performance on Arithmetic Word Problems of Disadvantaged and Deaf Students', *Educational Studies in Mathematics* **5**, 371–384.
(x) With M. Zanotti. 'Stochastic Incompleteness of Quantum Mechanics', *Synthese* **29**, 311–330.
　　The aim of this article is to characterize a stochastic sense of incompleteness for quantum mechanics in its standard form. The sense of incompleteness meant is given concreteness by examining the time-dependent distribution of position for the linear harmonic oscillator and the free particle. The additional conditions required to make the quantum mechanical theory of the harmonic oscillator a genuine stochastic process are considered. In addition, the time-dependent joint distribution of position and momentum for the harmonic oscillator is derived. The statistical independence of position and momentum is explained in terms of the motion of a classical oscillator and independent normally distributed fluctuations of position and momentum.

1975

(a) 'Approximate Probability and Expectation of Gambles', *Erkenntnis* **9**, 153–161.
(b) 'From Behaviorism to Neobehaviorism', *Theory and Decision* **6**, 269–285.
　　This article considers extensions of the author's earlier work on stimulus-response theory of finite automata. The move from behaviorism to neobehaviorism is characterized by the recognition that the observable data are behavioristic, but that it is reasonable at the same time to postulate a variety of internal structures to account

for memory and language. An appropriate learning theory for such a neobehavioristic position is sketched. Emphasis is placed on the importance of the kind of reinforcement admitted, and a stimulus-response theory admitting only nondeterminate reinforcement is outlined. The importance of having both an internal hierarchy of structure and an external hierarchy of problems is emphasized. An argument is given against any possibility of reduction of psychology to physiology, and consequently to physics.

(c) 'Impact of Computers on Curriculum in the Schools and Universities' in *Computers in Education*, pt. 1 (ed. by O. Lecarme & R. Lewis), North-Holland, Amsterdam, pp. 173–179.

(d) 'A Probabilistic Analysis of Causality' in *Quantitative Sociology* (ed. by H.M. Blalock, A. Aganbegian, F.M. Borodkin, R. Boudon, & V. Capecchi), Academic Press, New York, pp. 49–77.

(e) 'The School of the Future: Technological Possibilities' in *The Future of Education: Perspectives on Tomorrow's Schooling* (ed. by L. Rubin), Allyn & Bacon, Boston, pp. 145–157.

(f) With J. D. Fletcher and M. Zanotti. 'Performance Models of American Indian Students on Computer-assisted Instruction in Elementary Mathematics', *Instructional Science* **4**, 303–313.

(g) With B. Searle. 'The Nicaragua Radio Mathematics project', *Educational Broadcasting International*, September, 117–120.

(h) With H. Warren. 'On the Generation and Classification of Defence Mechanisms', *The International Journal of Psycho-Analysis* **56**, 405–414.

Following suggestions in the literature concerning the need for systematic treatment of psychoanalytic theory, we have attempted to introduce new means for generating and classifying the defense mechanisms. The classification results from a consideration of the elementary transformations that may be applied to unconscious propositions of the form actor-action-object. Elementary transformations on the actor, the action, or the object of the unconscious proposition are introduced, and the defense mechanisms are then systematically generated by applying one or more of the transformations to unconscious propositions. The relation of the mechanisms thus generated to more classic work is examined, as are several different recent proposals for the study of the defense mechanisms.

1976

(a) With B. Searle and J. Friend. *The Radio Mathematics Project: Nicaragua 1974–1975*, Institute for Mathematical Studies in the Social Sciences, Stanford University, Stanford, California.

(b) 'Elimination of Quantifiers in the Semantics of Natural Language by Use of Extended Relation Algebras', *Revue Internationale de Philosophie* **117–118**, 243–259.

To develop a more computational view toward the model-theoretic semantics of context-free languages, a restricted algebraic semantics of extended relation algebras is proposed and developed. This proposal gives a direct method for eliminating quantifiers in the semantic representation of many natural language sentences. A proof is given that the kind of grammatical production rules often used by linguists for quantifiers as part of noun phrases, in contrast to the ones given in the article, lead to an undesirable escalation of logical type in the underlying set-theoretical semantics. In particular, such a simple case as that of the propositions of the classical syllogism cannot have a Boolean semantics under weak assumptions about the quantifiers being part of noun phrases.

(c) 'Syntax and Semantics of Children's Language' in *Origins and Evolution of Language and Speech* (ed. by W.R. Harnad, H.D. Steklis, and J. Lancaster) (*Annals of the New York Academy of Sciences* **280**, 227–237), New York Academy of Sciences, New York.

(d) 'Testing Theories and the Foundations of Statistics' in *Foundations of Probability Theory, Statistical Inference, and Statistical Theories of Science*, vol. II (ed. by W.L. Harper and C.A. Hooker), Reidel, Dordrecht, pp. 437–455.

(e) With J. D. Fletcher. 'The Stanford Project on Computer-assisted Instruction for Hearing-impaired Students', *Journal of Computer-Based Instruction* **3**, 1–12.

(f) With J. D. Fletcher and M. Zanotti. 'Models of Individual Trajectories in Computer-assisted Instruction for Deaf Students', *Journal of Educational Psychology* **68**, 117–127.

In this article a quantitative theory of student trajectories in a computer-assisted-instruction course for deaf students is developed and tested. The theory rests upon certain qualitative assumptions about information processing, from which a stochastic differential equation can be derived. The differential equation is characteristic of the course, but the constants of integration are estimated separately for each student. The fit of data to theory is reported in terms of the standard scale of grade placement. The mean of the mean standard errors averaged across the approximately 300 students participating in the experiment was .046, which represents a relatively close fit of data to theory.

(g) With A. Goldberg. 'Computer-assisted Instruction in Elementary Logic at the University Level', *Educational Studies in Mathematics* **6**, 447–474.

(h) With D.T. Jamison, J.D. Fletcher, & R.C. Atkinson. 'Cost and Performance of Computer-assisted Instruction for Education of Disadvantaged Children' in *Education as an Industry* (ed. by J. Froomkin, D.T. Jamison, and R. Radner), Cambridge, Mass., NBER, Ballinger, pp. 201–240.

(i) With M. Léveillé. 'La Comprehension des Marques d'Appartenance par les Enfants', *Enfance* No. 3, 309–318.

(j) With E. Macken, R. van den Heuvel, and T. Suppes. *Home Based Education: Needs and Technological Opportunities*. U.S. Department of Health, Education, and Welfare, National Institute of Education.

(k) With B. Searle. 'Survey of the Instructional Use of Radio, Television, and Computers in the United States', *Journal of the Society of Instrument and Control Engineers* **15**, 712–720.

(l) With B. Searle. 'The Radio Mathematics Project', *The Mathematics Teacher* (India) **11A**, 47–51.

(m) With M. Zanotti. 'On the Determinism of Hidden Variable Theories with Strict Correlation and Conditional Statistical Independence of Observables' in *Logic and Probability in Quantum Mechanics* (ed. by P. Suppes), Reidel, Dordrecht, pp. 445–455.

(n) With M. Zanotti. 'Necessary and Sufficient Conditions for Existence of a Unique Measure Strictly Agreeing with a Qualitative Probability Ordering', *Journal of Philosophical Logic* **5**, 431–483.

Using extended indicator functions, which are built up from indicator functions for events by closure under functional addition, and also using necessary and sufficient conditions for the existence of a numerical representation of extensive measurement, the authors are able to give very simple necessary and sufficient conditions for the existence of a finitely additive probability measure strictly agreeing with a qualitative probability ordering. The use of extended indicator functions shows the desirability of going beyond the usual algebra of events in order to obtain appropriate qualitative conditions. The results already in the literature show that there is not likely to be a satisfactory formulation of necessary and sufficient conditions for the existence of a measure stated purely in terms of the algebra of events.

1977

(a) 'The Distributive Justice of Income Inequality', *Erkenntnis* **11**, 233–250.

(b) 'Is Visual Space Euclidean?', *Synthese* **35**, 397–421.

(c) 'Learning Theory for Probabilistic Automata and Register Machines, with Applications to Educational Research' in *Structural Models of Thinking and Learning* (ed. by H. Spada and W.F. Kempf), Hans Huber Publishers, Bern, pp. 57–79.

(d) 'Some Remarks about Complexity', in *PSA, 1976*, vol. II, Philosophy of Science Association.

(e) 'Some Remarks on the Concept of Resiliency', *Journal of Philosophy* **74**, 713–714.

(f) 'A Survey of Contemporary Learning Theories' in *Foundational Problems in the Special Sciences* (Part 2 of the Proceedings of the Fifth International Congress of Logic, Methodology and Philosophy of Science, Canada, 1975) (ed. by R. E. Butts and J. Hintikka), Reidel, Dordrecht, pp. 217–239.

(g) With B. Searle. 'Computer Usage in the Nicaragua Radio Mathematics Project' in *Proceedings of the International Conference on Computer Applications in Developing Countries*, vol. I (ed. by J.A. Jordan, Jr., and K. Malaivongs), Asian Institute of Technology, Bangkok, pp. 361–374.

(h) With B. Searle and J. Friend. 'The Nicaragua Radio Mathematics Project' in *Radio for Education and Development: Case Studies*, vol. 1 (ed. by P. L. Spain, D.T. Jamison, and E. McAnany), A Document of the Education Department of the World Bank, Washington, D.C., pp. 2–32.

(i) With R. Smith and M. Beard. 'University-level Computer-assisted Instruction at Stanford: 1975', *Instructional Science* **6**, 151–185.

(j) With M. Zanotti. 'On Using Random Relations to Generate Upper and Lower Probabilities', *Synthese* **36**, 427–440.

1978

(a) 'A Philosopher as Psychologist' in *The Psychologists: Autobiographies of Distinguished Living Psychologists*, vol. III (ed. by T. S. Krawiec), Clinical Psychology Publishing Company, Brandon, Vt., pp. 261–288.

(b) 'The Future of Computers in Education' in *Computers and the Learning Society* (Hearings before the Subcommittee on Domestic and International Scientific Planning, Analysis and Cooperation, of the Committee on Science and Technology, U.S. House of Representatives, Ninety-fifth Congress, First Session, October 4, 6, 12, 13,

18, and 27, 1977 [No. 47]), U.S. Government Printing Office, Washington, D.C., pp. 548–569.
(c) 'La Informática en la Educación', *Nonotza, Revista de Difusion Cientifica, Tecnologica y Cultural* **13,** IBM de Mexico.
(d) With I. Larsen and L. Z. Markosian. 'Performance Models of Undergraduate Students on Computer-assisted Instruction in Elementary Logic', *Instructional Science* **7,** 15–35.
(e) With E. Macken. 'The Historical Path from Research and Development to Operational Use of CAI', *Educational Technology,* April 1978, 9–12.
(f) With E. Macken. 'Steps toward a Variable-free Semantics of Attributive Adjectives, Possessives, and Intensifying Adverbs' in *Children's Language* (ed. by K. Nelson), Gardner Press, New York, pp. 81–115.

In this article we give a model-theoretic semantics for some adjective and noun phrases drawn from a corpus of speech collected from 15 children ranging in age from 6 to 7 years. The set-theoretical semantics developed by the first author in previous publications is restricted here to a variable-free semantics that increases the computational and algebraic character of the semantics. The semantic analysis concentrates on intensive adjectives like *big* or *little*, possessives, and intensifying adverbs.

(g) With E. Macken and M. Zanotti. 'The Role of Global Psychological Models in Instructional Technology' in *Advances in Instructional Psychology,* vol. I (ed. by R. Glaser), Erlbaum, Hillsdale, N.J., pp. 229–259.
(h) With B. Searle. 'Achievement Levels of Students Learning Primary-school Mathematics by Radio in Nicaragua', *Studies in Science and Mathematics Education* (India) **1,** 63–80.
(i) With H. Warren. 'Psychoanalysis and American Elementary Education' in *Impact of Research on Education: Some Case Studies* (ed. by P. Suppes), National Academy of Education, Washington, D.C., pp. 319–396.

In assessing the impact psychoanalytic theory has had on American education, we limit ourselves to the education of normal children and the period from 1900 to 1957. From detailed analysis of a variety of historical data, our summary conclusions are the following:

(i) Psychoanalysis has had a significant impact on 20th century elementary education; the most important psychoanalytic ideas incorporated into educational thought concern the importance of the early years of childhood, the fact of childhood sexuality, and the role the defense mechanisms play in internal life.

(ii) In broad terms, the nfluence of psychoanalysis on education grew throughout the entire first half of this century, but the slow development of the impact is evidence of the complicated way in which new ideas come to have an impact in education.

(iii) Throughout the period studied, ambivalence toward psychoanalysis was continually exhibited in a number of ways. The almost uniform theoretical eclecticism of textbook authors toward theory in general was amplified in the present case by the fact that psychoanalytic theory ran contrary to the prevailing educational ideas and concepts.

(iv) To a considerable extent the channels through which the influence of psycho-analysis spread were not professional ones. Main sources of dissemination were apparently the public press and the large literature addressed to parents.

(v) A salient feature of psychoanalytic thinking about education has been the stress on the natural limitations of what can be achieved and what should be expected. This view stands in strong contrast to the writings of John Dewey and other progressive thinkers.

In press

(a) 'The Logic of Clinical Judgment: Bayesian and Other Approaches' in *Clinical Judgment: A Critical Appraisal* (ed. by H. T. Engelhardt, Jr., S. F. Spicker, and B. Towers), Reidel, Dordrecht.

(b) 'Variable-free Semantics for Negations with Prosodic Variation' in *Festschrift* for Jaakko Hintikka, Reidel, Dordrecht.

(c) With M. Léveillé and R. Smith. 'Probabilistic Modeling of the Child's Productions' in *Studies in Language Acquisition* (ed. by P. Fletcher and M. Garman).

(d) With M. Zanotti and B. Searle. 'Nicaragua Radio Mathematics Project: The Role of Probabilistic Models in Data Analysis' in *Proceedings of the 41st Session of the International Statistical Institute, New Delhi, 5–15 December 1977.*

(e) *Set-theoretical Structures in Science*, forthcoming.
This is a book in the philosophy of science that the author has been in the process of writing for a number of years. Mimeographed copies have been fairly widely circulated. The emphasis throughout is on using set-theoretical structures to characterize scientific theories and a wide range of philosophical problems associated with standard theories or with standard philosophical issues, such as those concerned with causality and the analysis of evidence in support of hypotheses or theories. Several examples of scientific theories are cast in set-theoretical form to provide a framework for detailed discussion. The examples are mainly drawn from physics and psychology.

(f) 'Current Trends in Computer-assisted Instruction' in *Advances in Computers*, vol. 18 (ed. by M. C. Yovits), Academic Press, New York.

(g) 'Past, Present and Future Technologies' in *Proceedings of the International Conference on Developing Mathematics in Third World Countries* (held in Khartoum, 6–9 March 1978) (ed. by M. El Tom), North-Holland, Amsterdam.

Books Edited

With L. Henkin and A. Tarski. *The Axiomatic Method with Special Reference to Geometry and Physics* (Proceedings of an international symposium held at the University of California, Berkeley, December 16, 1957 – January 4, 1958), North-Holland, Amsterdam, 1959.

With K. J. Arrow and S. Karlin. *Mathematical Methods in the Social Sciences, 1959: Proceedings of the First Stanford Symposium*, Stanford University Press, Stanford, Calif., 1960.

With E. Nagel and A. Tarski. *Logic, Methodology and Philosophy of Science: Proceedings of the 1960 International Congress*, Stanford University Press, Stanford, Calif., 1962.

With J. H. Criswell and H. Solomon. *Mathematical Methods in Small Group Processes*, Stanford University Press, Stanford, Calif., 1962.

With J. Hintikka. *Aspects of Inductive Logic*, North-Holland, Amsterdam. 1966.

With L. J. Cronbach. *Research for Tomorrow's Schools: Disciplined Inquiry for Education*, Macmillan, New York, 1969.

With S. Morgenbesser and M. White. *Philosophy, Science, and Method: Essays in Honor of Ernest Nagel*, St. Martin's Press, New York, 1969.

With J. Hintikka. *Information and Inference*, Reidel, Dordrecht, 1970.

With K.J.J. Hintikka and J.M.E. Moravcsik. *Approaches to Natural Language: Proceedings of the 1970 Stanford Workshop on Grammar and Semantics*, Reidel, Dordrecht, 1973.

Space, Time and Geometry, Reidel, Dordrecht, 1973.

With L. Henkin, Gr. C. Moisil, and A. Joja. *Logic, Methodology and Philosophy of Science IV: Proceedings of the Fourth International Congress for Logic, Methodology and Philosophy of Science, Bucharest, 1971*, North-Holland, Amsterdam, 1973.

With D. H. Krantz, R. C. Atkinson, and R. D. Luce. *Contemporary Developments in Mathematical Psychology*, vol. I: *Learning, Memory, and Thinking*, W. H. Freeman, San Francisco, 1974.

With D. H. Krantz, R. C. Atkinson, and R. D. Luce. *Contemporary Developments in Mathematical Psychology*, vol. II: *Measurement, Psychophysics, and Neural Information Processing*, W. H. Freeman, San Francisco, 1974.

Logic and Probability in Quantum Mechanics, Reidel, Dordrecht, 1976.

Impact of Research on Education: Some Case Studies, National Academy of Education, Washington, D.C., 1978.

INDEX OF NAMES

Adams, E.W. 15
Ambler, S. 156
Arbib, M.A. 163
Aristotle 5, 6, 250
Arnold, B. 5, 51
Arrow, K. 51, 192
Atkinson, R.C. 9, 28, 41–42, 45, 53, 158, 181, 193, 202

Balch, M. 101
Banks, W. 178
Bartlett, W. 218
Batchelder, W. *149–186*, 223–229
Blackwell, D. 48–49
Bloomfield, L. 160, 249
Boscovich 6, 9, 250
Bower, G.H. 156
Bowker, A. 52, 53
Bradley, F.H. 5
Bridgman, P. 41
Brown, R. 33, 167
Bush, R.R. 150, 153

Campbell, N. 15, 41, 249
Carathéodory, C. 65
Carnap, R. 17, 22, 61, 64, 76, 140
Cartwright, N. 25
Chomsky, N. 160, 173, 180, 229, 246, 249
Crothers, E. 30–31
Culicover, P.W. 167, 182, 227

Davison, D. 14, 16, 49, 53, 100, 101

Descartes 6, 9, 250
Dewey, J. 5, 45, 232, 257
Donio, J. 29, 45, 51

Eddy, M.B. 3, 4
Eilenberg, S. 5
Estes, W.K. 9, 26, 27, 28, 49, 50, 53, 150, 152–154, 181, 182

Falmagne, J.C. 102
Farmer, J. 54
Fechner, G. 149
de Finetti, B. 149
Frankmann, R. 28
Frege, G. 33, 38, 40, 251
Freud, S. 232

Ginsberg, R. 29–30
Girshik, M. A. 8, 48–49
Good, I.J. 105, 125, 126
Grandy, R. *131–147*, 220–223
Greeno, J. 156, 157
Groen, G. 178

Hamburger, H. 32, 167, 227
Hamel, G. 65, 71, 235
Harsanyi, J. C. 128
Hawley, N. 29
von Helmholtz, H. 15, 149
Hempel, C. 17, 18, 60
Henkin, L. 10
Hering, E. 149
Hermes, H. 71–73

Hilbert, D. 65
Hintikka, J. 17, 54, 123
Holland, P. 25, 51
Hölder, O. 13, 15, 98
Hull, C. 26–27, 150, 151
Hume, D. 246

Ioanid, M. x
Inkeles, A. 203

Jamison, D. *187–206*, 230

Kahneman, D. 216
Kant, I. 6, 7, 9, 250
Kieras, D.E. 163–164, 225
Knuth, D.E. 36
Koopman, B.O. 21, 121
Kraemer, H. 51
Krantz, D. 14, 17, 53, 77, 101
Kreisel, G. 25, 46, 54
Kristeller, P.O. 7
Kuhn, T. 60, 79

Lamperti, J. 28
Léveillé, M. 33
Levine, M. 29, 51
Luce, R.D. 9, 11, 14–15, 17, 51, 53, *93–110*, 212–215, 223

Macken, E. 33, 39
Mackey, G.W. 12, 82
McCarthy, J. 41
McKeon, R. 5
McKinsey, J.C.C. 8–9, 16, 26, 38, 48, 50
Miller, G. 246
Millward, R.B. 157
Minsky, M. 178, 180
Montague, R. 14
Moravcsik, J. 54
Morgenstern, O. 5, 100, 101–102, 236
Morrisett, L. 41
Mosteller, F. 101–102, 150, 153
Moulines, C.U. *59–91*, 207–212

Nagel, E. 5–7
Narens, L. 98, 106

Nelson, R.J. 84, 164, 225
von Neumann, J. 5, 12, 100–102, 113, 236
Newell, A. 224
Newton, I. 6, 9, 65
Nogee, P. 101–102
Noll, W. 10
Nolman, F. 51, 156, 182

Papert, S. 178, 180
Pavlov, I.J. 150
Piaget, J. 249
Plato 225–226
Popper, K. 60, 83, 104

Rabin, M.O. 161
Ramsey, F.P. 67, 70, 79–80, 100–101, 112–114, 236
Randall, J.H. 7
Reichenbach, H. 22, 40
Restle, F. 26, 156, 178
Roberts, F. 15
Robinson, A. 98
Robinson, R.E. 96
Rosenkrantz, R. *111–129*, 216–219
Rottmayer, W.A. 166, 178
Rouanet, H. 29
Royden, H. 17
Rubin, H. 9, 49
Russell, B. 45

Savage, L.J. 100, 104, 107, 121, 236
Scott, D. 14, 50, 99, 104, 106, 161, 223
Sen, A.K. 127
Shaw, M. x
Sieber, J. 54
Siegel, S. 16
Simon, H. 71–76, 235
Simonides 225
Skala, H.J. 98
Skinner, B.F. 150, 151, 156, 249
Smith, C.A.B. 105
Smith, R. 33, 36
Sneed, J. *59–91*, 207–212
Spohn, W. 101
Steenrod, N. 5

Stevens, S.S. 96

Tarski, A. 8, 10, 15, 26, 33, 38, 48, 251
Thomas, L.H. 5
Thorndike, E. 150, 151, 231
Truesdell, C. 75, 77
Tversky, A. 14, 17, 53, 99, 104, 216

Walsh, K. 17

Wexler, K. 32, *149–186*, 166, 182, 223–229
Wigner, E. 84
Winet, M. 14, 101

Zanotti, M. 12, 20–21, 88
Zeeman, E.C. 10
Zinnes, J.L. 14, 28, 96, 107

INDEX OF SUBJECTS

Arrow's paradox 117
automata
  and S–R models 161–167, 224–226
  and Representation Theorem 163–167, 225
axiom
  structural 97, 111–112
  rationality 111–112
axiomatization
  in psychology 152–154, 181
  set-theoretic 63–70 *see also* set-theoretic
  of classical particle mechanics 70–81
  of empirical theories 63–67, 150
  of finite systems 98–99
  of Minkowskian chronometry 10–11
  of probability 103–106

Bayes' Theorem 122–123
Bayesian
  view of belief 17–18, 104
  view of confirmation 18
  view of decision 18
  learning from experience 122–124, 218–219
behaviorism 34–36, 179–180
Boolean algebra 38, 39, 98, 134
Boolean semantics 38–39, 133, 220

causality 23–26, 124–126, 219
  probabilistic def. 24, 124–125
  and experimentation 25
classical particle mechanics

internal structure 71–74
  semantics 74–82
  dynamics vs. kinematics 71, 73, 209
  Simon's axiomatixation 71–76
  Hamel's axiomatization 71
  Hermes' axiomatization 71–73
  MSS axiomatization 70–76, 209–210
concept
  quantitative 63, 68–70, 81
  qualitative 63, 68–70
  theoretical/nontheoretical 67–70, 76–78, 210
concept formation
  in induction 18
  in mathematics 29–30
conditionalization 22, 122–123
congruence
  in geometry 139
  phrasal 144–146, 222
  see meaning
curriculum
  elementary school 193–194
  university 194–195

decision theory 16–19, 99–102, 111–120
  testing of 102, 214–216

education 187–206
  and computers 40–45, 190–196
  evolution/of 188
  performance evaluation 42–43
  and instructional radio 196–197
  evaluation 200–201

theoretical research 197–202, 230–232

optimal teaching 201–202

evidence
total 17–18

expectation 217

force 77–80

game
two person 157–158

grammar
theory of 134–138
probabilistic 33, 135–138, 167–179, 220–221, 227–230
context-free 36, 136, 140, 168, 175, 227
children's *see* learning language
and frequency of utterance 170–179, 227–228
and simplicity 172–173, 229
competence vs. performance 172, 227
grammaticality judgments 174

income
distribution of 19

indicator function 20–21, 120–121

induction 18, 122–124

inertia 80

inference
logical 39
probabilistic 17

internal states 161–167, 225

invariance 96–97, 132, 212–213

joint distribution
of position and momentum 11, 84–85

justice 19, 126–128

language
philosophy of 36–40
and computers 32
see learning language

learning
theory 26–29, 151–159, 160–167
language 30–33, 43, 138, 166–167, 173–177, 226–228, 229

and conceptual change 122–124, 218–219
and induction 123–124
mathematical models of 152–158
mathematical learning 178
item component analysis of 198–199
trajectories of 200
Hull's theory of 26–27

logic
of empirical theories 131–134
nonclassical 84–88, 132–134

Lorentz transformations 10, 12, 13

mass 80–81, 208

mathematical learning theory 151–159, 179–180, 224

meaning 33, 37–38
and congruence 37–38, 138–147, 221–223
of physical concepts 74–82, 210

meaningfulness
empirical 96–97, 132–133, 213

meaning postulates 76–77, 141

measurement
of non-commuting observables 84–85
of physical quantities 208
theory of 13–16, 93–110
in psychology 15, 17
in physics 68–69, 78–81, 203
and semantic interpretation 68–69, 78–81
and finite systems 98–99, 213–214

mechanics *see* classical and quantum mechanics

model
for a continuum of responses 155–157
linear 153–154
Markov 156–158
stimulus-response 161–167, 225
of visual perception 179
for scientific theories 65–70, 74, 209–210

operationalism 71–73, 76–82

optics 11

ordering 94, 96

Pareto ordering 126–127

preposition
analysis of 39–40
probability 19–23
axiomatization of 14, 20–21, 103–106,
120–121
in quantum mechanics 11–13
qualitative 104–105
subjective 14, 16
comparative 120–121, 217
conditional 21–22
lower/upper 19–20, 216
Popper's view of 104
psychology 26–36, 149–186
formal theories of 149–150
axiomatization of 152–154, 181
cognitive 159–178, 180, 224
and automata 159–167
and linguistics 160
reductionist approach to 34–35
psycholinguistics 30–34

quantifiers 38–39
quantum mechanics 11–13, 82–89, 210–
211
Mackey's axiomatization 82
von Neumann's axiomatization 82
Popper's view 83
Copenhagen interpretation 84, 211
and probability 83–88, 103–104, 211
time dependent 88

Ramsey-eliminability 67, 70, 79–80
Ramsey model see utility
reinforcement 162–168, 226
relativity 10–11, 13
representation theorem 77, 94–96, 121,
163–167, 225

science

philosophy of 45–48, 59–63
semantics
of natural language 38–40, 138–147
of physical theories 62–63, 68–70,
207–209
model-theoretic 33, 36–38, 176, 228
semantic tree 140–142, 144–145
set-theoretic
methods 46–47, 150
predicate 71
axiomatization 63, 71
stimulus-response
theory 32, 34–36, 155–156, 160–167,
179–180, 219
and automata 161–167, 225–226
stimulus sampling theory 26–27, 42,
118, 122, 152–154, 162–167
and mathematical concept formation
30
and language learning 30

time 10–11
theories
inter-theoretical relations 77–80
Turing machine 35, 165

uncertainty relation 83–85
uniqueness theorem 95–96, 121
utility 16–17, 20, 111–119
axiomatization of 14, 100–101, 111
experiments on 101–103, 112–120
Ramsey model 100–101, 112–114
von Neumann-Morgenstern model
100–102, 113
Mosteller–Nogee experiments 101–
102

wave functions 211
wave–particle duality 83

PROFILES

Further volumes in this series which are in preparation include profiles of:

JAAKKO HINTIKKA

HENRY E. KYBURG and ISAAC LEVI

KEITH LEHRER

DONALD DAVIDSON

PETER T. GEACH